STUDIES IN CHRISTIAN HISTORY AND THOUGHT

Ratzinger's Augustinianism and Evangelicalism

Ratzinger's Augustinianism and Evangelicalism

An Exploration in Ecumenical Rapprochement

Patrick G. McGlinchey

Foreword by Canon Dr Christina Baxter

Copyright © Patrick G. McGlinchey 2017

First published 2017 by Paternoster

Paternoster is an imprint of Authentic Media
PO Box 6326, Bletchley, Milton Keynes, MK1 9GG

authenticmedia.co.uk

The right of Patrick G. McGlinchey to be identified as the Author of this Work has been asserted by him in accordance with the Copyright, Designs and Patents Act 1988.

All rights reserved. No part of this publication may be reproduced, stored in a retrieval system, or transmitted, in any form or by any means, electronic, mechanical, photocopying, recording or otherwise, without the prior permission of the publisher or a license permitting restricted copying. In the UK such licenses are issued by the Copyright Licensing Agency, Barnard's Inn, 86 Fetter Lane, London, EC4A 1EN.

British Library Cataloguing in Publication Data
A catalogue record for this book is available from the British Library

ISBN 978-1-84227-934-2
978-1-84227-935-9 (e-book)

Printed and bound for Paternoster
by Lightning Source

STUDIES IN CHRISTIAN HISTORY AND THOUGHT

Series Preface

This series complements the specialist series of Studies in Evangelical History and Thought and Studies in Baptist History and Thought for which Paternoster is becoming increasingly well known by offering works that cover the wider field of Christian history and thought. It encompasses accounts of Christian witness at various periods, studies of individual Christians and movements, and works which concern the relations of church and society through history, and the history of Christian thought.

The series includes monographs, revised dissertations and theses, and collections of papers by individuals and groups. As well as 'free standing' volumes, works on particular running themes are being commissioned; authors will be engaged for these from around the world and from a variety of Christian traditions.

A high academic standard combined with lively writing will commend the volumes in this series both to scholars and to a wider readership.

Series Editors

Alan P.F. Sell	Visiting Professor at Acadia University Divinity College, Nova Scotia
D.W. Bebbington	University of Stirling, Stirling, Scotland
Clyde Binfield	Professor Associate in History, University of Sheffield, UK
Gerald Bray	Anglican Professor of Divinity, Beeson Divinity School, Samford University, Birmingham, Alabama, USA
Grayson Carter	Associate Professor of Church History, Fuller Theological Seminary SW, Phoenix, Arizona, USA
Dennis Ngien	Professor of Theology, Tyndale University College and Seminary, Founder of the Centre for Mentorship and Theological Reflection, Toronto, Canada

This book is dedicated to my wife Helen and our three children, Paul, Patrick and Timothy.

Contents

Foreword by Canon Dr Christina Baxter	xi
Acknowledgements	xiii
Abbreviations	xiv
Introduction and Methodology	1
Chapter 1	
The Life and Thought of Joseph Ratzinger	5
Introduction	5
Bavarian Origins	6
War Experience	9
Theological Formation	11
Academic and Ecclesiastical Progress	15
The Papacy of Benedict XVI	21
Chapter 2	
Ratzinger's Credibility as a Dialogue Partner	26
Introduction	26
Ratzinger's Theological Method	28
Critical Insights	33
Francis Schüssler-Fiorenza	33
The Halbfass Affair	34
Ratzinger as a Dogmatic Theologian	36
The Christological Articles of the Creed	43
Conceived of the Holy Ghost, born of the Virgin Mary	43
Suffered under Pontius Pilate, was crucified, dead and buried	46
Rose again from the dead	50
From thence he shall come to judge the living and the dead	54
Ecclesiology and the Second Vatican Council	59
Conclusion	66

Chapter 3
Ratzinger and Augustinianism   **69**

Introduction   69
Ratzinger's Augustinianism and Evangelical Protestantism   70
The Debate about Ratzinger's Augustinianism   72
Ratzinger as an Augustinian Scholar   77
Gaudium et Spes   87
The Love of God   92
Reason   98
Augustine and the Evangelical Tradition   103
Protestant Augustinianism   103
The Ecumenical Possibilities of Augustine's Theology   105

Chapter 4
Ratzinger and Soteriology   **110**

Introduction   110
The Dispute over the True Nature of Augustine's Soteriology   112
Augustine's Theology of Grace and his Teaching on Justification   114
Ratzinger and Justification   120
Ratzinger and Küng   121
Justification in Ratzinger's Reflections on Vatican II   125
Ratzinger's Critique of Luther   128
Papal Addresses on Justification   131

Chapter 5
Obstacles to Rapprochement   **144**

Introduction   144
The Contours of Ratzinger's Soteriological Ecclesiology   146
An Evangelical Critique of Ratzinger's Ecclesiology   154
Christ as One Single Subject with the Church   154
Christ as a Corporate Personality in Scripture   156
Webster and Communio Ecclesiology   164
Baptism, Conversion and Faith in Ratzinger   163
Baptism   165

Conversion/*Metanoia*	167
The Church and the Mediation of Faith	168
The Critical Reverse Test	171
Purgatory	172
The Place of Mary in Ratzinger's Thought	179
Theological and Personal Context	179
Ratzinger's Defence of Mariology	180
Ratzinger's Mariology and Evangelicalism	185
Mary as Co-redemptrix	185
Conclusion	**190**
Bibliography	**197**
Index of Names	**212**
Index of Subjects	**218**

Foreword

Ecumenical theology as practised in the last century was at an impasse; needing to find fresh ways to enable progress in mutual understanding which might facilitate new models of being Christian together or making Christ known collaboratively. Dr McGlinchey's work is an important study because it presents areas for creative discussion where there is as yet unrecognised close alignment and the possibility of mutual learning.

Despite the landmark agreement between Roman Catholics and Lutherans on Justification, the formal consultations between the World Evangelical Alliance and the Roman Catholic Church, and the informal group 'Evangelical and Catholics Together', in many parts of the world there remains suspicion or hostility between these two groups which is deeply regrettable and potentially dangerous. It is perhaps not surprising that this piece of work has arisen in Ireland where misunderstanding and misrepresentation have wrought such havoc. And yet, there is much to be gained in mutual understanding and collaboration in the face of Western ignorance of the Gospel, and increased liberalism among Christian scholars.

In response to these challenges, Dr McGlinchey has explored in significant sympathetic detail whether Ratzinger's theology could be a basis for deeper agreement and mutual enlightenment than has hitherto been possible. I welcome this work because it has shown a way forward which will be capable of bearing fruit in dialogue, fellowship and mission. It has a universal reach both on account of its substance and its method.

The study works creatively to overcome two major challenges to its success. The first is to explain the influences and movement in Ratzinger's theology, which are not universally agreed. Here Dr McGlinchey's study of Ratzinger's Augustinianism is important, as he demonstrates both the consistency and rationale for Ratzinger's stance before, during and after the Second Vatican Council. Secondly, Dr McGlinchey has to engage the breadth of Evangelicalism whilst seeking to find its central tenets. Before exploring the interface between Ratzinger and Evangelicalism, Dr McGlinchey is offering an answer to the question as to whether there can be said to be theological coherence within the broad stream of Evangelicalism which is notorious for its divisions which self-define one sub-group by wrong-footing another. evangelicals will find it challenging reading as they rethink their essentials.

The Lord's command that we love our neighbour (including our enemy) requires of Christians that we should begin by understanding them. This is a major attempt to obey the Lord's command by understanding the leading proponent of the Roman Catholic faith in dialogue with that way of being Christian known as Evangelical. In both areas the reader is treated to detailed and sympathetic probing which lays out the debates before presenting reasoned conclusions. The discussion is both comprehensive and persuasive.

But it is the bold attempt to explore the thought of Ratzinger as a potential dialogue partner for evangelicals which offers hope for the future, since Dr McGlinchey shows that there is sufficient consonance to encourage further work. Indeed there is even the suggestion that in this more demanding work of dialogue both sides may have wisdom and mutual correctives to offer the other. Perhaps it is not surprising that an author who practices and teaches Missiology, is able to set out the relationship between salvation and ecclesiology in a way which enables fresh approaches for mission. Even in the classic struggles of the past – over purgatory or the role of Mary, about which the author is realistic, new opportunities for convergence are shown to be possible. Dr McGlinchey has shown this may be attributed to closer attention both to Scripture and to hermeneutics as well as to a lively emphasis on the need for a deep personal commitment to Christ which he finds both in Ratzinger and Evangelicalism.

One can only hope that this study will resource further mutual understanding between the two traditions as well as offering a way of engagement which may help other ecclesial traditions in their ongoing ecumenical exploration and collaboration.

Canon Dr Christina Baxter
Nottingham
May 2016

Acknowledgements

I would like to take this opportunity to express my thanks to all those who have played a part in the development of this writing project. I owe my doctoral supervisor, Rev. Professor Stephen N. Williams a huge debt of gratitude for his encouragement, wise counsel and thorough academic rigour throughout. I have also greatly appreciated the input of Dr. Cindy Bennett, my second supervisor, who was involved in some of the final supervisions prior to submission of the thesis. It is also fitting to acknowledge Rev. Dr. James Corkery S.J., an outstanding Ratzinger scholar, whose helpful and appreciative comments gave me greater confidence in my own reading of Benedict's Augustinian theology. My thanks also go to Rev. Professor Vincent Twomey S.V.D., Rev. Dr. Robin Stockitt and Canon Dr. Christina Baxter for their helpful comments at various points in the project. Finally, I would like to thank my wife Helen for her loving support and the valuable time willingly given to proof-reading.

Abbreviations

CDF	Congregation for the Doctrine of the Faith
DLT	Darton, Longman & Todd
ECNT	Exegetical Commentary on the New Testament
JETS	Journal of the Evangelical Theological Society
NICNT	New International Commentary on the New Testament
NPNF	A Select Library of the Nicene and Post-Nicene Fathers of the Christian Church, First Series (Buffalo: Christian Literature Co., 1886; reprint Grand Rapids: Eerdmans, 1980)
PG	Patrologia Graeca (Paris: J. –P. Migne 1857-66)
PL	Patrologia Latina (Paris: J. –P. Migne, 1841-64)
SCM	Student Christian Movement
TWNT	Theologisches Wörterbuch zum Neuen Testament (ed. Gerhard Kittel; Stuttgart: W. Kohlhammer,1960)
VHG	Volk und Haus Gottes in Augustins Lehre von der Kirche (Seiton: Eos Verlag, 1979)
WA	Weimarer Ausgabe. D Martin Luthers Werke: Kritische Gesamtausgabe (Weimar: Hermann Böhlaus Nachfolger, 1883-)
WBC	Word Biblical Commentary

Introduction and Methodology

My own theological journey from Roman Catholicism to Evangelicalism has been the main inspiration behind this study of Joseph Ratzinger's thought. A recurring question for me since that transition began is whether these distinctive traditions are capable of any form of meeting or rapprochement. The sheer plurality of theological outlook within Catholicism has meant that few expressions of contemporary Catholic theology naturally present themselves as bridges to the evangelical tradition.[1] Arguably, it is theological contributions emanating from the charismatic wing of the Catholic church which are the most obvious sources for the type of project that I have in mind. However, as it is shared charismatic experience which often acts as the driver for theological engagement with Evangelicalism or Pentecostalism, it might be argued that this is essentially an *insider* theology too focused on a particular type of religious encounter to warrant wider ecumenical significance.[2] Moreover, the charismatic movement has seemingly passed the heyday of its influence upon the church.

Joseph Ratzinger, Pope Emeritus Benedict XVI, emerges as a much more weighty dialogue partner. He was not only leader of the Roman Catholic church but is someone whose theological and ecclesiastical pedigree mark him out as having an authoritative voice when it comes to measuring the potential inherent in any ecumenical proposal. Ratzinger was an influential peritus at Vatican II and along with Rahner, Küng and de Lubac was among the chief architects of the Council. His long-term role as senior doctrinal advisor to John Paul II confirms his ability not only to articulate Catholic doctrine but to assess accurately the parameters within which orthodox doctrine may be expressed. One could legitimately assert that any model for rapprochement between Catholics and evangelicals which was broadly commensurate with Ratzinger's theology would have significant ecumenical potential.

The possibility of creating a credible bridge between the two traditions turns on the definition of Evangelicalism. It would be disingenuous to ignore the fact that most historic expressions of Evangelicalism have been deeply suspicious of the Roman Catholic church and that ecumenical progress has been slow on that account. However, it is my contention that parts of Evangelicalism have undergone an ecumenical thaw and that a new situation

---

[1] For examples of the diversity of perspective within Catholicism see the following range of disparate publications: Hans Küng, *On Being A Christian* (London: Fount, 1977); Gustavo Gutiérrez, *A Theology of Liberation: History, Politics and Salvation* (Maryknoll NY: Orbis Books, 1988); Paul F. Knitter, *No Other Name?: A Critical Survey of Christian Attitudes Toward the World Religions* (Maryknoll NY: Orbis Books, 1985) and Scott Hahn and Kimberley Hahn, *Rome Sweet Home* (San Francisco: Ignatius Press, 1993).

[2] While publications from the charismatic tradition such as Leon-Joseph Suenens' *A New Pentecost* (London: DLT, 1975) display a broader ecumenical vision, many of the writings from this stable focus on issues which are mainly of interest to charismatic evangelicals and Pentecostals.

obtains.³ Thus, while some key voices within Evangelicalism still regard Catholicism with a substantial measure of mistrust⁴, and this outlook is magnified amongst Fundamentalists who query the definition of Roman Catholicism as a Christian denomination⁵, there is an increasing number of individuals who are actively supportive of an ecumenical rapprochement between the two traditions.⁶ It is to this already existing constituency that one would seek to construct an ecumenical bridge.

From a methodological perspective, I would propose that Evangelicalism be understood as a system of belief and practice with identifiable historical and theological distinctives that are acknowledged by all. This line has been followed because there is no contemporary figure within Evangelicalism who can adequately represent such a disparate grouping or be perceived as the quintessential theological embodiment of the tradition.

Historian Mark A. Noll speaks for many when he suggests that amid the bewildering diversity of Evangelicalisms there are four characteristic marks of the tradition which fundamentally describe most of those who call themselves evangelicals or who are identified as such by outside observers.⁷ These four marks are derived from David Bebbington's classic study, *Evangelicalism in Modern Britain*, and are said by that author to collectively 'form a quadrilateral of priorities that is the basis of Evangelicalism.'⁸ Bebbington neatly sums up these defining characteristics as Conversionism, Activism, Biblicism and Crucicentrism. These categories will inform my critique of Ratzinger at various points (particularly the closing chapter of the study which explores the ecumenical barriers in Ratzinger's theology) as well as function as a working definition of Evangelicalism throughout the work.⁹ All

---

³ See Mark A. Noll's account of changing attitudes to Catholicism within Evangelicalism in his 'History of the Encounter: Roman Catholics and Protestant Evangelicals' in *Evangelicals and Catholics Together: Working Towards A Common Mission* (ed. Charles Colson and Richard Neuhaus SJ; London: Hodder & Stoughton, 1996), pp. 81-114.
⁴ See R. Albert Mohler Jr's contribution, 'Confessional Evangelicalism' in *Four Views on the Spectrum of Evangelicalism* (ed. Stanley N. Gundry, Andrew David Naselli and Collin Hansen; Grand Rapids: Zondervan, 2011), pp. 84-86.
⁵ See Kevin T. Bauder, 'Fundamentalism' in *Four Views on the Spectrum of Evangelicalism*, pp. 31-2.
⁶ This outlook is exemplified in the Agreed Statement 'Evangelicals and Catholics Together' published in Colson and Neuhaus (ed.), *Evangelicals and Catholics Together*, pp. xv-xxxiii.
⁷ Noll, 'History of the Encounter' in *Evangelicals and Catholics Together*, p. 104.
⁸ David W. Bebbington, *Evangelicalism in Modern Britain: A History from the 1730s to the 1980s* (Grand Rapids: Baker House, 1992), p. 3.
⁹ The publication *Four Views on the Spectrum of Evangelicalism* helpfully delineates the main schools of contemporary Evangelicalism as Fundamentalism, Confessional Evangelicalism, Generic Evangelicalism and Postconservative Evangelicalism. Whilst the writers representing the first two approaches do not acknowledge the possibility of theological rapprochement with Roman Catholicism, John Stackhouse (articulating the 'generic evangelical' outlook) is ecumenically open and defines Evangelicalism in terms

this is not to suggest that personalities or theological constructs are irrelevant to the characterization of Evangelicalism. Landmark figures in the evangelical historical consciousness, Luther and Calvin in particular, are given consideration, as is a core doctrinal conviction (the doctrine of imputed righteousness) which many evangelicals view as essential to orthodoxy.[10]

The focus on Augustinianism as a defining characteristic of Ratzinger's theology may be justified on two counts. First, it is a matter of record that Ratzinger is a thoroughgoing Augustinian and therefore any consideration of his theology must give due weight to the decisive influence exerted by Augustine on his thought. Second, Augustine is the figure in pre-Reformation church history whose theology has had the most profound impact on evangelicals and who is claimed by some as one of their own.[11] It would be reasonable to conclude that if ecumenical potential were to be sought in Ratzinger's theology, the Augustinian emphases would be the natural starting point for any enquiry.

The publication itself follows a logical order in that the question being examined demands a series of investigations which allow certain judgments to be made of Ratzinger.

Chapter one offers an overview of his life and thought with particular attention paid to biographical and academic influences which helped form his own unique theological outlook. At the close of the chapter it will be intimated to the reader that Joseph Ratzinger has followed a consistent theological vision and that particular critical 'moments' in his theological journey ('milestones' as he referred to them in his autobiography) were to determine the eventual shape of his theology. Some of the currents and impulses identified in this opening chapter will reappear at various points in the study.

Chapter two explores Ratzinger's credibility as a dialogue partner with the evangelical tradition. Arguably, an erstwhile liberal whose conservatism is contingent upon which way the ecclesiastical wind is blowing cannot be a fitting candidate for serious ecumenical consideration. The chapter provides evidence from Ratzinger's biography, theological method and the key publication of his so-called progressive period that he was essentially orthodox and that many of his core convictions were mirrored in the 'five fundamentals' associated with the Fundamentalist controversy of the 1920s. However, the point is made that his articulation of these views is coloured by the theological milieu in which he was working. The chapter closes with an exploration of Ratzinger's ecclesiology in which a substantial change of outlook did occur. It is suggested that the shift in perspective came about as the result of an

---

similar to those set out in this introduction. If there is a type of Evangelicalism to which Ratzinger is a bridge, it is closest in description to this one. See John G. Stackhouse Jr., 'Generic Evangelicalism' in Gundry et al (ed.), *Four Views*, pp. 118-142.

[10] See John Piper, *The Future of justification: A Response to N.T. Wright* (Nottingham: IVP, 2008), pp. 21-25.

[11] See James Buchanan, *The Doctrine of Justification* Reprint (Edinburgh: Banner of Truth Trust, 1997).

underlying theological conservatism which had been with him since the early days of his academic formation.

Chapter three engages with the question of Ratzinger's Augustinianism. The aim is to explore the nature of his Augustinian outlook and gauge its significance for evangelicals. It is demonstrated that some of his theological instincts mirror those of Protestant Augustinianism and that he has a markedly anti-Pelagian soteriology. Consideration of his early doctoral thesis on Augustine underscores where he is at variance with a strongly individualistic view of salvation, and a brief treatment of reason highlights a second area of his Augustinian thought that is at odds with traditional Evangelicalism. The section on the love of God highlights where there are remarkable points of convergence with evangelicals, whilst the concluding section explores Augustine's impact on the evangelical tradition in order to identify ecumenical possibilities.

Chapter four addresses the subject of soteriology in greater depth. Here, Augustinian themes come to the fore as I explore a number of issues associated with the topics of grace and justification. Questions regarding whether a Protestant reading of Augustine is warranted and whether Ratzinger agrees with Küng on the matter of justification form the backdrop to my own assessment of Ratzinger's perspective on soteriology. The discussion ends on a paradoxical note in that I observe an apparent contradiction in Ratzinger's approach to the sacraments.

Chapter five highlights those elements in Ratzinger's theology most likely to prove to be impediments in terms of ecumenical rapprochement. The first of these is his doctrine of the church which seems to have been profoundly influenced by two Augustinian themes: 'pure relations' and the *totus Christos*. The discussion addresses the issue of how congenial these themes are to a mainstream evangelical ecclesiology. The other main area of projected difficulty, his theology of the sacraments, is explored with specific reference to his understanding of conversion and faith. It is here that Ratzinger's thought evidences some ambivalence over the interplay between sacramentalism and the existential act of faith. It is my contention that ecumenical progress will be predicated on a mining of the ambivalences. The chapter ends with a critical reverse test in which I measure Ratzinger's commitment to a theology of grace against his published thought on two themes of Catholic theology deemed to be inimical to Evangelicalism: Purgatory and Mariology.

The study concludes with a brief overview of my findings and some suggestions for fruitful ecumenical dialogue. No reference is made to Benedict's resignation or the final months of his Papacy as virtually the entirety of the study was written prior to these events taking place.

CHAPTER 1

The Life and Thought of Joseph Ratzinger

Introduction

Joseph Ratzinger has provoked controversy and inspired admiration in almost equal measure over the course of his long career. In the first English-language biography of his life a comparison drawn between his experience and that of Christ sums up the public impact of the man destined to be Pope. John L. Allen comments that '[l]ike another child whose parents were Joseph and Mary, [Joseph] Ratzinger grew up to become a sign of contradiction, a scandal to some and a sort of savior to others.'[1]

These polarized responses relate mainly to his role as Prefect of the Congregation for the Doctrine of the Faith. This was a watchdog body responsible, among other things, for ensuring that heterodox opinions were not promoted in the name of the Catholic church. This high profile post, which he held for 23 years of John Paul II's pontificate, catapulted him to worldwide prominence but also earned him a media reputation that was to dog the early years of his papacy. Tabloid epithets such as 'God's Rottweiler' and 'Panzerkardinal' presented to the general public the image of a one-dimensional character who rabidly prosecuted heresy with little regard for tact, subtlety or even due process.

Irrespective of this media portrayal, even his fiercest critics concede that Ratzinger possesses remarkable theological expertise as well as a thorough understanding of the opinions over which his Consistory had sat in judgment.[2] The problem with him lay not in his competence, but rather in a sense that he had compromised his own liberal convictions for the sake of a prominent position within the church hierarchy. Tracey Rowland probably overstates the case when she characterizes the negative perception of Ratzinger as that of a 'Vicar of Bray, a tergiversator who tacks to and fro with changes in the theological breeze in order to advance his place in the hierarchy.[3] However, there is little question that his detractors see him as having made at least one dramatic sea change during the period of his academic career. For this reason, it has been asserted that

---

[1] John L. Allen Jr., *Cardinal Ratzinger: The Vatican's Enforcer of the Faith* (New York: Continuum, 2000), p. 2.
[2] Ratzinger's high level of attainment as a theologian is evidenced by Hans Küng's commendation of him as an equal. See Hans Küng, *My Struggle for Freedom: Memoirs* (Grand Rapids: Eerdmans, 2003), p. 452.
[3] Tracey Rowland, *Ratzinger's Faith: The Theology of Pope Benedict XVI* (Oxford: Oxford University Press, 2008), p.11.

[p]erhaps the biggest question facing a commentator on Joseph Ratzinger's career is why he renounced the liberal instincts that made him a champion of reform at the Second Vatican Council (1962-1965) for the ardent conservatism that marked his long tenure as Prefect of the CDF.[4]

Whether one has to see Ratzinger's life in such a straightforward light is a moot point. Commentators favourable to him will cite his own radical disclaimer that it was counterparts in the world of *Concilium* who changed and not he[5], while some of those on the extreme fringes of traditionalist Catholicism will parade his later theological work as evidence of a continued liberal bias.[6] The opinions about him are so diverse and contradictory that consensus may never be achieved. Nevertheless, the price of accepting agnosticism as to the true nature of Ratzinger's theology is something which no serious student should be willing to pay. A decision must be reached, however tentative, about the consistency of the former Pontiff's theological legacy.

With that goal partially in mind, the following introduction will pay particular attention to how his regional background, war experience, early theological formation and on-going academic and ecclesiastical progress shed light on what are his core theological convictions and whether or not these have changed. I am deliberately devoting least space to his role as Prefect of the CDF as this period of his life was largely marked by disputes with dissident theologians.[7] This initial orientation to Ratzinger's thought will influence the development of later chapters in which I explore his theology with reference to the evangelical tradition. It will also pave the way for the second chapter which focuses largely on his most seminal publication, *Introduction to Christianity*[8], a work which tells us much about his core theological orientation in the wake of the Second Vatican Council.

Bavarian Origins

Joseph Aloys Ratzinger is the product of one of the most distinctively Catholic regions in the world. Commenting on the Bavaria of what would have been the theologian's early childhood, historian Ian Kershaw describes a thriving religious culture marked by

---

[4] Rupert Shortt, *Benedict XVI: Commander of the Faith* (London: Hodder & Stoughton, 2005), p.1.
[5] Joseph Ratzinger and Vittorio Messorri, *The Ratzinger Report* (San Francisco: Ignatius Press, 1985), pp. 18-19.
[6] See Patrick J. Pollock, '101 Heresies of Antipope Benedict XVI,' http://www.patrickpollock.com/101heresiesofbenedictxvitract2.html (accessed May 10, 2008).
[7] Here Ratzinger spoke in his formal capacity as policeman of the church and for this reason it is difficult to draw conclusions about his own personal outlook.
[8] Joseph Ratzinger, *Introduction to Christianity* (San Francisco: Ignatius Press, 1990).

> ... an extraordinary degree of inner strength, cohesion, unity and vitality ... Student organisations flourished as never before, Parents' Associations and Mothers' Unions furthered the vital emphasis laid upon Catholic education and youth work. 'The Catholic Press Association for Bavaria' supplied 660 public libraries in Bavaria with over half a million volumes on Catholic matters, and distributed brochures and pamphlets, laid on films and lectures, and shared in the publication of thirteen daily newspapers. Catholic values were also reinforced through an upsurge of popular missionary activity, much of it carried out by the still expanding religious orders.[9]

It was into this profoundly Catholic milieu that the young Joseph Ratzinger was born on Holy Saturday, April 16th, 1927. His birth, sandwiched between Good Friday and Easter Sunday, presaged a life that was to find its meaning entirely within the parameters of the church. His autobiography offers a clue as to why religion should have played such a key role. More than anything else it was a love affair with the liturgy. His early exposure to the Eucharist, made accessible to him by a series of missals in which the Latin Mass was translated into German, profoundly moved him and set the course of his future life.

> Every new step into the liturgy was a great event for me. Each new book I was given was something precious to me, and I could not dream of anything more beautiful. It was a riveting adventure to move by degrees into the mysterious world of the liturgy, which was being enacted before us and for us on the altar. It was becoming ever more clear to me that here I was encountering a reality that no-one had simply thought up, a reality that no official authority or great individual had created.[10]

Apart from the marked influence of Catholic worship, it is impossible to consider Ratzinger's Bavarian roots without reference to the impact of Nazi rule on someone who was six years of age when Hitler became Chancellor. The issue is touched upon indirectly by Ratzinger himself when he refers to his policeman father's refusal to co-operate with the Nazi authorities in the harassment of local clergy.[11] This suggests that there was little, by way of family influence, that would have encouraged him to view Nazism as anything other than an insidious ideology. Moreover, the attitude of the local parish priest may only have intensified the young Ratzinger's unease with the regime. The words of the following sermon, preached by Fr Josef Stelzle on the Feast of Epiphany 1934, are preserved in a police report written after his arrest.

---

[9] Ian Kershaw, *Popular Opinion and Political Dissent in the Third Reich: Bavaria 1933-1945* (Oxford: Oxford University Press, 1983), p. 184 cited in Aidan Nichols OP, *The Thought of Pope Benedict XVI: An Introduction to the Theology of Joseph Ratzinger* (London: Burns & Oats, 2007), p. 9.

[10] Joseph Ratzinger, *Milestones: Memoirs 1927-1977* (San Francisco: Ignatius Press, 1998), pp. 19-20.

[11] Joseph Ratzinger, *Milestones*, p.14.

> Christ was born for all and died for all, white, yellow and black. Today there are movements who do not want this to be true, who want a falsified Aryan Christ. These populist movements preach a so-called positive Christianity, a German Christianity which gives the overlords credibility, and which brings disease over the people. Beware of these false prophets! Ask yourself whether they mean the real Christ, the child of Jews, who was born in Bethlehem.[12]

Ratzinger's memoirs hint that his ability to avoid seduction by the regime might also have been aided by the classical education he received in the *Gymnasium* at Traunstein. The fact that none of the Classics teachers could be prevailed upon to join the party, and that two of the headmasters had been removed from office by the Nazis, are taken as indicators by the mature Ratzinger that the study of Greek and Roman antiquity is a form of insulation against ideological brainwashing. He notes in passing that he was one of the final group of students to be allowed to complete their education at the *Gymnasium* under the old classical system.[13]

What theological inspiration might the young Ratzinger have drawn from these experiences and how might they have had an influence on his later thought? Whilst it is difficult to speculate, I would suggest that there are two possible inferences one can make. First, with regard to his encounter with the liturgy: if the comments from *Milestones* reflect accurately his state of mind at the time, we may be privy to what could be defined as the formation of a mindset or an orientation. The young Ratzinger's earliest religious instinct seems to have been an intuitive sense of the church as the repository of something divinely given. Whilst this took place in regard to the liturgy itself, it may be suggested that it had much further ramifications, since a strong bond exists between liturgy and dogmatic belief. An anecdotal illustration which might support this contention is a remark made by his erstwhile colleague, Hans Küng. Writing in the first volume of his *Memoirs*, Küng notes that some deep-seated pious instinct was at work 'inhibiting' Ratzinger's theology. After having asked rhetorically, '... how so gifted, friendly, open a theologian as Joseph Ratzinger can undergo such a change: from progressive Tübingen theologian to Roman Grand Inquisitor,'[14] Küng concludes that
'even in Tübingen my colleague, who for all his friendliness always seems distant and cool, had kept something like an unenlightened "devotional corner" in his Bavarian heart.'[15]

What this might have amounted to is fleshed out in comments Küng makes on his colleague Hermann Häring's work on Ratzinger:

---

[12] Cited by Allen in *Cardinal Ratzinger* (p. 21.) The priest was temporarily banished but returned to the locale within the year and remained there throughout the war.
[13] Ratzinger, *Milestones*, p. 24.
[14] Küng, *My Struggle for Freedom*, p. 457.
[15] Küng, *My Struggle for Freedom*, p. 457..

> In an acute analysis of more than 200 pages, Professor Hermann Häring, my assistant in Tübingen at the time, shows how from the beginning "Theology and Ideology in Joseph Ratzinger" (2002) have been interwoven. He simply didn't put certain questions to himself; he always had a skeptical attitude towards modern exegesis [i.e. historical critical], and was open to historical arguments only to a limited degree.[16]

Although this point will need further development later, one can see how his early liturgical experiences may have played a part in Ratzinger's thought never trespassing too far beyond orthodoxy. One might also note that his encounter with the Liturgy stimulated a more devotional approach to the practice of theology than that of some of his more *avant-garde* colleagues. This, too, will have contributed to him being set apart from those who were willing to question the whole 'Roman package', as it were. Hans Küng's early memories of him conjure up the impression of someone whose theology is intimately linked to his spirituality.

> He seems to me very friendly, though perhaps not completely open, whereas to him I possibly seem all too spontaneous and direct. For me he is more a *"timido"* with an invisible spiritual anointing, whereas to him I perhaps seem audacious, with more worldly charms.[17]

Second, his high estimation of the value of a classical education in a time of upheaval, the other outcome of his Bavarian experience, offers a clue as to why Ratzinger seems always to have been doctrinally orthodox. Perhaps the lesson of his educational background under the Nazis was that regard for antiquity leaves one much less susceptible to the spirit of the age. Whether or not this can be established, however, it is a matter of record that Ratzinger the theologian was opposed to attempts at supplanting credal definitions by recourse to 'modern exegesis.'[18]

War Experience

Ratzinger's experience of war has been understood in largely negative terms by critical biographers such as John L. Allen.[19] The standard complaint made is that his family kept a low profile during the Nazi years and failed to actively oppose the regime. This is in contrast to some Communists, Jehovah's Witnesses, and even fellow Catholics in the district who are said to have openly challenged the Nazi authorities.[20] It is difficult to know how much credence to

---

[16] Küng, *My Struggle for Freedom*, p. 458.
[17] Küng, *My Struggle for Freedom*, p. 229.
[18] Ratzinger, *Milestones*, pp. 125-26.
[19] See also David Gibson, *Rule of Benedict: Pope Benedict XVI and His Battle with the Modern World* (New York:HarperSanFrancisco, 2006), pp. 137-8 and Shortt, *Commander of the Faith*, pp. 15-17.
[20] Allen, *Cardinal Ratzinger*, pp. 17-21.

give such an interpretation of events, as Ratzinger has alluded to at least one occasion on which his father's hostility to the regime placed his life in jeopardy.[21] Where Allen may be on more certain ground, however, is his contention that the war had helped nurture in Ratzinger a particular perspective on church and culture. The manner in which Allen characterizes this development is not intended to give the reader confidence in Ratzinger's judgment. The lesson the future Prefect is said to have learnt is that political totalitarianism can only be effectively countered by ecclesial totalitarianism.

What is interesting about such a barbed criticism is that the same core idea, communicated in less pejorative language, approximates quite closely to the outlook that Joseph Ratzinger had as Prefect of the CDF. He clearly did feel that when the faithful were in danger of being seduced by a powerful and insidious *Zeitgeist*, and theologians had aided such a state of affairs, the church's only recourse was to restrict the freedom of the theologians so that what the church taught remained utterly unambiguous. Allen may be correct, therefore, that living through such apocalyptic times as Germany in the Third Reich would have helped instill in Ratzinger a sense that the church's message had to be preserved at all costs even if this entailed keeping a tight rein on the pronouncements of theologians.

The impact of Ratzinger's teenage military experience on his theology is difficult to gauge. Perhaps the most telling fact is that his circumstances enabled him to avoid the sort of compromising moral situations that tainted other future Catholic priests.[22] His exposure to military life began at age 16 when he was drafted, along with several other junior seminarians, into the batteries of the anti-aircraft defence in Munich. Even here he seems to have had little personal animosity towards the Allies and speaks of himself and his classmates coming to look at the imminent invasion of France as a 'sign of hope.'[23] His army service proper began on September 20th 1944 when he was attached to a labour detail in Burgenland. Here he rubbed shoulders with a number of fanatical Nazi ideologues who victimized him on account of his aspirations to the priesthood. His posting lasted three months and after a hiatus of a further few months he was assigned to the infantry barracks at Traunstein. At the end of April 1945 he left the barracks and made for home, having effectively chosen to desert the German army. Ratzinger's house was to become the Allied Headquarters after the invasion of Germany and the

---

[21] An incident is referred to in *Milestones* (pp. 36-37) in which his father openly expressed his ire against Hitler to two SS men who had been billeted at their home during the war. Additionally, prior to Hitler's assumption of power, Ratzinger's father (as a policeman) took positions against Nazi violence at public meetings. See Ratzinger, *Milestones*, p. 12.

[22] In 1969 it was disclosed that the auxillary bishop of Munich, Matthias Defregger, while a captain in the Wehrmacht, enforced an order to execute civilian hostages. See Allen, *Cardinal Ratzinger*, p. 30.

[23] Ratzinger, *Milestones*, p. 32.

teenager, having been identified as a soldier, was made a prisoner of war for a few months. He was eventually released on June 19th 1945.

Theological Formation

It is impossible to appreciate how Joseph Ratzinger was formed as a theologian without setting German Catholic theology in its historical context. For centuries Catholicism had functioned as a minority faith within Germany and this meant that over time it had adapted itself to the wider culture in which it subsisted.[24] This accommodation was nowhere more prevalent than in the field of theological training. Church historian Thomas Bokenkotter outlines how the impact of rationalism within the dominant Protestant culture had a profound effect on the way Catholic theology developed. He notes that,

> As the only Catholic community in the world with theological schools located in the secular universities, they [German Catholics] were forced to keep in touch with scientific developments and so were acutely aware of the need of the Church to face realistically the problems raised by modern culture. They saw that the Church could only deal effectively with the arguments raised by the rationalists by emulating their spirit of scientific impartiality. And so the German Catholic scholars broke away from the obsolete Scholastic texts and developed new scientific methods to defend the faith, with intellectual freedom presupposed as a sine qua non.[25]

Bokenkotter's analysis of the Catholic theological scene is borne out by Ratzinger's own reminiscences of his early days in the seminary at Freising. Here an avid spirit of intellectual enquiry prevailed amongst the seminarians as they explored the latest currents in scientific and philosophical thought. Ratzinger highlights their excitement at breakthroughs in the natural sciences by Planck, Heisenberg, and Einstein which were thought to open up the world of science again to the possibility of God[26] as well as the profound impact made by the philosophy of personalism.[27] Indeed, Ratzinger himself describes the encounter with personalism as a spiritual experience that left an essential mark.[28] It is not surprising that in the face of such exciting developments he found the thought of Thomas Aquinas, as it was siphoned through neo-

---

[24] Gibson, *Rule of Benedict*, p. 124.
[25] Thomas Bokenkotter, *A Concise History of the Catholic Church* (New York: Doubleday, 2004), p. 309 cited in Gibson, *Rule of Benedict*, p. 124.
[26] Ratzinger, *Milestones*, p. 43. He cites, in particular, Aloys Wenzel's *Philosophy of Freedom* 'which tried to show that the determinist worldview of classical physics, which had left no room for God, was now dispelled by an open conception of the world in which there was room for something new, unforeseen and incalculable.'
[27] Ratzinger, *Milestones*, p. 44.
[28] Ratzinger, *Milestones*, p.44. It is relevant, in terms of Ratzinger's future collaboration with John Paul II, that the latter was also profoundly impacted by personalism.

Scholastic texts books, to be 'too closed in on itself, too impersonal and ready-made.'[29]

After a two year study of philosophy in the seminary at Freising, Ratzinger proceeded to the Theology Faculty at Munich where his aim was 'to become more fully familiar with the intellectual debates of the time ... so as to be able to devote [himself] to teaching theology as a profession.'[30]

The grounding he received here marked all of his later thought and fitted perfectly with the picture of German theological education presented by Bokenkotter. Dogmatic Theology was taught by Michael Schmaus whose approach owed little to the neo-Scholastic way of doing things but was deeply indebted to Scripture and the study of the Church Fathers. One must note the obvious similarities between Schmaus and those theologians associated with 'back-to-the-sources' *ressourcement* Catholicism.

The star of the Munich Faculty was Friedrich Wilhelm Maier, a New Testament scholar who, decades previously, had been dismissed from his chair on the grounds of modernism. Ratzinger notes that this had left Maier with a permanent distaste both for Rome and the Archbishop of Munich. The elderly but popular Professor remained an ardent practitioner of the historical critical method and the mature Ratzinger was to acknowledge his debt to that form of teaching.

> [T]he candid questions from the perspective of the liberal-historical-critical-method created a new directness in the approach to Sacred Scripture and opened up dimensions of the text that were no longer perceived by the all-too-determined dogmatic reading. As a result the Bible spoke with a new immediacy and freshness.[31]

However, engagement with the thought of Romano Guardini had also alerted him to a deficiency in Maier's approach. It became clear to him that it was not enough to 'look on dogma ... [as only] a shackle, a negation, and a limit in the construction of theology.'[32] With his mentor, he saw the value of the history of dogma and began to question the prevailing assumption among many in the Munich Faculty that dogmatic constraints hindered the development of Christian thought. Given this early dissatisfaction with the liberal approach, it makes sense that at some future point Ratzinger might find himself at odds with representatives of Catholic theology who wished to sever the link with dogma and develop a schema for Christian faith that was entirely dependent on the historical critical method. Indeed, in a striking passage from *Milestones* in which he questions the way in which certain notions about the 'material completeness of Scripture' had been developed at Vatican II, we are given a

---

[29] Ratzinger, *Milestones*, p. 44.
[30] Ratzinger, *Milestones*, p. 47.
[31] Ratzinger, *Milestones*, p. 52.
[32] Ratzinger, *Milestones*, p. 52.

glimpse of what Ratzinger thought was the fundamental difficulty of subjugating theology to the vagaries of biblical scholarship.

> There was talk [at the Council] of the material completeness of the Bible in matters of faith. This 'catchword' which was regarded as a great new realization, just as quickly became detached from its point of departure in the interpretation of the Tridentine decree. It was now asserted that the inevitable consequence of this realization was that the church could not teach anything that was not contained in Scripture.
> [However] ... since the interpretation of Scripture was identified with the historical-critical method, this meant that nothing could be taught by the Church that could not pass the scrutiny of the historical-critical method. This new theory meant that exegesis became the highest authority in the Church; and since, by the very nature of human reason and historical work, no agreement among interpreters can be expected in the case of such difficult texts, all of this meant that faith had to retreat into the region of the indeterminate and constantly changing that characterizes historical or would-be historical hypotheses. In other words, believing now amounted to having opinions and was in need of constant revision.[33]

The influence of Guardini, though profound in Ratzinger's life, was eclipsed by that of the great Latin Church Father, Augustine.[34] What was to become his doctoral thesis, *The People and the House of God in Augustine's Doctrine of the Church*, had been a topic originally suggested to him by Gottlieb Söhngen, the Professor of Fundamental Theology in Munich. It was completed in the run-up to his ordination to the priesthood on the Feast of St Peter and St Paul in 1951 and is the root of much of his subsequent theology.[35] Also significant at this time was his engagement with Henri de Lubac's book *Catholicism* which not only shed more light on Augustine but familiarized the young Ratzinger with the themes of *ressourcement* theology. Vincent Twomey, writing with Ratzinger's later struggles in mind, suggests that it was this

> Early research into Augustine's view of the Church that provided the inspiration he later needed to combat various misunderstandings of the Council, not least the mistaken attempt to view the Church as the People of God in more or less empirical or sociological terms.[36]

---

[33] Ratzinger, *Milestones*, pp. 125-6.
[34] In a 1969 publication, Ratzinger acknowledges the pre-eminent place this Church Father had even then in his theology: 'Augustine has kept me company for more than twenty years. I have developed my theology in dialogue with Augustine, though naturally I have tried to conduct this dialogue as a man of today.' J. Ratzinger, 'Glaube, Geschichte und Philosophie. Zum Echo Auf *Einführung in das Christentum*', *Hochland* 61 (1969), p. 543 cited in Nichols, *The Thought of Pope Benedict XVI*, p. 17.
[35] D. Vincent Twomey, *Pope Benedict XVI: The Conscience of our Age* (San Francisco: Ignatius Press, 2005), p. 51.
[36] Twomey, *Conscience of our Age*, p.51.

This judgment is significant, if true, because it would indicate that from an early stage of Ratzinger's work as a theologian he was wary of the idea that only the majority opinion among those currently still alive is the *sensus fidelium*. Given that such an 'empirical' or 'sociological' view of the 'people of God' was a defining attitude of many who sought change in the wake of Vatican II, one can clearly see grounds for future disagreement between Ratzinger and them. The real issue, though, in terms of whether Ratzinger changed or not, is how much correlation or continuity there was between the views of the later Ratzinger and the mindset of the young graduate student studying Augustine. The submission of Ratzinger's *Habilitation* thesis, the mandatory second thesis required for anyone wishing to secure a university Professorship in Germany, was to be an occasion of great consternation to him. Contrary to expectations, he was informed by Michael Schmaus that his work had failed to meet the necessary academic standards. This was a disastrous outcome, given that failure meant the end of Ratzinger's hopes of an academic career. With the support of Söhngen, he was given permission to re-submit the thesis in a radically revised form. The work was completed in an astonishingly short space of time and in February of 1957 his *Habilitation* was duly granted.

Ratzinger concluded that Schmaus had not only taken personal affront at the thesis[37], but had also been affected by rumours about the student's modernism.[38] An explanation about the background to the thesis will put Schmaus' concerns in perspective. Having done substantial work in Patristics, Söhngen, his supervisor, had felt that it would be helpful for Ratzinger to focus on the Middle Ages. The latter agreed and settled on the theme of revelation to complement the work previously done on ecclesiology. At that time, 'Salvation History', an idea originally developed within Protestantism, was an important area of Catholic theological enquiry and Ratzinger's task was to explore whether anything corresponding to it was present in the work of Bonaventure (another Augustinian!) and, if so, whether this had any bearing on the idea of revelation.

The project was an implicit criticism of the prevailing notion of revelation which Ratzinger had already believed to be too limited. His conclusion was that nothing in Bonaventure bore much reference to the idea of revelation that was currently in vogue within Catholicism. For in the high Middle ages, he asserted,

> "revelation" is always a concept denoting an act. The word refers to the act in which God shows himself, not to the objectified result of this act. And because this is so, the receiving subject is also part of the concept of revelation. Where there is no-one to receive revelation, no re-*vel*-ation has

---

[37] Ratzinger, *Milestones*, p. 108. Ratzinger's work had presumed that certain stances *vis-à-vis* Medieval Studies promoted by Schmaus were now outmoded.

[38] Ratzinger, *Milestones*, p. 109.

occurred, because no *veil* has been removed. By definition, revelation requires a someone who apprehends it.[39]

His understanding of the implications of Bonaventure's theology, as seen in the following quotation, serves to both canonize some of the presuppositions of the 'salvation history' school, as well as offer a new starting point for a defence of the 'two sources of revelation' theory defined at Trent. Ratzinger suggests that if Bonaventure is right,

> ... then revelation precedes Scripture and becomes deposited in Scripture, but is not simply identical with it. This in turn means it is always something which is greater than what is merely written down. And this means there can be no such thing as pure Sola Scriptura, because an essential element of Scripture is the church as understanding subject, and with this the fundamental sense of tradition is already given.[40]

Whilst Schmaus read these conclusions as opening the door to a dangerous subjectivising of revelation, and acted accordingly, Ratzinger clearly wants his readers to understand the argument as securing tradition a place within the act of revelation itself and therefore a legitimate Catholic idea to have pursued. Seen in that light, one can read his intentions as orthodox, that, as he put it in his first interview with Peter Seewald, his 'impulse [had been] to free up the essential kernel of the faith from encrustations and to give this kernel strength and dynamism.'[41] However, that should not lead anyone to the conclusion that he was perceived as orthodox at the time. His willingness to question and his pioneering stance *vis-à-vis* a major theme of Fundamental Theology would have left him deeply suspect. Even Twomey, who is an unequivocal supporter of Ratzinger's, acknowledges that 'compared to the established theology of the day, he was liberal and progressive, not to say revolutionary.'[42] However, the point must not be lost that this was in contrast to a pre-Vatican II neo-Scholastic theology which at that time appeared set in stone.

Academic and Ecclesiastical Progress

After successfully obtaining his *Habilitation* he began work on January 1st 1958 as Professor of Fundamental Theology and Dogma in the college at Freising. Ratzinger, commenting on that period, notes that the frosty relationship with

---

[39] Ratzinger, *Milestones*, p. 108. Ratzinger's memories of his argumentation as they are recorded in the autobiography.
[40] Ratzinger, *Milestones*, p. 109. We shall later re-visit the question of 'Sola Scriptura' and the degree to which Ratzinger may be deemed to be at odds with this first principle of evangelical theology.
[41] Joseph Cardinal Ratzinger, *Salt of the Earth: The Church at the End of the Millennium [An Interview with Peter Seewald* (San Francisco: Ignatius Press, 1997), p. 79.
[42] Twomey, *Conscience of our Age*, p. 47.

Michael Schmaus had the effect of bolstering his friendship with Karl Rahner.[43] Indeed, Ratzinger seems to have been somewhat in awe of Rahner until the close of Vatican II when he had become less comfortable with the theology of his former mentor.[44] His stay in Freising was surprisingly brief and on April 15th 1959 he was appointed Professor of Fundamental Theology at the University of Bonn. Here he won the respect of Cardinal Frings, the Archbishop of Cologne, and was to become the Bishop's theological advisor (*peritus*) at Vatican II (1962-65), earning with that other precocious academic, Hans Kung, the nickname 'the teenage theologian.'[45]

His memories of Vatican II, outlined in *Milestones,* clearly understate the pivotal progressive role that he played there. Protestant observer at the Council, Robert MacAfee Brown, refers to a crucial anti-curial speech made by Cardinal Frings which had the effect of not only 'blowing the dome off St Peter's' but de-railing the entire conservative agenda at the outset.[46] Whilst not claiming that Ratzinger necessarily penned the speech[47], it is clear that he would not have demurred from the Cardinal's sentiments. In fact, it will be argued later that he lobbied for reform in a way that his own subsequent account fails to sufficiently acknowledge.

The high water mark of Ratzinger's progressivism was to be the Third Session of Vatican II when his scholarly comments served to advance an agenda which he later diligently opposed as Prefect. However, Aidan Nichols is probably right to suggest that Ratzinger's negative reactions to the hierarchical church were short-lived and that even before the close of Vatican II there were signs of a change of mindset.[48] The catalyst for this was the French inspired draft document *Gaudium Et Spes* which Ratzinger felt portrayed an altogether too optimistic assessment of the world. We can see in retrospect that this was when his Augustinian instincts first seriously came into play. In an impassioned piece of writing at the time he claimed that the authors of *Gaudium Et Spes* had

> ...unfortunately dragged beyond the protecting walls of the theology faculty building just those affirmations which theology shares anyhow with any spiritual-ethical picture of man whatsoever. Whereas what is proper to

---

[43] Ratzinger, *Milestones*, p. 113.

[44] According to Ralph M. Wiltgen's history of German influence on Vatican II, *The Rhine flows into the Tiber;* 'Fr Ratzinger ... had seemed to give almost unquestioning support to the views of [Fr Rahner] during the Council. But as it was drawing to a close he admitted that he disagreed on various points, and said he would begin to assert himself more after the Council was over.' Ralph M. Wiltgen, S.V.D., *The Rhine Flows into the Tiber: The Unknown Council* (New York: Hawthorn Books, 1967), p. 285.

[45] Ratzinger was just 35 years old when he travelled to Rome as *peritus.*

[46] Robert MacAfee Brown, *Observer in Rome: A Protestant Report on the Vatican Council* (New York: Doubleday,1967), p. 150 cited in *Cardinal Ratzinger*, p. 46.

[47] As Allen hints in his biography of Ratzinger (pp. 52ff) and Seewald states directly in *Salt of the Earth*, p. 71.

[48] See forthcoming discussion later in this chapter

theology, discourse about Christ and his work, was left behind in a conceptual deep-freeze, and so allowed to appear, in contrast with the understandable part, even more unintelligible and antiquated.[49]

The marked dissonance between Ratzinger and his erstwhile colleagues highlights a fault line between two factions in the progressive camp which may have hitherto gone unnoticed. Ratzinger, with his Augustinian and biblical emphasis, had always seen reform in terms of a return to the original sources so that the Church might be renewed and re-energised. His more liberal colleagues – those identified with *aggiornamento* as opposed to *ressourcement* – were looking in an entirely different direction and sought to make peace, so to speak, with modernity. *Gaudium Et Spes* was the means of unveiling the chasm that was already present. It confirmed that the reforming impulse at Vatican II consisted of two very diverse theological orientations that happened to share the same agenda. Indeed, much of the later conflict between Ratzinger and the post-Conciliar liberals can probably be traced back to this discovery even though the battle lines were only drawn up later.

His career did not remain stationary during the time of the Council. In the summer of 1963 he took up a Professorship at Münster. In *Milestones*, he characterises the Münster period as a time when he first had serious reservations about developments at the Council.[50] He instances a lecture he gave at the University on true and false renewal which had failed to make an impact on his reformist audience, and then details how that message had been repeated in a more forceful way at the Bamberg Catholic Congress of 1966.[51] Interestingly, Cardinal Döpfner of Munich is said to have voiced his surprise at detecting a 'conservative streak' in the young Professor.[52]

However, his time at Münster was also to come to a premature end when, through the strenuous efforts of Hans Küng, he was appointed Professor of Dogma in the Catholic Faculty of Tübingen in the summer of 1966. His experiences here were to be the final catalyst in his movement from Council liberal to ecclesiastical conservative. This is not to say, however, that every indication from the Tübingen years suggested that he was losing his liberal instincts. In his autobiography he states that he looked forward to the collaboration with Küng[53] (who was later to become his nemesis) and, as late as 1968, he was to sign the Nijmegen Declaration on the freedom and rights of the

---

[49] J. Ratzinger, *Ergebnisse und Probleme der dritten Konzilsperiode* (Cologne, 1965), p. 34 cited in Nichols, *The Thought of Pope Benedict XVI*, p. 70.
[50] Ratzinger, *Milestones*, p. 134.
[51] For a translation of this address see Josef Ratzinger, 'Catholicism after the Council' in *The Furrow*, Vol. 18, No. 1 (1 Jan, 1967), pp. 3-23.
[52] Ratzinger, *Milestones*, p. 134.
[53] In *Milestones*, p. 135, he states that the collaboration with Küng remained a possibility for him because he thought that 'the fundamental consensus to be expected among Catholic theologians would remain untouched.'

theologian.[54] Yet even with these counter indicators, it was still clear that Ratzinger was becoming disillusioned with the liberal project. This was highlighted, particularly, by a series of lectures on the Creed which later became *Introduction to Christianity*, his best-selling book and the one in which he took most pride. In the preface, Ratzinger re-tells a German folk tale, *Hans im Glück* ('Lucky Jack') in which a man carrying a burdensome lump of gold exchanged it successively for a horse, a cow, a goose and a whetstone, 'which he finally threw into the water without losing much; on the contrary, what he now gained in exchange, so he thought was the precious gift of freedom.' The warning being communicated was that *avant-garde* theology was in danger of doing a similar thing to the substance of the faith.

However, commentators are agreed that the major factor in thoroughly disillusioning Ratzinger with liberal reform was the student disturbances of 1968. At that tumultuous time the governing intellectual paradigm within the University of Tübingen had become Marxist virtually overnight (previously it had been existentialist) and the two theology faculties were themselves the unlikely locus of unrest. Lecturers suffered verbal abuse and there was an air of revolution which profoundly traumatized Ratzinger. Hans Küng comments that, 'Even for a strong personality like me this was unpleasant. For someone timid like Ratzinger, it was horrifying.'[55] The upshot of these disturbances was that Ratzinger sought a more peaceful locale for the development of his theology.

Fortuitously, a second chair in Dogma had opened up at the new university of Regensburg in Bavaria and this coincided with the fact that his brother Georg was choir master at the city's cathedral. Here was the ideal opportunity, and one of which he happily availed, to find relief from the front-line battle 'against existential reductionism ... in the doctrine of God [as well as] ... the pernicious Marxist threat dressed up in the guise of theology.'[56]

The new and final chapter in his university career was to be the defining one. His eight years at Regensburg (1969 – 1977) witnessed a massive cutting of ties with the liberals with whom he had previously taught and collaborated. This was nowhere more marked than his 1972 resignation from the board of *Concilium*. Reading between the lines it seems that a coterie of previously reform-minded academics who worked alongside him on the International Theological Commission summoned by Paul VI might have played a part in that defection. Certainly de Lubac, and pre-eminently Von Balthasar, have been profound influences on him ever since and it was with these and other former *Concilium* theologians such as Walter Kasper and Karl

---

[54] The actual declaration signed by 1,360 Catholic theologians including Küng, Rahner, Schillebeeckx, Congar, J.B. Metz and Ratzinger asserted that the teaching office of popes and bishops 'cannot and must not supersede, hamper and impede the teaching task of theologians as scholars.' Allen, *Cardinal Ratzinger*, p. 67. For fuller details see 'Scholars Plead For Theological Freedom', *National Catholic Reporter*, January 1, 1969.
[55] Allen, *Cardinal Ratzinger*, p. 116.
[56] Ratzinger, *Milestones*, p. 137.

Lehman that he helped found the rival journal *Communio* in 1974. This realignment with more conservative thinking was further cemented by some writings of a polemical nature which criticised publications by the likes of Hans Küng and Johann Baptist Metz.[57] It seems fairly clear that by this stage the battle lines had been drawn and Ratzinger perceived himself as struggling for the traditional faith in a milieu that was deeply antagonistic to it. In *Milestones* his description of the path trod by Henri de Lubac would very nearly approximate his own. The one who had suffered under the narrowness of the neo-Scholastic regime had shown himself to be 'a decided fighter against the fundamental threat to the faith that now was changing all previous theological positions'.[58]

His elevation to the Archbishopric of Munich and Freising in the summer of 1977 came unexpectedly and it served only to reinforce the image of a doughty conservative. During his brief tenure as Cardinal Archbishop he was to assert the value of truth in a way reminiscent of him in his later role as Prefect of the CDF. Following his mentor Augustine, who was likewise an academic turned Bishop, he was to engage strenuously with any theological viewpoint which he deemed suspect or dangerous. As he stated to Peter Seewald with reference to his Episcopal calling,

> The words of the Church Fathers rang in my ears, those sharp condemnations of shepherds who are like mute dogs; in order to avoid conflicts, they let the poison spread. Peace is not the first civic duty, and a bishop whose only concern is not to have any problems and to gloss over as many conflicts as possible is an image I find repulsive.[59]

His behind-the-scenes role in the Hans Küng affair[60] and his successful attempt to block J.B. Metz from taking up a chair at Munich were to demonstrate that these sentiments were heartfelt.[61] His reputation as a stout defender of the

---

[57] See Ratzinger's criticism of Moltmann and Metz in Joseph Ratzinger, *Eschatology: Death and Eternal Life* (Washington: Catholic University of America Press, 1988) pp. 57-66 cf. *Milestones* p. 135 and his indictment of Küng in Hans Urs von Balthasar et al, *Diskussion über Hans Küngs "Christ sein"* (Mainz: Matthias-Grünewald, 1976). Here Ratzinger speaks of *On Being A Christian* as expressing 'a school certitude, a party certitude, not a certitude for which one can live and die, a certitude for comfortable times in which the ultimate is not demanded.' (*Cardinal Ratzinger,* pp. 128-29.)
[58] Ratzinger, *Milestones*, p. 142.
[59] Ratzinger, *Salt of the Earth*, p. 82.
[60] Allen, *Cardinal Ratzinger*, pp. 129-130. The author cites an interview Ratzinger gave to a German Catholic news agency following a meeting he and other West German cardinals had with Pope John Paul II in Rome. It was in this context that the suggestion was first mooted that Küng might lose his *Missio canonica*. Allen infers from this that Ratzinger may have been involved in the decision to withdraw Küng's licence to teach as a Catholic theologian.
[61] See Karl Rahner's public censure of Ratzinger for this action in *Cardinal Ratzinger*, pp. 125-26. Karl Rahner, 'Ich Protestiere', *Süddeutsche Zeitung*, November 14, 1979.

Papacy was thus assured during his three and a half years as Archbishop and it was not a complete surprise that John Paul II should effectively head-hunt him for the top doctrinal post in the church: Prefect of the Congregation for the Doctrine of the Faith.

During this period Ratzinger was to famously discipline major Catholic theologians who were deemed to have promoted error in the name of the church. Among the most significant of these figures were the following: Charles Curran who lost his position at Catholic University of America as a consequence of his teaching on sexual ethics; Tissa Balisuriya, who was excommunicated for questioning the tenability of belief in original sin and the Marian dogmas (this was the only case of excommunication); Leonardo Boff, who was silenced on account of his approach to ecclesiology and his flirtation with Marxism; and Jesuit, Roger Haight, whose *Missio canonica* was withdrawn as a result of promoting a seemingly Unitarian view of Christ.[62] However, the image of Ratzinger conjured up by this litany of censure is somewhat mitigated by certain background details pertaining to some of these cases. It seems clear that he was less proactive in his prosecution of heresy than the media caricature would lead anyone to believe. For example, with regard to Charles Curran, it was Ratzinger's predecessor at the CDF, Franjo Seper, who had opened the case.[63] Moreover, even the withdrawal of Curran's *Missio canonica* might have been forestalled if Curran had recanted the particular teachings on birth control, masturbation, pre-marital sex and homosexuality which had been the cause of the investigation. According to Shortt, a compromise had been proposed 'under which Curran's "errors" would be enumerated, and he would stop teaching sexual ethics'.[64] The dissident moral theologian ultimately refused to back down and was subsequently stripped of his office.[65] In the case of Balisuriya, the excommunication ban was lifted within a matter of months and was probably less retributive than some might have assumed. Ambivalence also surrounds the case of Leonardo Boff, whose initial appeal to Ratzinger for support, had been the stimulus for the CDF's direct involvement in the situation.[66] Indeed, even the decision to impose a temporary ban of penitential silence on Boff came at the insistence of the Prefect of the Congregation for the Religious Orders (Cardinal Jerome Hamer) and not Ratzinger himself.[67] These lesser known details provide more of a context for the grudging concession made by Rupert Shortt about the tone of Ratzinger's prefecture.

If the profile of the Congregation between 1982 and 2005 were judged simply by how much use was made of the stiffest penalties, then one might

---

[62] See the discussion in Rupert Shortt's, *Commander of the Faith*, pp. 61ff.
[63] Ratzinger, *Cardinal Ratzinger*, p. 257.
[64] Shortt, *Commander of the Faith*, p. 70.
[65] Shortt, *Commander of the* Faith, p. 70.
[66] Shortt, *Commander of the Faith*, pp. 66-67.
[67] The view of Rome correspondent H.J. Fischer in *Pope Benedict XVI: A Personal Portrait* (New York: Crossroad Publishing Company, 2005), p. 37.

conclude that Ratzinger had taken a relaxed approach to doctrinal enforcement.[68]

However, the real unease about Ratzinger lay not in the perception that his judgments were excessive and extreme. The issue was much more to do with the manner in which the CDF executed its responsibilities. A case in point was the Belgian theologian, Jacques Dupuis, who was investigated on account of his teaching concerning religious pluralism.[69] The general feeling was that an ageing and respected theologian, such as Dupuis, should not have been subjected to the sort of scrutiny imposed by the CDF. Most vocal in his condemnation of Ratzinger was the retired Archbishop of Vienna, Cardinal König, who engaged him in public debate about the issue through an article published in the English Catholic weekly, the *Tablet*. König cast the CDF's move as 'a sign, an indication, that mistrust, suspicion and disapproval are being prematurely spread about an author who has the highest intentions, and has earned himself great merits in the service of the Catholic Church.'[70] This very public act of censure highlights what we might term the problem of Ratzinger. His activities in his role of Prefect of the CDF have been deeply contentious and forced people to make judgments about him. Indeed, that acknowledgment leads us full circle to the observation made at the beginning of this chapter: that people tend to perceive Ratzinger as either a scandal to the church or something of a saviour. But who is the real Joseph Ratzinger and what conclusions may we legitimately draw regarding him? A work of this nature does not afford the space to embark on that form of investigation. Arguably, though, a realistic picture of Ratzinger's character and spirituality might emerge from a study of the impressions of those reporters and biographers who have spent time with him or are conversant with the workings of his consistory.

The Papacy of Benedict XVI

Joseph Cardinal Ratzinger was elected Pope on April 19th 2005 and took on the Papal name Benedict XVI. This was in honour of Benedict of Nursia, the Patron Saint of Europe, and communicated to the world the central place that Europe would have in Benedict's own priorities.[71] Pundits trace his election partly to the conservative make-up of the College of Cardinals and partly to a stirring address he had given on the eve of the Conclave warning about the dangers of relativism. His election was to be a relief to traditionalists and a profound disappointment for progressives. Thus it evoked simultaneously both high hopes and dark suspicions.

---

[68] Shortt, *Commander of the Faith*, p. 66.
[69] See Jacques Dupuis S.J., *Toward a Christian Theology of Religious Pluralism* (Maryknoll, NY: Orbis Books, 2002).
[70] Cited in Gibson, *Rule of Benedict*, p. 202.
[71] For an understanding of Benedict's focus on Europe see Joseph Ratzinger, 'Europe in the Crisis of Cultures', *Communio* 32 (2005), pp. 345-356.

A dispassionate account of his eight year papacy would have to acknowledge the degree to which it was overshadowed by controversy and public relations gaffes. The early successes, characterised as they were by larger papal audiences and a form of truce on the part of the world's press, were diminished and undermined over time. Thus, whilst many of his overseas trips (not least that to the UK) were rapturously received and most of his literary publications lauded for their depth and substance, there was also another darker story unfolding in the media history of this papacy which served to weaken Benedict.

An assessment of the first five years of Benedict's reign in the German daily, *Der Spiegel,* went so far as to describe his papacy as an outright failure.[72] Whilst this was arguably an unfair judgment, there were a number of critical areas in which Benedict's words or actions could have been seen as undermining his credibility as leader of the Catholic church. These include his perceived mishandling of the clerical sex abuse scandal; the effects on the dialogue with Islam following the Regensburg address; the muted indignation of the Jewish community over his reintroduction of prayers for their conversion; the highly publicised reinstatement of schismatic Bishops associated with the Society of Pius X, most notably Holocaust denier Bishop Richard Williamson; the uneasy relationship with the Anglican Communion following the sudden offer of an Ordinariate to disaffected clergy and congregations; and the alleged linking of condom use with the increased spread of AIDS.[73] Taken collectively, and read at face value, these depict a Pontiff who had significant difficulty in promoting his own message and values. Indeed, the challenge to secularism's hegemony in the West (Benedict's primary agenda) was blunted and sometimes muted as a result of those troubling and de-stabilizing factors.

Whilst such issues cannot be the focus of this dissertation, three general comments may offer some perspective on Benedict's perceived shortcomings. First, it seems that severe and unnecessary damage has been done to his reputation as a result of the ineptitude of his own advisors. A recent Italian study by two Vatican journalists entitled *Attack on Ratzinger: Accusations and Scandals, Prophesies and Plots*[74] suggests that whilst

---

[72] Fiona Ehlers et al, 'The Failed Papacy of Benedict XVI', *Der Spiegel* (2010) http://www.spiegel.de/international/germany/0,1518,687374,00.html (accessed March 26, 2011).

[73] Comments made during an interview on a flight to Cameroon on March 17, 2009 about prophylactics only increasing the problem of AIDS were a media disaster for the Pope. Interestingly, in a recent interview with Peter Seewald, Benedict amended his position on condoms by suggesting that on some occasions their use might be the lesser of two evils. Joseph Ratzinger, *Light of the World: The Pope, the Church, and the Signs of the Times [A Conversation With Peter Seewald]* (San Francisco: Ignatius Press/Catholic Truth Society, 2010), p. 119.

[74] Andrea Tornielli and Paolo Rodari, *Attacco a Ratzinger*: *Accuse e scandali, profezie e complotti* (Casale Monferrato:Piemme, 2010) cited in John L. Allen Jr., 'Attack on

Benedict's papacy has been under attack from both secularists and liberal Catholics, the most potent 'enemies' have at times been his own aides with their abysmal failure to understand modern communications. The Regensburg remarks concerning Islam and violence, whilst being legitimate in the context of an academic lecture, lent themselves too much to misunderstanding when reported in sound-bite form to the Muslim world. Wise media advisors would have alerted Benedict to the danger of such remarks. Similarly, the failure to examine the background of Richard Williamson in the run-up to the reinstatement of clerics associated with the Society of Pius X, meant that a huge media disaster was not forestalled: a fact which Benedict acknowledged in his last interview with Peter Seewald.[75] Indeed, John L. Allen, stimulated by the argument of the two Italian journalists, speculates that even Benedict's comments about condoms making the AIDS problem in Africa worse might have enabled him to challenge the current Western AIDS strategy, had these comments been appropriately nuanced and properly managed. Regrettably for the Pope Emeritus, his advisors had lacked such foresight and that deficiency was never fully redressed.

Second, Benedict's positive attempts to deal with clerical sex abuse and cover-up were given less weight by the media than they might have deserved. This observation comes from an unlikely but reliable source. John L. Allen, Vatican correspondent for the *National Catholic Reporter*, suggests that the media charge that Ratzinger co-ordinated a large scale cover-up of sexual abuse stretching over decades[76], is quite simply wrong. His real responsibility for dealing with the crisis only began in 2001 and this was followed by a more rigorous handling of the problem than had hitherto taken place. Allen characterised him as the first high-ranking prelate to grasp the magnitude of clerical sexual abuse and suggested that there was ample evidence that he was not only appalled by what was going on but that his policies marked a change of course on the part of the Vatican.[77] However, Allen is not minded to absolve Benedict of all responsibility for the issue. He acknowledges that questions still remain over his knowledge of child abuse in the diocese of Munich, and also that prior to becoming acquainted with the scale of the problem, he 'came off as just another Roman Cardinal in denial.'[78]

Ratzinger: Italian book assesses Benedict's papacy.' *National Catholic Reporter* (2010) http://ncronline.org/blogs/all-things-catholic/attack-ratzinger-italian-book-assesses-benedicts-papacy (accessed 2 October, 2010).
[75] Joseph Ratzinger, *Light of the World*, p. 121.
[76] As evidenced by Hans Küng's 'Open Letter to Catholic Bishops.' (2010) http://fratres.wordpress.com/2010/04/20/full-text-open-letter-to-bishops-by-hans-kung/ (accessed 4 November, 2010).
[77] John L. Allen, 'Keeping the record straight on Benedict and the crisis' *All Things Catholic* (2010)
http://ncronline.org/blogs/all-things-catholic/keeping-record-straight-benedict-and-crisis (accessed Jan 28 2011).
[78] John L. Allen, 'Keeping the record straight on Benedict and the crisis.'

Thirdly, and finally, it should be noted that some of Benedict's innovations, though unpopular in terms of political correctness, corresponded to his understanding of core Catholic beliefs. For example, his reintroduction of prayers for the conversion of the Jews underscored his view that Christ was the fulfilment of Judaism and the Saviour of the Jewish people.[79] Whilst John Paul's comments about the Jewish people having their own covenant with God gave grounds for optimism that Catholic theology had changed position[80], Benedict was merely reiterating the traditional view based on both Scripture and tradition. Even his rehabilitation of the Latin Mass was based on a long-held opinion that liturgical development should be gradual and organic rather than abrupt as was the case with suppression of the Tridentine Mass.[81] In making it an option again he was underscoring its legitimacy rather than trying to undo the vernacular liturgy. Indeed, given his emphasis on the primacy of truth, there may have been a sense in which Benedict was less worried about popularity and political correctness than most people occupying such a visible public position.

In concluding this final section of the chapter, it is appropriate to comment briefly on his most recent theological publications, focusing particularly on how these might relate to the forthcoming chapters of the monograph. The three papal encyclicals (centring on charity[82], hope[83] and 'charity in truth'[84] respectively) have met with widespread approval[85], although American neo-conservative Catholics such as George Weigel have been unhappy with the apparent attack on Capitalism in the most recent of the encyclicals.[86] All of them reflect Augustinian themes and highlight Benedict's own passions and concerns. His two volume work on Christology (*Jesus of Nazareth*) has also elicited fulsome praise though in this case this has been

---

[79] This occurred in July 2007 when Benedict restored the traditional Latin Mass as one of the two approved forms of the Mass.

[80] This perspective has been traced to an address given by John Paul II in Rome on October 31, 1997 though Dulles does not believe that such an interpretation of his words does justice to his meaning or the stance of the Catholic Church. See Avery Cardinal Dulles, 'The Covenant With Israel', *First Things* November 2005.

[81] Ratzinger, *Milestones*, pp. 146-47.

[82] Pope Benedict XVI, *Deus Caritas Est: First Encyclical Letter* (London: CTS, 2006).

[83] Pope Benedict XVI, *Spe Salvi: Encyclical Letter on Christian Hope* (London: CTS, 2007).

[84] Pope Benedict XVI, *Caritas in veritate: Charity in Truth* (Dublin: Veritas, 2009).

[85] See Hans Küng's positive response to *Deus Caritas Est* reported on the Jimmy Akin blog. Jimmy Akin, '*Caritas Deus Est:* The Küng Perspective.' http://jimmyakin.com/2006/01/deus_caritas_es.html (accessed 9 June, 2009).

[86] George Weigel, 'Caritas in Veritate in Gold and Red.' (2009) http://www.nationalreview.com/articles/227839/i-caritas-veritate-i-gold-and-red/george-weigel (accessed 8 June 2009).

counter-balanced by intense criticism on the part of some.[87] This is not surprising, given that these works constitute a major attack on the dominance of the historical critical method. Essentially, the Pope Emeritus seems to have been attempting to mark out a new hermeneutical pathway, or possibly advocate a return to an older one in which a credible link is felt to exist between the Jesus of history and the Christ of faith. Either way, his views are remarkably in sympathy with more nuanced evangelical approaches to Scripture and hint at a much wider common vision. Indeed, the sheer Christocentrism of Benedict's spirituality, revealed in these volumes, as well as the soteriological musings found in his papal addresses on St Paul, prompts the question with which the rest of this monograph will be concerned: is there a potential bridge between Catholicism and moderate Evangelicalism in Joseph Ratzinger's Augustinian theology? Certainly, there is present in the Pope Emeritus' writings a concern for mission[88], a passion for personal faith[89], and a willingness to engage with the doctrine of justification[90], which might augur well in terms of finding a positive answer to this question.

---

[87] For example, Geza Vermes' article in *The Guardian*, 12 March 2011. http://www.guardian.co.uk/books/2011/mar/12/jesus-nazareth-pope-benedict-review?INTCMP=SRCH (accessed 16 March 2011).

[88] Note the desire expressed in the Foreword to *Jesus of Nazareth Part Two: Holy Week: From the Entrance into Jerusalem to the Resurrection* (San Francisco: Ignatius Press, 2011), p. xvii, 'I...hope that I have been granted an insight into the figure of our Lord that can be helpful to all readers who seek to encounter Jesus and believe in him.'

[89] In the Foreword to the first volume, *Jesus of Nazareth: From the Baptism in the Jordan to the Transfiguration* (New York: Doubleday, 2007), p. xxiv, he speaks of '...the most urgent priority [being] to present the figure and message of Jesus ... [and] so to help foster the growth of a living relationship with him.'

[90] Not only does Benedict engage with this theme in his papal addresses, but he had previously made a significant (behind closed doors) contribution to the historic Lutheran/Roman Catholic Joint Declaration on Justification made in 1999, when still Cardinal Ratzinger (see chapter 4).

CHAPTER 2

Ratzinger's Credibility as a Dialogue Partner

Introduction

The survey of Ratzinger's life and thought in the opening chapter has garnered some of the evidence to suggest that his basic theological orientation was conservative. However, there has been a consistent chorus amongst some of his critics that he embraced theological conservatism more for reasons of expediency than conviction.[1] Given this continued question mark surrounding the true nature of his theology, this chapter will aim to locate Ratzinger more assuredly as a conservative theologian and *ipso facto* a credible dialogue partner with the evangelical tradition. The focus of the study will be his early career because, whatever may be said about the older Ratzinger, there is still a commonly held view that the younger Ratzinger was essentially liberal in outlook.

Advancing this task will involve enquiring into Ratzinger's early academic period from a variety of vantage points. The goal will be to demonstrate that from whatever perspective we choose to view Ratzinger, there are consistent indicators that an underlying orthodoxy determined his approach to theology and doctrine. Indeed, even in the matter of key doctrinal shibboleths associated with the evangelical tradition, there is evidence of significant common ground despite the differences in vocabulary and theological milieu. To substantiate these claims, I shall focus on four areas of enquiry which, when taken collectively, throw considerable light on Ratzinger's theological orientation at this formative point in his career.

The first concerns theological method. Drawing on the work of writers who have commented extensively on the presuppositions undergirding Ratzinger's theology and giving primacy to material relating to his early career, I shall argue that he was fundamentally a conservative who not only understood the dynamic of liberal theological method but found it increasingly unsatisfactory. Indeed, his experience of teaching Fundamental theology early in his career was to foster within him convictions which were significantly at odds with the outlook of many of his colleagues in Catholic theological faculties.

Second, alongside theological method one must also consider significant biographical events and/or insights of contemporaries which might shed light on the state of his thinking at the time. In Ratzinger's case, there is much to indicate that his association with reformist centres of theology such as

---

[1] See Hans Küng, *My Struggle for Freedom: Memoirs* (New York: Continuum, 2003), p. 429 cf. Peter Seewald, *Benedict XVI: An Intimate Portrait* (San Francisco: Ignatius Press, 2007), p. 110.

Münster or Tübingen did not entirely mask or blunt his conservatism. Two examples (one of which concerns the recollections of a former student and the other an event at Tübingen) will demonstrate the degree to which he was independent of the prevalent liberal ethos. The student memoir, deriving from the less turbulent Münster period, draws attention to the huge continuity in Ratzinger's thought and casts doubt on theories which suggest he was traumatised into a fundamental change of view by the events of 1968. What makes these observations most telling is that the author, Francis Schüssler Fiorenza, is a theological moderate without a conservative axe to grind.[2] The event concerned a theological controversy involving the Tübingen faculty (the so-called Halbfass affair) which succeeded in unveiling a visceral passion for orthodoxy on Ratzinger's part. His actions at the time were to earn him unpopularity among faculty and students alike.

Third, the centrepiece of the chapter is a study of Ratzinger as a dogmatic theologian during his so-called liberal phase which ended with his departure from Tübingen in 1969. Here I shall attempt to lay to rest the view that there was a sufficient distancing from traditional or orthodox positions during this period to demonstrate that any later conservatism was at odds with what had gone before. It is my contention that a survey of seminal sections from his best known 1960s publication, *Introduction to Christianity*[3], will offer a fairly clear picture of what were his early priorities. Moreover, I shall highlight important areas of commonality with evangelicals in the matter of certain fundamental convictions related to the Creed. The reader should note in advance that the 'five fundamentals of Evangelicalism' (which will be the focus of this discussion) are treated in two distinct sections of the chapter. The three which are directly creedal are dealt with in some detail by Ratzinger in his explication of the Christological articles of the Creed (*Introduction to Christianity*, pp. 205-251) and this seemed the best location for my own treatment of them. Christ's deity and the inerrancy of Scripture seemed to belong more naturally to the preceding discussion of Ratzinger as a dogmatic theologian.

The fourth and final vantage point of this chapter will be Joseph Ratzinger's ecclesiology. What all commentators will agree upon is that a radical shift of some kind took place in the late 1960s which transformed Ratzinger from being a Council radical to an ecclesiastical conservative. The question is why this was the case. To formulate an answer entails exploring his role in Vatican II and moving the focus of our investigation back in time to the pre-Tübingen period. Whilst this interrupts the biographical flow of the chapter, it is necessary for one vital reason. The reader will have become aware at this

---

[2] In the article he describes himself as theologically closer to Rahner and Metz than to Ratzinger. See Francis Schüssler Fiorenza, 'From Theologian to Pope: A Personal View Back, Past the Public Portrayals.' *Harvard Divinity Bulletin* Vol. 33, No. 2. [Autumn 2005] http://www.hds.harvard.edu/news-events/harvard-divinity-bulletin/articles/from-theologian-to-pope (accessed 9 October, 2009).
[3] Joseph Ratzinger, *Introduction to Christianity* (San Francisco: Ignatius Press, 1990).

stage that a genuine case can be made for Ratzinger's underlying conservatism. That knowledge will prepare the ground for the final argument of the chapter and make its conclusions more credible. I shall attempt to demonstrate that where movement did occur in Ratzinger's thinking, this involved no fundamental altering of his basic theological orientation. Indeed, it may even have been his core theological convictions which partially prompted the change that did occur in the domain of ecclesiology.

Ratzinger's Theological Method

How might one characterise the essence of Joseph Ratzinger's theological outlook? According to former student, Vincent Twomey, his thought seems always to have been a merging of reason *and* revelation with revelation exercising the more determinative role.[4] Whilst this could arguably be taken as only reflecting the later Ratzinger, there is interesting corroborating evidence from Hans Küng that such an outlook had always prevailed. In an interview with Peter Seewald, Küng indicates that Ratzinger was consistently reluctant to allow the claims of reason (at least when defined by the standards of the Enlightenment) to limit or determine the content of revelation. Küng's words may be somewhat disparaging of Ratzinger, not to say repetitive[5], but they confirm that he had always suspected that some form of 'superstition' had inhibited Ratzinger from accepting the hegemony of rationalism. Note particularly, his view that this outlook went deeper than any 'change of perspective' on Ratzinger's part during the Tübingen years.

> There is a break in his biography, no question. This change is of course only contingent. I believe there must still have been, somewhere in his heart, an unenlightened shrine to an old-fashioned God. I should say that in my case there is no belief on which I have not actually cast the light of reason. But somewhere or other, he still has his Bavarian shrine to an old-fashioned God, where reason ceases.[6]

Whilst Küng attributes Ratzinger's outlook to a naïve faith, the reality is more complex and nuanced. It was through his theological studies, and particularly under the influence of the works of St Augustine, that the young Ratzinger had become convinced of the compatibility of reason with revelation. It was this which allowed him to feel no obligation to follow Küng in subjecting the claims of revelation to the constraining demands of Enlightenment rationalism. Rather, for him, the fusion of revelation and reason properly understood was

---

[4] D. Vincent Twomey, *Benedict XVI: Conscience of our Age* (San Francisco: Ignatius Press, 2005), pp. 38-39.

[5] In another context, as noted on page 8, Küng refers to an 'unenlightened devotional corner' in Ratzinger's 'Bavarian heart.' Here on page 28 we are given a further explication of what this means for Küng and how it determined his understanding of whether or not Ratzinger underwent a fundamental change in outlook.

[6] Peter Seewald, *An Intimate Portrait* (San Francisco: Ignatius Press, 2007), p. 109.

justified in that Christianity was the true philosophy and Christ the Logos personified.

This perspective can be detected as early as his inaugural lecture at the University of Bonn where he challenged Emil Brunner's assertion that the revealed, personal God depicted in Holy Scripture was an image in tension with the picture of God bequeathed by Greek philosophy.[7] In Ratzinger's view they complemented one another, and this union of natures, so to speak, was what secured Christianity's place as the true religion. James Corkery SJ, commenting on the lecture, confirms for us the reason why Ratzinger should have set such store by Greek rationality. His view is that this was the outworking of an Augustinian instinct which saw a deep compatibility between the Christian faith and the truest and highest insights afforded by reason.

> Ratzinger's solution to the dilemma [created by Brunner] is to say that the one and the other belong together: the one personal, addressable, named God of biblical revelation *is* the One, the Absolute of Greek philosophy, the metaphysical One beside whom there is not and cannot be another. Underneath this lies an Augustinian facial feature[8]: Augustine's refusal to erase the connecting line (the *Bindestrich* or 'dash') between Neo-platonic ontology and Christian faith, knowing that to do so would be to fail to give the radical monotheism of the Bible its most adequate expression.[9]

Interestingly, Corkery concludes his discussion by suggesting that Ratzinger's equating of the philosophical concept of God with the God of faith is a pillar of his whole theological system from start to finish.[10] Whether or not this can be stated definitively is a moot point. However, one can certainly argue that it was on account of this theological premise that Ratzinger felt under no compulsion to pit reason against revelation.

A second fundamental aspect of Ratzinger's theological method, and one which distances him considerably from *avant-garde* theology, is his consciously diachronic approach to matters of truth. As Twomey observes, his writing has consistently been influenced by the whole sweep of theological and philosophical history and not primarily by those intellectual assumptions which were currently in vogue.[11] The outworking of this stance is perhaps most evident in his understanding of the legacy of Vatican II. More progressive scholars such as Karl Rahner have viewed the Council as an absolute watershed

---

[7] I am indebted to James Corkery SJ for the reference to Ratzinger's Bonn lecture as well as to his subsequent analysis. See James Corkery, *Joseph Ratzinger's Theological Ideas: Wise Cautions and Legitimate Hopes* (New York: Paulist Press, 2009), pp. 30ff.
[8] In Corkery's own attempt to build a picture of Ratzinger's theological method he has drawn on the metaphor of the face which speaks of that which is a characteristic feature.
[9] Corkery, *Joseph Ratzinger's Theological Ideas*, p. 30.
[10] Corkery, *Joseph Ratzinger's Theological Ideas*, p. 31.
[11] Twomey, *The Conscience of our Age*, p. 39

in the history of Catholic theology[12] and venture the opinion that it may be more determinative for the future of the church than anything that has happened up to the point of the Council's commissioning in 1961. However, Ratzinger finds such a synchronic perspective impossible to accept because he is committed to the essential continuity of revealed truth expressed through the church's dogmatic tradition. To his mind there is no privileged epoch, barring the definitive witness of the early centuries, which has the capacity to frame or re-frame the faith.

His viewpoint is particularly nuanced and his early interpreter, Aidan Nichols, captures something of its subtlety.[13] Nichols' comments are based mainly on a work published in Italian in 1971 which is probably reflective of Ratzinger's earlier period teaching Fundamental Theology.[14] The crucial point to note about Ratzinger's perspective is that he is convinced of a deep-seated problem in the realm of contemporary dogmatic theology. This was the prevailing assumption that *all being* (and this is where Nichols is drawing extensively on Ratzinger's own nomenclature) is *'Gewordensein'* which is translated as 'having becomeness.'[15] When that language is applied to the mindset of Vatican II progressives, what it suggests is that truth is perceived as still developing or evolving, and coming into being. Indeed, its nature as *Gewordensein* mitigates against the permanence or fullness of previous definitions of belief.[16] That this is how Ratzinger understands 'Gewordensein' is confirmed by the comparison he draws between contemporary attitudes to truth and that of nineteenth century Catholic theology.

> The Christian reality [in the context of the nineteenth century] had been conceived as the Absolute, the self-manifestation of immutable, divine truth. But now it has let itself be interpreted in terms of the categories of history, and of historicity – and in such a way that, the more it involves itself in the problem of historicity, the more it seems that the absolute character of Christian truth is resolved into the process of historical becoming.[17]

---

[12] Rahner compares its impact to the Council of Jerusalem's impact on the first Jewish Christians. Karl Rahner, 'Towards a Fundamental Theology of Vatican II,' *Theological Studies 40* (December 1979): pp. 726-727.

[13] The following discussion is indebted to Nichols' chapter, 'Back to the Foundations' in Aidan Nichols, *The Thought of Benedict XVI: An Introduction to the Theology of Joseph Ratzinger* (London: Burns & Oats, 2007), pp. 160-171.

[14] It will be shown later in the chapter that this mindset was already firmly in place during the Tübingen years and thus probably established during his time teaching Fundamental theology in Bonn and Münster.

[15] Nichols, *The Thought of Benedict*, p. 160.

[16] As Nichols puts it, 'Thought no longer leads back the process of historical transformation to the permanent truth of God, but turns even what is apparently stable into the process of historical transformation', *The Thought of Benedict*, p. 161.

[17] J. Ratzinger, *Storia e dogma* (Milan, 1971), p. 14 cited in Nichols, *The Thought of Benedict*, p. 160.

The solution to such a crisis of understanding is said to lie in two pivotal declarations of the doctrinal magisterium which are believed to provide an exit from the blind alley of historicism.[18] The first is Vatican I's repudiation of theological evolutionism and its affirmation that the dogmas of the church are to be preserved 'in perpetuity' according to the sense in which they were originally given by the church.[19] The other magisterial pronouncement which Ratzinger understands to be crucial in the plotting of future Catholic theology is the decree *Lamentabili,* issued during the modernist crisis.[20] Its essential value is deemed to be the same as that of the teaching of the First Vatican Council (namely, the repudiation of a 'radically evolutionist and historicist direction' for the interpretation of doctrine.)[21]

Whilst this stance marks a very fundamental fracture with the Council liberals, it should be noted that Ratzinger's position was not a knee jerk bow to the forces of tradition. His submission to the magisterium was imaginative and subtle as opposed to uncritical and naïve. He was not unaware that it had been excesses on the part of Liberal Protestant theology (in particular, work on the history of dogma by Adolf von Harnack) which had led the Catholic authorities to assume the tone that they had in their response to modernism.[22] In affirming the magisterial teaching he was in no way suggesting that dogma remained utterly static or that there was no place for doctrinal development. Nichols gives evidence of this in two respects. First, he cites Ratzinger to the effect that Newman's theology[23], even with its limitations, offered a positive perspective on the notion of historical change.[24] This was clearly an admission of the legitimacy of some form of historical development. Second, whilst acknowledging that for Ratzinger the church was eternally tied to a fixed interpretive norm, Nichols also made clear that there was a place for an ever deepening appreciation of the truths of the faith.[25] Thus the younger Ratzinger

---

[18] Nichols, *The Thought of Benedict,* p. 161
[19] H. Denzinger and A. Schonmetzer, *Enchiridion Symboloram, Definitionum et Declarationum de rebus fidei et morum* (Freiburg, 1967), 3020 cited in Nichols, *The Thought of Benedict XVI,* p. 161.
[20] See Denzinger and Schonmetzer, *Enchiridion Symboloram,* 3421-3422.
[21] Ratzinger, *Storia e Dogma,* p. 15 cited in Nichols, *The Thought of Benedict,* p. 161.
[22] Nichols, *The Thought of Benedict,* p. 161. Nichols reminds his readers that in *Story and Dogma,* Ratzinger charges the Catholic authorities of '[assuming] a defensive position in a precipitate and inflexible fashion.' (Ratzinger, *Storia e Dogma,* p. 16)
[23] John Henry Newman, *Essay on the Development of Christian Doctrine* (Cambridge: Cambridge University Press, 2010)
[24] Nichols, *The Thought of Benedict XVI,* p. 163
[25] Nichols, *The Thought of Benedict,* p. 163. Nichols summarises Ratzinger's outlook in these terms:'Again, in the theology of *revelation,* the biblical revelation is best thought of as an event which both happened once for all in the past, and yet happens again repeatedly, constantly, for faith. For the believer, the God-Man relationship has reached its ultimate perfection already, in Christ. It cannot be transcended, yet it can be re-received time and again. In accepting the rule of faith, and the canon of Scripture, the Church submits herself for ever to a fixed interpretive norm. Yet the affirmations of the

offered a nuanced perspective which both allowed for growth in understanding as well as for clearly defined doctrinal truths which were unalterable.

A few comments must be made in conclusion with regard to the important question of Scripture within Ratzinger's theological method. It has been demonstrated that the early Ratzinger was committed to the compatibility of reason with revelation and that by at least as early as 1971 he was fundamentally opposed to an historicist understanding of the revelatory process. Was there anything in his employment of Scripture which might cause us to query this emerging picture of a theology which was essentially orthodox? The indications are that the same basic orientation present in his treatment of revelation was repeated in his handling of Scripture. This is evident from some of his early engagements with the documents of Vatican II. Here the biblical text was sufficiently normative for him to function as a corrective even to trends in Conciliar thought which he deemed at odds with the biblical revelation. The most striking example of this is his intense criticism of the anthropology emanating from *Gaudium et Spes*. This will be discussed in detail later in the chapter on Augustinianism.

None of this, however, warrants the conclusion that Ratzinger is an unconscious adherent of *Sola Scriptura*. He explicitly disavows such a perspective, believing that the receptive church is uniquely connected to the revelation event (see the earlier discussion of his *Habilitationschrift* pp. 14-15). and that the Church exercises a role in the economy of God far in excess of any which the theologians of the Reformation would accord it. Notwithstanding these important caveats, it is clear that Ratzinger is still content to make the Bible central to the formation of his own theology[26] and accords its revelation a finality (at least in terms of the language he uses) with which supporters of *Sola Scriptura* might not take issue.[27] One might legitimately conclude with Twomey that his theology is profoundly influenced by the Bible and that there appears to be no other point of departure for it.[28] Ratzinger's words cited in *Salt of the Earth* serve to underline the primary role played by the Word in his theological deliberations.

Creed and the Bible are not themselves the revelation, but its explication in the words of men.'

[26] This has been demonstrated in the devotional/exegetical work, *Jesus of Nazareth: From the Baptism in the Jordan to the Transfiguration* (New York: Doubleday, 2007) and the homily delivered to the College of Cardinals on the eve of the Conclave. Joseph Ratzinger, 'Jesus Christ: "The Measure of True Humanism",' Translation online 'Cardinal Ratzinger's Homily in Mass Before Conclave' *Zenit* (2005). http://www.zenit.org/article-12791?l=english (accessed 10 June, 2010).

[27] Ironically, this viewpoint was expressed most powerfully when the later Ratzinger, in a discussion about the theological significance of Fatima, contrasts the binding nature of public revelation against any illumination of that public revelation which might be vouchsafed through private revelation. See pp. 185-186 of the monograph.

[28] Twomey, *The Conscience of our Age*, p. 39 n.1.

That we believe the Word of God, that we try really to get to know it and understand it, and then as I said, to think it together with the great masters of the faith. This gives my theology a somewhat biblical character and also bears the stamp of the Fathers, especially Augustine.[29]

Critical Insights

This brief section affords a unique insight into the life of Joseph Ratzinger during that period when he was most identified with the progressive wing of the Catholic church. The memories of his former student, shared recently in the *Harvard Divinity Bulletin*, take us back almost to the beginning of his academic career and demonstrate how distanced the media portrayal of the early Ratzinger was from the reality. In a similar vein, the 'Halbfass affair' reveals strong conservative instincts in Ratzinger at a point when he was dean of the Tübingen faculty.

Francis Schüssler Fiorenza

Francis Schüssler Fiorenza is the Stillman Professor of Roman Catholic Theological Studies at Harvard Divinity School and the husband of renowned feminist theologian, Elizabeth Schüssler Fiorenza. He studied under Ratzinger in the Catholic faculty at Münster prior to the latter's move to Tübingen in 1966. In 2005 he wrote a retrospective reflection entitled 'From Theologian to Pope (A personal view back, past the public portrayals)'[30] in which he challenged the view that traumatic experiences in Tübingen during the student disturbances had transformed the young Ratzinger from a progressive theologian to a conservative one. Schüssler Fiorenza's conclusion is that such perspectives 'overlook [the fact] that Ratzinger has from early days had a consistent theological vision.'[31]

Although the article also focuses on aspects of his later theology, there are a number of examples given of his early theological thinking which were entirely consistent with what might be described as his later 'conservative' period. For example, students from Münster had challenged the Vatican Council's use of Scripture as not sufficiently cognizant of the historical critical method. Ratzinger defended the church's position and, in the process, revealed what Schüssler Fiorenza thought was a key characteristic of his own theological orientation. Not only did he argue that the role of historical criticism in exegesis ought to be limited, but under the influence of a former Bultmanian

---

[29] Ratzinger, *Salt of the Earth*, p. 66.
[30] Francis Schüssler Fiorenza, *Harvard Divinity Bulletin* Vol 33 No.2 (Autumn 2005)
[31] Schüssler Fiorenza, 'From Theologian to Pope.' (2005)
http://bulletin.hds.harvard.edu/articles/autumn2005/theologian-pope

turned Catholic, Heinrich Schlier, he repudiated the existentialist interpretation of Scripture championed by Rudolf Bultmann.[32]

Why did Ratzinger adopt the particular stances he did? Schüssler Fiorenza's conclusion is that this is best explained by his association with the movement known as *La Nouvelle Théologie* (the new theology).[33] As outlined in the previous chapter, its aim was to reform the dominant neo-scholastic theology of the time by retrieving the theology of the patristic period, particularly the thought of St Augustine. Most striking in Schüssler Fiorenza's assessment of this movement is his account of the purpose behind the retrieval of the scriptures. 'This retrieval focused not on the historical criticism of the scriptures, but on the multiple senses of the scriptures that the fathers of the church elaborated.'[34]

Ratzinger, claims Schüssler Fiorenza, was a progressive only to the extent that he challenged the reigning neo-scholastic paradigm. His over all theological vision, particularly his employment of Scripture in the realisation of that vision, placed him in an altogether different category to those associated with a more progressivist approach to theology. Schüssler Fiorenza's summary statement of Ratzinger's essential theological orientation accords very closely with the picture that emerged in the opening chapter of this dissertation. It was that of a Catholic thinker of fundamentally orthodox disposition whose '... emphasis on ecclesial authority in the interpretation of scripture, ... critique of the dominance of the historical method, and ... appeal to patristic resources for the interpretation of scriptures have remained constant features of his theological writings.'[35]

The Halbfass Affair

This event was recorded in John L Allen's biography, *Cardinal Ratzinger*, and it involved disciplinary action taken by the Episcopal authorities against ordained Catholic theologian, Hubertus Halbfass.[36] Whilst teaching at a *Hochschule* in Reutlingen, Halbfass had authored a book entitled *Fundamentalkatechtik: Sprache und Erfahrung in Religionsunterricht* (Fundamentals of catechetics: Speech and experience in religious instruction) which caused a furore on account of its questioning not only of Christ's bodily

---

[32] For more on Schlier's rejection of Bultmanianism see H. Schlier, 'A Brief Apologia' in K. Hardt S.J. e.a., *We Are Now Catholics* (Dublin: Mercier Press, 1958), pp. 193-214.

[33] Whilst some of this analysis reflects claims already made in chapter one, the point to note is that much of the argument there was based on material from Ratzinger's own memoirs. Schüssler Fiorenza's account offers independent corroboration that the subject's claims about his early theological instincts were trustworthy and reliable.

[34] Schüssler Fiorenza, 'From Theologian to Pope.'

[35] Schüssler Fiorenza, 'From Theologian to Pope.'

[36] See John L. Allen, Jr., *Cardinal Ratzinger: The Vatican's Enforcer of the Faith* (New York: Continuum, 2000), pp. 221-24.

resurrection but also the church's understanding of missionary activity.[37] For Halbfass the goal of mission was not to make converts but to enable members of the world religions be better adherents of their own religion. The effect of this publication was that the church authorities blocked Halbfass' appointment to a *Hochschule* in Bonn and revoked his *Missio canonica* as a Catholic theologian.

The general response to these actions on the part of German-speaking theological students and lecturers was one of outrage. Various demonstrations were staged in university towns and significant pressure was put on the Catholic faculty in neighbouring Tübingen to support their colleague. Hans Küng recollects that there was a widespread consensus among virtually all the faculty that some action should be taken in defence of Halbfass. The single exception was Ratzinger who was then serving as dean of the faculty. During a subsequent meeting between Halbfass and members of the Catholic faculty at Ratzinger's home, the dean was to affirm the author's right to advance the positions he had in his recent book but not as a Catholic theologian! Interestingly, Allen notes that Halbfass was not surprised that Ratzinger took the position he did since he was aware that as early as 1966 the future Prefect had written in a monograph on the fourth session of the Vatican Council: 'The prevailing optimism, which understands the world's religions as in some way salvific agencies, is simply irreconcilable with the biblical assessment of these religions.'[38]

Küng notes that in the faculty meeting following the interview with Halbfass, Ratzinger remained adamant that the faculty should not express any support for Halbfass nor intervene on his behalf with the Diocesan Bishop. However, aware that there was widespread disapproval of his actions in the university, Ratzinger later gave a public lecture to 700 students outlining his reasons for taking the position he did. One of that audience, Ratzinger graduate student Charles MacDonald, remembered the defining moment being when he commented about the way in which Halbfass understood a particular doctrine: 'If I believed that I could no longer honestly say the creed.' This was to reveal to MacDonald how 'deeply existential'[39] the issue was for Ratzinger.

A short historical cameo such as this underscores the view that Ratzinger was willing to defend theological positions with which the majority of progressive theologians would have taken issue. Moreover, he is shown to have risked unpopularity for the sake of credal beliefs which he felt to be sacrosanct. This is an unlikely *modus operandi* for someone whose theological loyalties were allegedly held as lightly as Ratzinger's were. Was it not more suggestive of a theologian with deeper convictions?

---

[37] This was the primary ground of the church's reaction to Halbfass although his teaching on the resurrection would also have been unacceptable to the Episcopate.
[38] Cited in Allen, *Cardinal Ratzinger*, p. 223.
[39] Allen, *Cardinal Ratzinger*, p. 223.

Ratzinger as a Dogmatic Theologian

Ratzinger's outstanding theological publication of the 1960s was the best selling *Introduction to Christianity*. In its original guise this was a lecture series on the Apostles' Creed delivered to students of all faculties at the University of Tübingen in 1967. In beginning to assess to what degree the book embraced a more progressivist theology, it is instructive to read the retrospective comments of Hans Küng who perceived the work as little more than an ideological attack on modern liberal scholarship.

According to Küng, Ratzinger 'had contented himself with a caricature of contemporary research into Jesus and here already showed the beginnings of the misinterpretations, insinuations, caricatures and condemnations of which he [was] capable.'[40] Nevertheless, the polemical edge to these lectures probably obscures what was a more positive intent. The project was obviously a labour of love for Ratzinger who had hoped that it would have a profound impact on the University. We get a hint of the pastoral and apologetic motivation that lay behind it when he speaks of the *Introduction* being 'able to open a door for many' through the content of the addresses.[41]

Certainly, Küng's dismissal of the work as reactionary conservatism fails to communicate the spirit in which the book was written. Ratzinger's theology had more depth, creativity and novelty than any work which might have passed in those days as 'traditional.' A more rounded judgment on it, yet delivered from a critical perspective, was offered by John L Allen. Allen writes,

> [A]s a sort of first-fruit of the Council, the book did not strike a defensive note with its audience. Instead, it was celebrated as daring, liberating, a model of the kind of searing honesty in Catholic intellectual life that Vatican II made possible. Ratzinger's book was no legalistic manual stuffed with rules and regulations; this was a meditation on faith that reached into the depths of human experience, that dared to walk naked between doubt and belief, in order to discover the truth of what it means to be a modern Christian. It marked, in short, a transformation in how theologians presented the Catholic faith.[42]

The opening chapter of *The Introduction* which explores the nature of contemporary belief enables us to witness firsthand not only the considerable breadth of Ratzinger's learning but also some of the fundamental convictions which underlay his later work and which in this publication find their most thorough justification.

The general tenor of his argument is that the liberal trajectory upon which post-Conciliar theology was travelling was largely a dead end. Using Kierkegaard's famous parable of the clown who had communicated a message of deadly seriousness but been taken only as play-acting, he suggests that this

---

[40] Küng, *My Struggle for Freedom*, p. 458.
[41] Ratzinger, *Milestones*, p. 139.
[42] Allen, *Cardinal Ratzinger* p.93

must also be the fate of the modern theologian.[43] However, the error of *aggiornamento* is the presupposition that as the clown's message of an impending fire might have been believed if he had discarded his clown's costume when communicating the message, similarly Christianity might become palatable again if one discarded the outmoded aspects of belief which modernity found unacceptable. Ratzinger's conclusion is that even in the short period of time since the Council, this viewpoint has been discredited.[44]

This does not mean, however, that he has no interest in building intellectual bridges with his audience. Acknowledging the central place of existentialism within the student mindset, Ratzinger in a manner hitherto unknown among Catholic theologians, acknowledges the oppressive power of doubt both within the believer and the unbeliever. However, rather than depict this in purely negative terms, he presents it as a potential avenue of communication and a way to ensure that the two groups do not remain in hermetically sealed worlds.[45] This more open approach illustrates the outlook of a theologian who at this point in his career is seeking strenuously to make a connection with those outside the faith.

From this juxtapositioning of doubt and belief, Ratzinger proceeds to ask the most fundamental question of theology: what does it mean to believe?[46] Here we are given the fruit of his lecturing work in history of dogma and history of religions. He begins by reminding his listeners of the error of presuming 'religion' and 'belief' are synonymous terms. It was not simply a foregone conclusion that 'belief' should have been the 'centre of gravity' of Christianity since other religions in history have had a different central axis. He cites the example of Roman civic religion where the issue was not a personal act of commitment but loyalty to the cult. So recognising the significance of 'belief' being at the heart of Christianity, Ratzinger asks 'what is involved in the act of believing?' and 'why do contemporary people find it so difficult?' His surprising response – and one that requires greater exploration elsewhere - is that the act of believing has always been problematic and that even during the heyday of Catholicism (the Medieval period), it was a small minority of people who embraced belief in wholly personal terms.[47]

Ratzinger's explanation for why things should be this way lies in his conviction that there is an existential distance between human beings and God, and that left to their own devices human beings can see no further than the limited horizons of human experience. The movement to what Ratzinger would

---

[43] Joseph Ratzinger, *Introduction to Christianity* (San Francisco: Ignatius Press, 1990), p. 16.
[44] Ratzinger, *Introduction to Christianity*, pp. 16-17.
[45] Ratzinger, *Introduction to Christianity*, pp. 17-21.
[46] Ratzinger, *Introduction to Christianity*, pp. 22 ff.
[47] His justification for that view is that historical research into the Medieval period has revealed '...that even in those days there was the great mass of fellow-travellers and a relatively small number of people who had really entered into the inner movement of belief.' See Ratzinger, *Introduction to Christianity*, p. 23.

define as the 'most real' is attained only through the biblical journey of conversion. Ratzinger outlines the stages of this movement and, although highlighting the radical nature of it, affirms that it must also be seen as a daily decision.

> Man's natural centre of gravity draws him to the visible, to what he can take in his hand and hold as his own. He has to turn around inwardly in order to see how badly he is neglecting his own interests by letting himself be drawn along in this way by his natural centre of gravity. He must turn around to recognize how blind he is if he trusts only what he sees with his own eyes. Without this change of direction, without this resistance to the natural centre of gravity, there can be no belief. Indeed belief **is** the con-version in which man discovers that he is following an illusion if he devotes himself only to the tangible. This is at the same time the fundamental reason why belief is not demonstrable: it is an about –turn; only he who turns about is receptive to it; and because our centre of gravity does not cease to incline us in another direction it remains a turn that is new everyday; only in a life-long conversion can we become aware of what it means to say "I believe".[48]

As the various pieces of the mosaic of belief continue to be fitted together, Ratzinger goes on to explain why the journey to belief is especially fraught with difficulty at this time in cultural history. Not only is it existential distance that constitutes a barrier to belief, but the fact that the concept of tradition itself has lost intellectual coinage and that everything associated with it, including belief, has been rendered suspect to the present generation.[49] Thus to Ratzinger, *aggiornamento* and the demythologizing programme are no solution since they are ultimately perceived as attempts to defend a belief system that is irrevocably wedded to tradition.[50]

However, underlying this immense problem for the church is the even more fundamental issue of the particularity of Christianity and its claims regarding the uniqueness of Jesus Christ as the God-man.[51] Whilst Ratzinger expresses some sympathy for the attractiveness of a more open-ended Asiatic viewpoint that does not limit the Eternal to the pinprick of a single human life, he affirms strongly his belief in the Incarnation and challenges the unbeliever to question the widely held assumption that only the empirically demonstrable is real.[52]

This assumption, which finds its expression in the movement towards historicism (the rejection of any meaning outside the realm of what can be demonstrated by human beings) is for Ratzinger a diminution of the human spirit and no foundation for living. Neither, indeed, is the emerging Marxism which seeks to bring its own meaning to the world through praxis. Marxism, or

---

[48] Ratzinger, *Introduction to Christianity*, p. 25.
[49] Ratzinger, *Introduction to Christianity*, pp. 26-27.
[50] Ratzinger, *Introduction to Christianity*, p. 27.
[51] Ratzinger, *Introduction to* Christianity, p. 27.
[52] Ratzinger, *Introduction to Christianity*, pp. 29-30.

indeed any human system, fails because without a meaning that is larger than himself, and one that is not reducible to empirical knowledge, man is said to remain homeless in the universe. Indeed, relying on knowledge and being dependent on what human beings may be able to make of the future is no better than Baron Münchhausen's futile attempts to pull himself out of the mire by his own hair.[53]

This under-cutting of the prevailing secular ethos leads to the culmination of Ratzinger's theology of belief. Rather than rely on knowledge that individuals can attain within the relatively closed system of human intellectual endeavour, and instead of trying to create self-generated meaning, the real breakthrough for human beings is to find a meaning which is greater than themselves and upon which they can rely. Thus Christianity, in Ratzinger's system, is the answer from the outside which provides the only solid foundation for living.[54] Even though it may be an affront to the prevailing materialistic ethos, it is for him the doorway to freedom. From the perspective of evangelical theology, it is interesting to note that for Ratzinger the heart of belief is intensely personal. He stresses that Christian belief is not acknowledgement of a vague spiritual ground to reality but faith in a person. '[The central formula of the Christian faith] is not *'I believe in something'* but *'I believe in thee.'* The 'thee' in question is Jesus Christ who is the meaning of the world encountered as a person.

> Thus faith is the finding of a 'You' that bears me up and amid all the unfulfilled – and in the last resort unfulfillable – hope of human encounters gives me the promise of an indestructible love which not only longs for eternity but guarantees it. Christian faith lives on the discovery that not only is there such a thing as objective meaning, but this meaning knows me and loves me, I can entrust myself to it like a child that knows all its questions answered in the 'You' of its mother. Thus in the last analysis believing, trusting and loving are one, and all the theses around which belief revolves are only concrete expressions of the all-embracing about-turn, of the assertion 'I believe in You' – of the discovery of God in the countenance of the man Jesus of Nazareth.[55]

Ratzinger, however, is acutely aware of the charge of fideism in promoting the Incarnate Christ as the answer to humanity's deepest needs and in other parts of the *Introduction* seeks to demonstrate the viability of such a claim. It is in that task that we can further identify Ratzinger's essential orthodoxy and also the reasons for Küng's strong disapproval. Essentially, Ratzinger is unconvinced by the historical critical method and believes that the naturalistic assumptions underlying it have skewed the whole development of Christological thinking and resulted in a series of wrong turns. He highlights for special attention the exegetical work of Adolf Von Harnack and Rudolf Bultmann. In different ways

---

[53] Ratzinger, *Introduction to Christianity*, p. 42.
[54] Ratzinger, *Introduction to Christianity*, p. 43.
[55] Ratzinger, *Introduction to Christianity*, p. 48.

they are said to have failed to address the necessary relationship that exists between the Jesus of history and the Christ of faith. In Harnack's case, the historical Jesus had been invested with all the admirable traits of the late 19th century liberal and transformed into someone who, in reality, was not the subject of his own proclamation.[56] Whilst recognizing that such a non-polemical Jesus eased tensions between warring Christians as well as with other practitioners of the world's religions, Ratzinger reminds his audience that such an historical reconstruction had failed to do justice to the Christ of the gospels. Speaking of Harnack's Christology, Ratzinger notes,

> One certainly cannot deny that these are impressive and stirring assertions which cannot lightly be dismissed. And yet – while Harnack was still proclaiming the optimistic message about Jesus, those who were to bury his work were already knocking at the door. At the very same time proof was produced that the plain Jesus of whom he spoke was a romantic dream, a *Fata Morgana* of the historian, a mirage induced by thirst and longing which dissolved as he approached.[57]

Bultmann, who opted for the opposing path, is charged with leading people up another blind alley. Ratzinger questions, in particular, his plea that all that should matter about Jesus is the bare fact of his existence in order that faith might no longer rest on uncertain historical reconstructions but 'only the verbal happening of the preaching of the Gospel, through which closed human existence is opened up to its true nature.'[58] Such a stance is deemed to be as doubtful as Harnack's because 'an empty event' is no more credible than one filled with content.[59]

> Is anything gained when the question who, what and how this Jesus was is dismissed as meaningless and man is tied instead to a mere verbal event? The latter certainly takes place, for it is *preached*; but this way its authenticity and content of reality remains extremely dubious.[60]

It is Ratzinger's view, however, that, 'this shuttle movement of the modern mind'[61] between the Jesus of history and the Christ of faith has not been an entirely wasted journey. It is an indicator that one cannot exist without the other and that, before any more reconstructions take place, it would be prudent to explore the traditional Christian synthesis of the two.[62] In any attempt to do this, however, Ratzinger is cognizant of the need to demonstrate that the

---

[56] Jesus' message was presented as focusing on the Fatherhood of God and brotherhood of man.
[57] Ratzinger, *Introduction to Christianity*, p. 147.
[58] Ratzinger's summary of Bultmann's position, Ratzinger, *Introduction to Christianity*, p. 147.
[59] Ratzinger, *Introduction to Christianity*, p. 147.
[60] Ratzinger, *Introduction to Christianity*, p. 147.
[61] Ratzinger, *Introduction to Christianity*, p. 148.
[62] Ratzinger, *Introduction to Christianity*, p. 148.

traditional high Christology has a foundation in history. As he notes, with reference to his own stirring evocation of the virtues of 'historic' Christology in the preceding discussion[63],

> Have we not perhaps raised ourselves aloft on a splendid system of ideas but left reality behind us, so that the indisputable coherence of the system is of no use to us because the foundation is missing? In other words, we must ask whether the findings of the Bible and its critical illumination of the facts empower us to conceive the Sonship of Jesus in the way we have just done and in the way Christological dogma does.[64]

His answer to such a rhetorical question is that an examination of Christ's Sonship in the gospels, followed dispassionately but without the naturalistic presuppositions of liberalism[65], will demonstrate that Christ perceived himself in precisely the same divine terms that were later enshrined in the ecumenical creeds. Thus belief in Christ, as it has been advocated throughout the book, finds its justification in an assessment of the gospels as credible historical documents.[66] Some of Ratzinger's later statements on specific articles of the Creed reinforce this impression of one who is committed to orthodoxy, but even to say this about his approach fails to do justice to certain aspects of his theological method. In the forthcoming sections I will demonstrate how Ratzinger reaches conservative conclusions about key Christian dogmas but does so with a method which is very much his own and which pays most attention to the existential situation of his readers.

Notwithstanding this acknowledgment of Ratzinger's creativity, the point must also be reiterated that my choice of credal themes is not incidental to the exercise. Their inclusion has a direct bearing on our examination of Ratzinger's suitability as a dialogue partner with evangelicals. A brief historical detour will illustrate the point. In the early decades of the twentieth-century conservative Protestantism in America found itself forced to define its core beliefs against an ascendant liberalism within the mainstream denominations.[67] Though this protest movement lapsed into obscurantism over time, it had at its inception (1910-1915) drawn on the support of moderate British scholar James Orr. This eminent Presbyterian was to contribute to a series of pamphlets entitled *The Fundamentals*, from which came the derogatory label, 'fundamentalist', that subsequently characterised the movement. What will

---

[63] Ratzinger, *Introduction to Christianity*, pp. 148-156.

[64] Ratzinger, *Introduction to Christianity*, p. 157.

[65] These amount to the ruling out of the possibility of the supernatural on the grounds that God cannot or will not contravene the natural order that he has put in place. Incarnation and bodily resurrection from the dead would be examples of such interventions.

[66] Ratzinger, *Introduction to Christianity*, pp. 169-170.

[67] Note the crucial historical account of this period in American evangelicalism written by George Marsden, *Fundamentalism and American Culture: The Shaping of Twentieth Century Evangelicalism 1870-1925* (Oxford: Oxford University Press, 1999).

become significant in terms of our analysis of Ratzinger's theology is that the conservative faction within the historic denominations (in this case influenced directly by Presbyterianism) identified five fundamental beliefs which were felt to sum up most acutely the essence of orthodox evangelical belief.[68] Whilst this list was very marginally amended over time[69], its relevance to our discussion is that it mirrors a number of the credal affirmations treated by Ratzinger in *The Introduction*. The 'five fundamentals' of conservative Protestantism were as follows:

1. The inspiration and inerrancy of Scripture
2. The deity of Jesus Christ
3. The virgin birth of Christ
4. The substitutionary, atoning work of Christ on the cross
5. The bodily resurrection and the personal bodily return of Christ to the earth.

Ratzinger's stance on these fundamental beliefs will offer insight into the common ground that exists between himself and evangelicals. In the previous pages, I have sought among other things to demonstrate Ratzinger's commitment to a robust orthodox Christology which the second of the 'fundamentals' also sought to affirm. With regard to the first, the inerrancy of Scripture, it must be conceded that Ratzinger holds a position that conflicts with the views of those traditional inerrantists who bear the label fundamentalist.[70] However, I would venture to say that subscription to strict inerrancy is no longer such a defining belief among evangelicals that one cannot legitimately claim the name without it. Not only was one of the key writers of *The Fundamentals* (James Orr) not inerrantist in outlook himself[71],

---

[68] In 1910 the Presbyterian General Assembly, partly in response to questions raised over the orthodoxy of certain graduates of Union Theological Seminary, 'adopted a five-point declaration of 'essential doctrines'. Summarised, these beliefs were: (1) the inerrancy of Scripture, (2) the Virgin Birth of Christ, (3) his substitutionary atonement, (4) his bodily resurrection, and (5) the authenticity of the miracles.' (Marsden, *Fundamentalism and American Culture*, p. 117.) Although not originally intended to be a creed or a definitive statement, it became known in the 1920's as 'the five points' and was the rallying position of the conservatives.

[69] See Marsden, *Fundamentalism and American Culture*, pp.117 and 262 n.30 where he explains that the fifth 'fundamental' from the early Presbyterian statement in 1910, 'the authenticity of the miracles' was replaced by 'the return of Christ.'

[70] See Ratzinger's lecture, 'Biblical Interpretation in Crisis: On the Question of the Foundations and Approaches of Exegesis Today' in which he calls the so-called Fundamentalist approach to Scripture into question. Whilst this was written during his tenure at the CDF, it is consonant with views he adopted during his theological training. Delivered on 27 January, 1988 at Saint Peter's Church in New York. http://www.christendom-awake.org/pages/ratzinger/biblical-crisis.htm (accessed 13 January, 2010)

[71] Interestingly, Mark A Noll in *Between Criticism and Faith: Evangelicals, Scholarship and the Bible* (Grand Rapids: Baker, 1991), p. 79 makes the point that recent research

but evangelical hermeneutics is now so nuanced that the sophisticated doctrines of inspiration advanced today by conservatives of all stripes bear little resemblance to the literalist model of inerrancy so popular in the past.[72] Thus given the growing subtlety in evangelical approaches to Scripture, one might argue that Ratzinger's vigorous opposition to central tenets of the historical critical method, whilst not making him a strict fundamentalist, qualifies him to be in a similar hermeneutical camp to those wishing to affirm Scripture's authority but likewise take the phenomena of the text seriously. His writings on hermeneutics would certainly indicate that this is the case.[73] These considerations of the first two of the 'fundamentals' are the necessary grounding to our investigation of the remainder of them as they are treated in *Introduction to Christianity*.

The Christological Articles of the Creed
Conceived of the Holy Ghost, born of the Virgin Mary

Here Ratzinger tackles the mystery of Jesus' origin from the Father. The classic statement of this is the idea of virginal conception found in the infancy narratives of Matthew and Luke. Ratzinger is aware that the stories are a 'thorn in the flesh' to rationalistic commentators and that a stock dismissal of the notion of virgin birth is prevalent among many scholars.[74] However, his study of the history of religions has brought home the differences between the traditional expression of the virgin birth myth (the one which rationalist theologians associate with the biblical accounts) and what we actually encounter in the New Testament. For Ratzinger, God's role in Jesus' conception is not primarily defined by the physical and biological.

> As we have seen, nothing of this sort appears in the New Testament: the conception of Jesus is new creation, not begetting by God. God does not become the biological father of Jesus, and neither the New Testament nor the theology of the Church has fundamentally ever seen in the narrative or in

---

surveys 'find no leading evangelical spokesmen who insisted upon a strict view of biblical inerrancy from the period after 1900 until World War II.'

[72] See the in-depth discussion of this issue in Noll, *Between Criticism and Faith*, pp. 142-161.

[73] The paper by Ratzinger cited previously, 'Biblical Interpretation in Crisis', demonstrates that the former Cardinal, though not Fundamentalist in outlook, was committed to an approach to Scripture which shared many of the same presuppositions as moderate Evangelicalism. Indeed, his concluding recommendations for proper exegesis of the biblical text would be heartily endorsed by most evangelicals.

[74] Ratzinger, *Introduction to Christianity*, p. 207. Ratzinger notes that critical scholars point to the general unhistorical thinking of the ancients which would allow them to speak in supernaturalist terms about a birth.

the event recounted in it the ground for the real divinity of Jesus, his 'Sonship' of God.[75]

Indeed, for Ratzinger, virginal conception is not absolutely required in order to hold to the deity of Christ.

> According to the faith of the Church the Sonship of Jesus does not rest on the fact that Jesus had no human father; the doctrine of Jesus' divinity would not be affected if Jesus had been the product of a normal human marriage. For the Sonship of which faith speaks is not a biological but an ontological fact, an event not in time but in God's eternity.[76]

However, this approach is clearly not for Ratzinger a subtle way of marginalizing the dogma of the virgin birth. It is more the case that some have understood the virgin birth as somehow constitutive of Jesus' nature as God's Son and he wishes to undo such a false impression. As he states, 'the contemporary aversion for both the tidings of the Virgin Birth and the full acknowledgment of the Sonship of Jesus rests on a fundamental misunderstanding of both and on the false connection between the two which seems to be widely assumed.'[77]

The question to be answered, however, is – given that Jesus' virginal conception by the power of the Spirit has nothing directly to do with his ontological Sonship, what meaning does it carry? Ratzinger suggests that its meaning is closely associated with the Messianic promises given to Israel. When one peruses salvation history, it becomes clear how central the concept of miraculous birth seems to be to the fulfilment of God's purposes.

> The Old Testament contains a whole series of miraculous births, always at decisive turning points in the history of salvation: Isaac's mother Sarah (Genesis 18), Samuel's mother (1 Sam 1-3), and the anonymous mother of Samson (Judg 13) are all barren and all human hope of their being blessed with children has been abandoned. With all three the birth of the child who eventually contributes to Israel's salvation comes to pass as a manifestation of the gracious mercy of God, who makes the impossible possible (Gen 18:14; Luke 1:37), elevates the lowly ... and pulls down the mighty from their thrones... With Elizabeth, John the Baptist's mother, this process is continued ... and reaches its climax and goal with Mary.[78]

---

[75] Ratzinger, *Introduction to Christianity*, p. 208.

[76] Ratzinger, *Introduction to Christianity*, p. 208. While these comments must be deemed unpromising from a traditional evangelical perspective, the point to bear in mind is that Ratzinger nevertheless affirms the virginal conception and in a later publication retracts his claim that Jesus' divinity would not have been compromised if he had had two human parents (see later discussion).

[77] Ratzinger, *Introduction to Christianity*, pp. 209-210.

[78] Ratzinger, *Introduction to Christianity*, p. 210.

Throughout the outworking of God's purposes what becomes clear, asserts Ratzinger, is that

> 'the salvation of the world does not come from man and from his own power; man must let it be bestowed upon him, and he can only receive it as a pure gift. The virgin birth is not a lesson in asceticism nor does it belong directly to the doctrine of Jesus' Sonship; it is first and last a theology of grace, a proclamation of how salvation comes to *us*: in the simplicity of acceptance, as the voluntary gift of the love that redeems the world.[79]

Jesus, in contrast to all those who were chosen before him, 'not only *receives* the spirit of God; in his earthly existence he *is* only through the spirit and therefore he is the fulfilment of all the prophets: he is the true prophet.' As we reflect on this type of reasoning it is possible to draw some comparison with the theology of Karl Barth. In a section entitled 'The Miracle of Christmas' in *Church Dogmatics*[80], one of the ways that Barth advocates the reasonableness of the virgin birth is to suggest that it demonstrates that the incarnation is all of grace, and that man is the passive partner unable to contribute to God's saving action. For Barth, like Ratzinger it would seem, if Jesus were the human child of Joseph and Mary, we would have a figure of humanity participating and contributing to the act which would bring about his own redemption.

The excursus on the Virgin Birth is concluded with a clear affirmation of its historicity. Ratzinger makes the point that all the assertions which have preceded what has gone before only have

> a meaning on the assumption that the happening whose meaning they seek to elucidate really took place. They are the interpretation of an event; if this event is removed they become empty talk which would have to be described not only as frivolous but as downright dishonest.[81]

Thus using a creative approach which does not entail defending the virginal conception on what he originally deemed to be spurious grounds, the young Professor is able to reassert the dogma from a study of salvation history and acknowledgment of the pre-eminence of grace in the scheme of salvation. Significantly, later in *Daughter Zion*, Ratzinger amends his position on the necessity of virginal conception as a result of von Balthasar's critique and acknowledges that the event has biological implications. His explanation for not initially affirming this was that he did not wish Jesus' ontological Sonship to seem dependent on an event in time.[82]

---

[79] Ratzinger, *Introduction to Christianity*, pp. 210-211.
[80] See Karl Barth, *Church Dogmatics* 1:2 (Edinburgh: T&T Clark, 1980), pp. 172-202.
[81] Ratzinger, *Introduction to Christianity*, p. 211.
[82] Joseph Ratzinger, *Daughter Zion* (San Francisco: Ignatius Press, 1983), p. 51. 'The virgin birth is the necessary origin of him who is the Son and who as Son first endows the messianic hope with a permanent significance extending far beyond Israel.' He adds in a footnote: 'With this statement I would like to emphasise clearly the limits of my

Suffered under Pontius Pilate, was crucified, dead and buried

An essential starting point for understanding Ratzinger's theology of atonement is his conviction that in theological discourse, an inappropriate wedge has been driven between Jesus' person and his work, between Christology and Soteriology. In his view, a true understanding of Christ's person is impossible when this is attempted in isolation from a consideration of his death and vice versa.[83] The ramifications of this position emerge in his treatment of Anselm's Satisfaction Theory which functions as the prelude to his own thoughts on atonement.

Ratzinger opens the discussion by reminding his readers of the degree to which the Satisfaction Theory has shaped the Western Christian consciousness and become the dominant model of atonement. However, he draws a distinction between the theory as it was originally enunciated by Anselm and the form that it has taken in the popular imagination. Whilst Anselm's first articulation of the idea is deemed to have some merit, he believes this has been eviscerated over time by the manner in which it has been popularised. His judgment is that 'even in its classical form [the theory] is not devoid of one-sidedness, ... [but] when contemplated in the vulgarised form which has extensively moulded the general consciousness it looks cruelly mechanical and less and less feasible.' [84]

His conclusion is that even though Anselm's theory possesses certain potential advantages[85], 'the perfectly logical divine-cum-human legal system [erected by the great theologian] ... can make the image of God appear in a sinister light.'[86] This is possible because 'God's unrelenting righteousness' which issues in a demand for a human sacrifice places the wrath of God and not the love of God at the centre of the redemptive action.[87] Indeed, the way

---

frequently cited observation in *Einführung in das Christentum* (Munich 1968), 225, that Jesus' divine sonship would not of itself exclude an origin in a normal marriage. I wanted only to emphasise very clearly the distinction of biological and ontological levels of thought and to clarify that the ontological statements of Nicaea and Chalcedon are not as such identical with the statements about the virgin birth. This should not be used to deny that, despite the distinction of levels, a deep, even an indissoluble correspondence exists between the two levels, between Jesus' unity of person with the eternal Son of the eternal Father and the earthly fatherlessness of the man Jesus. Yet I admit that I did not make the point clearly enough; to that degree von Balthasar's critique is justified.'

[83] 'That the two questions parted company, that the person and the work were made the subject of separate enquiries and treatises, led to both problems becoming incomprehensible and insoluble.' Ratzinger, *Introduction to Christianity*, p. 172.

[84] Ratzinger, *Introduction to Christianity*, p. 172.

[85] Ratzinger, *Introduction to Christianity*, p. 174. Ratzinger acknowledges that the theory 'takes account of crucial biblical and human perceptions' and '...will always command respect as an attempt to synthesize the individual elements and the biblical elements in one great all-embracing system.'

[86] Ratzinger, *Introduction to* Christianity, p. 174.

[87] This recoil from caricatured views of the atonement which are deemed to have impugned God's character, tells us little about how Ratzinger might have responded to

Anselm's theory has been subsequently configured is said to imbue the wrath with a certain ominous quality whilst making the love of God seem incredible and unbelievable.[88]

Ratzinger's rejoinder is that the cross is not portrayed biblically as 'a mechanism of injured right.'[89] Indeed, it is the very opposite of this if one stops to consider Jesus' person as well as his actions when contemplating the cross. In that light the cross is 'the expression of the radical nature of the love which gives itself completely, of the process in which one is what one does, and does what one is; it is the expression of a life that is completely being for others.'[90] He is able to make this judgment on the basis of a comparison between the biblical account of redemption and notions of expiation or redemption as they emerge in the non-Christian religions. In the latter case, the initiative stems from the side of humanity and the act of expiation is designed to change the divinity's attitude to the sinner. With the New Testament it is the Deity who takes the initiative and sets about the task of reconciliation. As Ratzinger expresses it,

> [I]n the New Testament the cross appears primarily as a movement from above to below. It does not stand there as the work of expiation which mankind offers to the wrathful God, but as the expression of that foolish love of God's which gives itself away to the point of humiliation in order thus to save man, it is *his* approach to us, not the other way about.[91]

However, it is significant that he goes on to acknowledge that the movement of the cross is not entirely downward, but that a host of texts speak of Jesus' act of expiation as a sacrifice made to the Father on humanity's behalf. This seems to reintroduce the emphasis that Ratzinger to this point has been repudiating. Must a choice therefore be made in favour of one over the other? Such an option is balked at by Ratzinger who believes that '… by doing so we should in the last analysis be elevating our own capricious opinion to the status of the criterion of faith.'[92] The solution to the relationship between the cross as the gracious initiative of God on the one hand, and an expiatory sacrifice offered to God on the other, is to examine how the New Testament utilizes the Old Testament liturgical texts on sacrifice in its discussion of the cross.[93] It is here that

---

more nuanced evangelical presentations of substitution which give full weight to the love of God. See, for example, John Stott, *The Cross of Christ* (Leicester: IVP, 1989) and Tony Lane 'The Wrath of God as an Expression of the Love of God' in Kevin J. Vanhoozer (ed.) *Nothing Greater Nothing Better: Theological Essays on the Love of God* (Grand Rapids: Eerdmans Publishing Company, 2001): pp. 138-167.

[88] Ratzinger, *Introduction to Christianity*, p. 214.
[89] Ratzinger, *Introduction to Christianity*, p. 124.
[90] Ratzinger, *Introduction to Christianity*, p. 214.
[91] Ratzinger, *Introduction to Christianity*, p. 215.
[92] Ratzinger, *Introduction to Christianity*, p. 216.
[93] Ratzinger, *Introduction to* Christianity, p. 216.

Ratzinger believes we will discover the proper balance between two seemingly opposed perspectives on what is happening in Jesus' passion.

It is to the Epistle to the Hebrews that Ratzinger turns in order to gain a biblical understanding of how the cross functions as an expiatory sacrifice. This is his text of choice because, here more than anywhere else, the writer '... connects the death of Jesus on the cross with the ritual and theology of the Jewish feast of reconciliation ...'[94] As he summarises the epistle's train of thought a quite individual perspective on the atonement emerges which is at the same time the product of detailed biblical exposition. Ratzinger is thus much less speculative than many developing innovative approaches in that his thoughts are tethered to the biblical text and not intended to be novel or revolutionary.

The substance of the writer to the Hebrews' argument, according to Ratzinger, is that sacrificial rituals of whatever kind are fruitless in effecting reconciliation with God. What is needed is something else. 'God does not seek bulls and goats but man; man's unqualified 'yes' to God can alone form true worship ... love's free yes is the only thing for which God must wait – the only worship or 'sacrifice' that can have any meaning.'[95]

Thus, it is in Jesus' sacrifice that true worship is taking place. Ratzinger says of this self-offering that, '... he who performed it broke through the confines of the liturgical act and made truth: he gave himself. He took from man's hands the sacrificial offerings and put in their place his sacrificed personality, his own 'I'.[96] It is at this juncture that the concept of representation or substitution (*Stellvertretung*) is shown to be dominant in Ratzinger's scheme. Jesus' self-offering of absolute love to the Father, in our place, is that which makes up for what human beings are by themselves powerless to do.[97] Intriguingly, it also speaks of the pointlessness of attempts to win justification by our own efforts.

> Christian worship consists in the absoluteness of love, as it could only be poured out by the one in whom God's own love had become human love; and it consists in the new form of representation included in this love, namely that it stood for us and we let ourselves be taken over by him. So it means that we can put aside our own attempts at justification ... It means that instead of indulging in the destructive rivalry of self-justification we accept the love of Jesus Christ that 'stands in' for us, let ourselves be united in it, and thus become worshippers with him and in him.[98]

---

[94] Ratzinger, *Introduction to* Christianity, p. 216.
[95] Ratzinger, *Introduction to Christianity*, p. 217.
[96] Ratzinger, *Introduction to Christianity*, p. 218.
[97] It is difficult to ignore the similarities between Ratzinger's view of Christ as the perfect worshipper, doing something in our place on the cross, and C. S. Lewis' portrayal of Christ as the perfect penitent. See chapter 4, 'The Perfect Penitent' in C. S. Lewis, *Mere Christianity* (London: Fount, 1983).
[98] Ratzinger, *Introduction to Christianity*, pp. 218-19.

This emphasis on the cross as worship, as Christ's self-offering of infinite love, begs the question which Ratzinger seeks to answer towards the close of his discussion of atonement. What is the relationship between sacrifice (or worship) and pain?[99] - a theme which is so central to the culture's appreciation of what was happening at Calvary. It is at this point that the exposition takes on a more abstract and impressionistic form. Christ is now viewed as a representative or substitute who, on the cross, not only offers infinite love but is stretched and torn apart in order to effect a reconciliation between human beings and God. Ratzinger admits that he is striving with some difficulty to articulate this idea and draws on the work of French Jesuit, Jean Daniélou, to help make firmer sense of it.[100] Although the author is writing on another theme, his reflections on what is happening through the cross are said to capture the heart of what Ratzinger was seeking to communicate.

> Between the heathen world and the threefold God there is only one link, and that is the cross of Christ. Yet when we move into this no-man's-land and try afresh to twitch the threads that link the heathen world and the threefold God, should we still be surprised that we can only do it in the cross of Christ? We must make ourselves resemble that cross, bear it within ourselves, 'always carrying in the body the death of Jesus', as St Paul says of the preacher of the faith (2 Cor 4:10). This feeling of being torn asunder, which is a cross to us, this inability of our heart to carry within itself simultaneously love of the most holy Trinity and a love of a world alienated from the Trinity, is precisely the death-agony of the only-begotten Son, an agony which he calls on us to share. He who bore this division within himself in order to abolish it within himself, and who could only abolish it because he had previously borne it within himself – he stretches from one end to the other. Without leaving the bosom of the Trinity he stretches out to the ultimate limit of human misery and fills the whole space in between. This stretching-out of Christ, symbolized by the four directions of the cross, is the mysterious expression of our own dismemberment and makes us like him.[101]

In Ratzinger's closing thoughts he reiterates once again that even this perspective on the cross is more about love than the accumulation and experience of pain. As he puts it,

> It is not pain as such that counts, but the breadth of love which spans existence so completely that it unites the distant and the near, bringing God-forsaken man into relation with God. It gives pain an aim and a meaning. Were it otherwise, then the executioners around the cross would have been the real priests; they who had caused the pain would have offered the sacrifice. But this was not the point; the point was that inner centre that bears and fulfils the pain, and therefore the executioners were not the priests;

---

[99] Ratzinger, *Introduction to Christianity*, p. 219.
[100] Ratzinger, *Introduction to Christianity*, pp. 220-21.
[101] Jean Daniélou, *Essai sur le mystère de l'histoire* (Paris, 1953)

the priest was Jesus, who re-united the two separate ends of the world in his love.[102]

From this overview it is clear that the early Ratzinger sought to remove from the reader's imagination any sense of a wrathful God demanding his pound of flesh through the slaughter of his Son. In that sense his thinking on the atonement is far distant from evangelical presentations which preserve and even glory in such formulations. Notwithstanding that, there are elements of Ratzinger's approach to the cross which resonate with a more moderate evangelical perspective. For example, he is uneasy with an individualistic and speculative soteriology, and seeks to anchor his view of the atonement in what Scripture actually says about it. It is also difficult to deny that he believes there is a certain necessity in what Jesus underwent during the crucifixion. One might go so far as to say that his death is portrayed as an objective, rather than a subjective, atonement. Moreover, substitution of one kind or other is present in much of what he writes. Christ offers the worship, in our place, which we were incapable of offering. Even more suggestively, as a substitute Christ enters on our behalf into the human state of God-forsakenness, being stretched to the very limit. These insights do not amount to a statement of traditional substitutionary atonement, but I would suggest that Ratzinger at this stage in his theological development has intuitively spoken words about the cross which some later evangelicals would deem full of promise. Certainly, they offer a platform for further developments of the notion of substitution in relation to God-forsakenness which could be ecumenically suggestive in relation to a dialogue with Evangelicalism.

Rose again from the dead

Ratzinger's treatment of the bodily resurrection of Christ brings to the fore the influence that personalism has on his theology. He presents the resurrection event as evidence of the truth found in Scripture (*Song of Sol 8:6*) that 'love is [as] strong as death.' While the original context for that saying is a poem in praise of the power of eros, Ratzinger does not diminish the significance of this because love itself, even love within the bounds of eros, is something which 'demands infinity, indestructibility ... and is, so to speak, a call for infinity.'[103] The tragedy from the human standpoint is that love fails to attain that which it demands and is itself part of the world of death. It is this tragic factum of human existence which, for Ratzinger, offers an insight into the meaning of the resurrection. Jesus' rising from the dead '*is* the greater strength of love in the face of death.'[104]

He lends force to this claim about the tragedy of human nature by suggesting that mankind's attempts at immortality, either via the notion of

---

[102] Ratzinger, *Introduction to Christianity*, pp. 221-22.
[103] Ratzinger, *Introduction to Christianity*, p. 230.
[104] Ratzinger, *Introduction to Christianity*, p. 230.

continued existence through offspring or the achievement of long-lasting fame, are doomed to failure since what continues to exist is merely an echo or shadow of what was there. If therefore humanity is to continue to exist in another, which seems the only possible option for an otherwise mortal life to be maintained, this *other* cannot be perishable as are progeny and fame. The only one capable of giving lasting stability and a life that would endure forever, is the one who has neither beginning nor end. As Ratzinger describes him, he is

> the God of the living, who does not hold just the shadow and echo of my being, whose ideas are not just copies of reality. I myself am his thought, which establishes me more securely, so to speak, than I am in myself; his thought is not the posthumous shadow but the original source and strength of my being. In him, I can stand as more than a shadow; in him I am truly closer to myself than I should be if I just tried to stay by myself.[105]

This same notion is then presented in a radically different form employing some of the vocabulary and concepts of Pierre Teilhard de Chardin, the famous Jesuit palaeontologist whose writings had been suppressed by the church up until his death in 1955.[106] Ratzinger, once more addressing the relationship between love and death, suggests that only in a situation where one places love above life itself, can one say that love is stronger than death. He then speculates that if this monumental task could be achieved in reality, and not just in aspiration, that it would mean that the power of love had proven itself superior to the power of that which is merely biological. Taking up the language of Teilhard, he attempts to demonstrate that Jesus' self-giving on the cross signalled a new stage in evolution which made possible the leap from merely human or biological existence to existence in the realm of the spirit.

> To use Teilhard de Chardin's terminology, where that took place [love being placed above life itself], the decisive complexity or 'complexification' would have occurred; *bios* too would be encompassed and incorporated in the power of love. It would cross the boundary – death – and create unity where death divides. If the power of love for another were so strong anywhere that it could keep alive not just the memory, the shadow of his 'I', but that person himself, then a new stage in life would have been reached. This would mean that the realm of biological evolutions and mutations had been left behind and the leap made on to a quite different plane, on which love was no longer subject to *bios* but made use of it. Such a final stage of 'mutation' and 'evolution' would itself be no longer a biological stage; it would signify the end of the sovereignty of *bios*, which at the same time is the sovereignty of death; it would open up the realm which the Greek Bible calls '*zoe*', that is definitive life, which has left behind the rule of death. The last stage of evolution needed by the world to reach its goal would then no

---

[105] Ratzinger, *Introduction to Christianity*, p. 232.
[106] Teilhard de Chardin, against his superiors' wishes, arranged for his works to be published posthumously.

longer be achieved within the realm of biology but by spirit, by freedom, by love. It would no longer be evolution, but decision and gift in one.[107]

The groundwork which Ratzinger has thus laid down allows him to relate the subject of love and death directly to the question of Jesus' resurrection. It is the risen Christ, as the revelation of the triune God, who provides the absolute permanence whereby our personal existence is upheld even beyond death. Indeed, he was uniquely placed to do this after the event of the incarnation by means of a supreme act of love which was greater in power than the power of *bios*. The transition from *bios* to *zoe* which up to this point is the explanation of what the victory of love over death means for the cosmos, is also the grid by which Ratzinger explores the resurrection as it is recounted in the gospels. He stresses that Jesus' risen life is not a return to *bios* and life in the biological realm as it had previously been known by him. It is a life of a different and superior order but one which was conceived nonetheless in history and which is itself a testimony to the fact that 'love has here broken through death and thus transformed fundamentally the situation of all of us.'[108] This definitive life, which is the prototype for the future existence of all believers, is no longer subject to chemical and biological laws but inhabits the realm of eternity. Thus given the newness of this life and its differentiation from the concrete physical existence of bios, Ratzinger wishes to define the post-resurrection encounters with the risen Jesus as 'appearances.' Jesus is not always recognised, he is both the same and quite different simultaneously, and whether or not he is recognised seems to lie more with his decision to 'reveal' himself than any obvious recognisability which one might associate with the post-resurrection state.[109] In this sense, the resurrection encounters are mysterious, lacking in clarity and not able to be measured by the same standards as we would measure other more conventional and mundane occurrences.

However, this reluctance to present the resurrection appearances according to the canons of any normal historical event does not mean that Ratzinger is resorting to a subjective interpretation of what happened. As he states with regard to the previous discussion in which he has highlighted the strangeness of these Resurrection 'appearances', 'Of course, all this is only half the story; to stop at this alone would mean falsifying the evidence of the New Testament.'[110]

In his view, the resurrection narratives

> testify to an approach which did not rise from the hearts of the disciples but came to them from outside, convinced them *against* their doubts and made them certain that the Lord had truly risen. *He who lay in the grave is no longer there; he – really he himself – lives.* He who had been transposed into the other world of God showed himself powerful enough to make it palpably

---

[107] Ratzinger, *Introduction to Christianity*, pp. 232-233.
[108] Ratzinger, *Introduction to Christianity*, p. 234.
[109] Ratzinger, *Introduction to Christianity*, p. 235.
[110] Ratzinger, *Introduction to Christianity*, p. 236.

clear that he himself stood opposite them again, that in him the power of love had really proved itself stronger than the power of death.[111]

Indeed, as if to banish any lingering uncertainty about what he might mean by the resurrection of Christ, Ratzinger closes the discussion by arguing that only by taking these recent statements with the same degree of seriousness as the earlier ones he made about the 'appearances', is one faithful to the New Testament witness. For him, it is impossible to hold to the Christian faith and to 'religion within the bounds of pure reason.'[112] One must choose between an objective resurrection and the worldview that dismisses such a possibility in an *a priori* fashion.[113]

---

[111] Ratzinger, *Introduction to Christianity*, p. 237 (italics mine).

[112] Ratzinger, *Introduction to Christianity*, p. 237.

[113] Contra Walter Kasper ('Das Wesen des Christlichen. B,' *Theologische Review* 65/3 (1969): pp. 182-188) and Patrick James Fletcher (*Resurrection and Platonic Dualism: Joseph Ratzinger's Augustinianism*, Catholic University of America, 2011 dissertation) who claim that Ratzinger demythologizes the resurrection in the closing section of *Introduction to Christianity* (pp. 273ff). The offending statement is the following: 'It now also becomes clear that the real heart of the faith in resurrection does not consist at all in the idea of the restoration of bodies, to which we have reduced it in our thinking; such is the case even though this is the pictorial image used throughout the Bible.' (p. 274) Fletcher treats this statement as Ratzinger's paradigmatic position on the resurrection (see *Resurrection and Platonic Dualism*, pp. 136-37) and concludes that at this point in his career he was demonstrably out of step with orthodoxy. However, three factors serve to undermine Fletcher's conclusion and support the view that Ratzinger remained essentially orthodox.1. Seven pages after the reference to resurrection not being about the 'restoration of bodies' we encounter the caption '*The question of the resurrected body*' under which Ratzinger tells his readers that the issue of whether a resurrection body exists still awaits address. It is clear from this that his actual position has not yet been stated and the earlier quotation cannot be taken as his definitive stance. 2. Ratzinger goes on to affirm that there is a resurrected body and that the resurrection involves the incorporation of matter: 'Has, then, the resurrection no relation at all to matter? ... If the cosmos is history and if matter represents a moment in the history of spirit, then there is no such thing as an eternal, neutral combination of matter and spirit; rather, there is a final 'complexity' in which the world finds its omega and unity. In that case there is *a final connection between matter and spirit* in which the destiny of man and the world is consummated, even if it is impossible for us today to define the nature of the connection.' (p. 277) Ratzinger's conclusion (based on 1 Corinthians 15) is that resurrection is not a return to the same physical conditions as existed prior to death, but induction into a new form of life that will have a material dimension which we are not yet in a position to define with any clarity. N.T. Wright (*The Resurrection of the Son of God*) reaches similar conclusions in his discussion of the same passage though he uses the term 'non-corruptible physicality' to help define the resurrected state. The difference, however, is only semantic in that non-corruptible physicality doubles for what Ratzinger would have meant by a resurrection that combines both matter and spirit and is not a reproduction of the old, corruptible, biological life. 3. The meaning of

From thence he shall come to judge the living and the dead

Ratzinger opens his discussion of eschatology in dialogue with the existentialist theologian, Rudolf Bultmann, who felt that the doctrine of Final Judgment was one of those disposable elements of faith rendered obsolete by current scientific knowledge. The problem Ratzinger has with such a view is that the biblical message about the end of the world has undoubted cosmological elements to it and it is unclear to what degree these are imagery and to what degree they are reality. Seen from another vantage point, the end of the world - as it is portrayed in the New Testament - is also an anthropological event. It is human history being brought to that end which has 'been dictated and achieved by God.'[114] How, therefore, do these cosmological and anthropological backdrops relate to each other within the wider context of the Bible?

Ratzinger's first observation is that there is a necessary relationship between the cosmos and humanity.

> [F]or the Bible the cosmos and man are not two clearly separable quantities, with the cosmos forming the fortuitous scene of human existence, which in itself could be parted from the cosmos and allowed to accomplish itself without a world. On the contrary, world and human existence belong necessarily to one another, so that neither a worldless man nor even a world without man seems thinkable.[115]

Ratzinger proceeds again to introduce the thought of Teilhard de Chardin as a means of making contemporary sense of a difficult credal doctrine. Using terminology similar to that which was employed to explain the meaning of the resurrection, he suggests that there is an essential union between the cosmos

---

Ratzinger's earlier reference to the resurrection not being a 'restoration of bodies' must also centre on his use of the word *Rückgabe* (return gift) which is translated 'restoration'. The original German can only mean a return to the old physical existence prior to death and Ratzinger is quite right to assert the difficulty with this common misapprehension about the nature of resurrection. Indeed, his statements in *Eschatology* about Paul's view of the resurrection fill out what has already been stated in *Introduction to Christianity* and illustrate that for him corporeality is essential to resurrection: '...Paul's unconditional rejection of the naturalistic approach [i.e. resurrection as the restoration of bodies] does not stop him from continuing to speak of the resurrection of the body, different though this is from the resuscitation of corpses as the world would conceive it. For Paul, the abandonment of naturalism does not mean abandoning the resurrection but illuminating it. To his mind, body exists not only in the Adamic mode of the ensouled body but also in the Christological mode prefigured in the resurrection of Jesus, a corporeality stemming from the Holy Spirit. In other words, what Paul opposes to a physicalist realism is not spiritualism but a pneumatic realism.' (Joseph Ratzinger, *Eschatology*, pp. 169-170 cf. Wright, *Resurrection of the Son of God*, (London: SPCK, 2003), pp. 348 ff.)

[114] Ratzinger, *Introduction to Christianity*, p. 244 (italics mine).

[115] Ratzinger, *Introduction to Christianity*, p. 244.

and humanity which will ensure that the end of the world or the coming of the Lord involves the renewal of both humanity and the cosmos.

> Cosmos and man, which already belong to each other even though they so often stand opposed to one another, will become one through their 'complexification' in the larger entity of that love that, as we said earlier, steps beyond and encompasses *bios*. Thus it becomes evident here once again that the New Testament rightly depicts this resurrection as *the* eschatological happening.[116]

The underlying process of thought going on in the development of Ratzinger's argument seems to be influenced to some degree by elements of both Idealism and evolutionary mysticism. He is at pains to disabuse his readers of any notion that the cosmos is simply a receptacle for history but yet somehow detached from it. For Ratzinger, '… the cosmos is movement; … it is not just a case of history *existing in* it, … the cosmos itself *is* history. It does not merely form the scene of human history; before human history began and later with it, it is itself '*history*'.[117]

The allusions to both Idealism and Teilhard become more obvious as he describes 'one single all-embracing world history' (combining both cosmos and humanity) which is developing purposefully. The emergence of *spirit* in this cosmic movement is not some accidental by product of progress but something which is essential to the *telos* towards which everything is moving. Ratzinger's thought at this point is extremely complex and owes much to the German audience for whom he was originally writing, who were conversant with both Idealism and the new evolutionary theology. But what he is essentially saying, as his own summary makes clear, is 'that nature and mind form one single history, which advances in such a way that mind emerges more and more clearly as the all embracing element and thus anthropology and cosmology finally in actual fact coalesce.'[118] He takes the argument a stage further when he suggests that the increasing 'complexification' of things through mind implies its coming together around a personal centre. In his view, 'mind' in its specific nature exists not just as some nebulous construct but as 'person in community,' the only true mode in which 'mind' can fundamentally exist. Thus the argument that the world is moving towards 'complexification' through mind 'also implies that the cosmos is moving towards a unification in the personal.'[119]

This vivid depiction of the world's movement towards an omega point is Ratzinger's innovative way of introducing Christology and relating it to the final culmination of the evolutionary process. Indeed the positivism of Christology in which one individual becomes the centre point of all history is the very thing which makes sense of the journey that cosmic and human history is on.

---

[116] Ratzinger, *Introduction to Christianity*, p. 245.
[117] Ratzinger, *Introduction to Christianity*, p. 245.
[118] Ratzinger, *Introduction to Christianity*, p. 246.
[119] Ratzinger, *Introduction to Christianity*, p. 246.

> The intrinsic necessity of this positivism here becomes apparent afresh: if it is true that at the end stands the triumph of the spirit, that is the triumph of truth, freedom and love, then it is not just some force or other that finally ends up victorious; what stands at the end is a countenance. The omega of the world is a 'you', a person, an individual. The all-encompassing 'complexification', the unification embracing all, is at the same time the final denial of all collectivism, the denial of the fanaticism of the mere idea, even the so-called 'idea of Christianity'. Man, person always takes precedence over the mere idea.[120]

Given the way this process of 'complexification' is described, it is necessary for Ratzinger to dispel one potential misconception which may have arisen. The breakthrough to what he describes as 'the ultra complexity of the final phase' is by no means a 'neutral cosmic drift.' As this final stage is itself characterised by 'freedom' or 'responsibility', it must be entered into (if one is to enter in) by means of personal choice. It is not in itself an inexorable process which human beings are caught up in irrespective of their own volition. Ratzinger, although couching the discussion in the relatively unfamiliar language of 'complexification', ultimately presents a fairly orthodox understanding of Final Judgment in which there is no automatic universalism at work but the solemn honouring of individual freedom. As Ratzinger puts it, 'There is a freedom which is not cancelled out even by grace and indeed is brought by it face to face with itself: man's final fate is not forced upon him regardless of the decisions he has made in his life.'[121]

There are two issues at this point which call out for further elucidation. The first is Ratzinger's extensive deployment of concepts developed by Teilhard de Chardin[122] and the second is his recourse to the language of Idealism. It might be asserted that in explicating credal themes by these means Ratzinger has in some way crossed the Rubicon and tethered himself to an essentially liberal outlook. I would suggest that such a criticism loses much of its force when we consider the overall context of his thought. Whilst it is undeniable that Teilhard de Chardin's ideas have been developed in very unorthodox directions (a tendency which Ratzinger has labelled 'Teilhardian'[123]), it is not at all clear that this has been the case with our subject. Two quotations (one of which pre-dates the writing of *Introduction to*

---

[120] Ratzinger, *Introduction to Christianity*, p. 247.
[121] Ratzinger, *Introduction to Christianity*, p. 247.
[122] Although this issue is addressed in the main body of the text, it is helpful to give some further context for Ratzinger's extensive use of Teilhard de Chardin. Fletcher (*Resurrection and Platonic Dualism*, p.134) notes a widespread tendency amongst mid-twentieth century Catholic theologians to 'situate whatever they are doing within an 'evolutionary framework' and suggests that Ratzinger would have found it difficult to frame his thought without paying heed to that established academic pattern.
[123] Note his comments in Joseph Ratzinger, *Theological Highlights of Vatican II* (New York: Paulist Press, 1966), p. 226.

Christianity) reveal his unease with liberal readings of Teilhard de Chardin. Commenting in 1966 on the theology of *Gaudium et Spes*[124], Ratzinger cites a German Lutheran scholar's use of a remark which had been attributed to the French mystic, 'You are all hypnotised by evil.' The scholar was to follow that statement by voicing approval of the sentiment,

> Isn't he right with his sovereign disdain for sin and evil, with his will to see the world as a good creation, to regard it positively and not overestimate what is negative... Teilhard is in agreement with Karl Barth ... Even for the Bible, sin is not the central idea to the extent it is for Teilhard de Chardin's critics. For Paul himself, to whom they appeal, sin has been overcome in Christ and has lost its domination; it belongs to the old aeon which is past.[125]

Ratzinger's response, however, is instructive in that he quite definitively repudiates the outlook attributed to Teilhard (though he raises questions in the footnotes about whether Daeke has been fair to the French theologian in the way he has drawn out his thought): 'Now the Council did not show a sovereign disdain for sin and evil and there is really no reason to do so, either from the Bible or our own experience (especially of the present century).'[126]

This sentiment is given fullest expression in a later work in which Ratzinger attacks 'Teilhardism's rejection of an historical fall. His language makes clear that his theological instincts are profoundly at odds with those who would reinterpret anthropology in the manner suggested by the most common reading of Teilhard de Chardin.

> In an evolutionist hypothesis of the world (which corresponds to a certain 'Teilhardism' in theology), there is obviously no place for an 'original sin'. This, at most, is merely a symbolic, mythical expression to designate the *natural* deficiencies of a creature like man, who, from the most imperfect origins, moves towards perfection, toward his complete realisation. Acceptance of this view signifies, however, turning the structure of Christianity on its head: Christ is displaced from the past to the future. Salvation would simply mean moving toward the future as the necessary development to the better. Man is but a product who has not yet been fully perfected by time. There has never been a 'redemption' because there was no sin on account of which man would need to be healed ...[127]

---

[124] Joseph Ratzinger, 'The Dignity of the Human Person' in Herbert Vorgrimler (ed), *Commentary on the Documents of Vatican II* (Vol. 5) (London: Burns & Oats/Herder and Herder, 1966), p.124.

[125] S.M. Daeke writing about Teilhard de Chardin and the Pastoral Constitution on the Church in the Modern World in J.C. Hampe, (ed) *Die Autorität der Freiheit III* (1967) pp. 98-112 cited in Vorgrimler, *Commentaries on Vatican II* (Volume 5), p. 124.

[126] Ratzinger, 'The Dignity of the Human Person' cited in Vorgrimler, *Commentaries on Vatican II* (Volume 5), p. 124.

[127] Joseph Ratzinger and Vittorio Messorri, *The Ratzinger Report* (San Francisco: Ignatius Press, 1985), p. 80.

Given these deep concerns with 'Teilhardism', it strikes me as more likely that Ratzinger at the time of the *Introduction* believed Teilhard de Chardin's ideas to be capable of application in ways which were not at variance with orthodox theology and which could be profitably used in the Tübingen context. This view is given further weight when it is noted that Ratzinger's mentor and fellow *ressourcement* theologian (Henri de Lubac) had at that time written a positive introduction to Teilhard's theology which emphasised the orthodox elements within it while also acknowledging the material's potential for abuse.[128]

As noted, the second question mark against his theology needing redress was his borrowing of the language of philosophical Idealism. Was Ratzinger here accepting the presuppositions of Hegel and other Idealists or was his thinking still within the bounds of mainstream Christian thought? Fortunately, we are not left in a quandary in that regard because in another section of the *Introduction* he engages in the debate between Idealism and philosophical materialism.[129] His goal is to show that neither gives an accurate account of reality and that the insights of the Christian faith proffer a better way forward. His closing summation provides a nuanced statement about the nature of creation which I believe to be commensurate with orthodox belief. Indeed, would we expect anything else from a theologian so wedded to the tradition and uncomfortable with the exercise of private judgment? Ratzinger writes,

> The Christian belief in God is not completely identical with either of these solutions [i.e. Idealism or philosophical materialism]. To be sure, it too will say, being is being-thought. Matter itself points beyond itself to thinking as the earlier and more original factor. But in opposition to idealism, which makes all being into moments of an all-embracing consciousness, the Christian belief in God will say: Being is being-thought – yet not in such a way that it remains only thought and that the appearance of independence discloses itself to him who looks more closely as mere appearance. On the contrary, Christian belief in God means that things are the being-thought of a creative consciousness, of a creative freedom, and that the creative consciousness that bears up all things has released what has been thought into the freedom of its own, independent existence. In this it goes beyond any mere idealism. While the latter explains, as we have just established, everything real as the content of a single consciousness, in the Christian view what supports it all is a creative freedom that sets what has been thought in the freedom of its own being, so that on the one hand it is the being-thought of a consciousness and yet on the other true self-being.[130]

---

[128] Henri de Lubac, *Teilhard Explained* (New York: Paulist Press, 1968), p. 74: 'We can observe in Père Teilhard beside eminent merits a certain number of tendencies which, freed by their isolation, could lead to abusive consequences.'

[129] See his discussion 'Faith in God Today' in pp. 105-110 of *Introduction to Christianity*.

[130] Ratzinger, *Introduction to Christianity*, p. 110.

Having considered the issues raised by the references to Teilhard and Idealism in Ratzinger's thought, it is appropriate to return briefly to the subject of Final Judgment. Although Ratzinger fairly comprehensively rejects universalism[131], it is interesting to note that he ends his discussion of Final Judgment with recourse to the New Testament's more optimistic perspective on the Parousia, summed up in the glorious cry recorded by Paul in 1 Corinthians of *'Marana Tha'*, 'Our Lord come.' In marked contrast to the Middle Ages designation of the Second Coming as *'Dies irae'*, this cry of longing focuses on the hope and joy associated with the meeting with the Lord and Ratzinger suggests that this note was not missing in the outlook of those who originally framed the Apostles Creed. He quotes this statement from the so-called Second Epistle of Clement to justify this perspective on the Creed, 'Brothers, we must think of Jesus as God, as him who judges the living and the dead. We must not think little of our salvation, for by thinking little of him we also think little of our hope.'[132]

Thus rather than labour the darker side of the Parousia, he is content to highlight the hopeful which he believes is already present in this article of the Creed since the judgment here described has been committed not to an unknown and fearsome deity, but to one who understands our condition from the inside.

> ... he has handed the judgment over to one who, as man, is our brother. It is not a stranger who judges us but he whom we know in faith. The judge will not advance to meet us as quite the other, but as one of us, who knows human existence from inside and has suffered.[133]

One might close this discussion about Ratzinger's perspective on judgment by reminding ourselves of two aspects of his theological method which are determinative for his discussion of this theme. The first is the recourse to personalism which consistently places any discussion of dogma within the context of our lives and needs as human beings. This in itself is an attempt to establish a genuine meeting point with the listener. Secondly, there is the central place of Jesus Christ himself, and the individual's relationship to him, which here and in so many other contexts is the culmination and summation of his theological enquiries.

---

[131] Ratzinger, *Introduction to Christianity*, p. 249. Note these unequivocal words towards the end of his discussion, 'To judge the living and the dead' – this also means that no one but *he* has the right to judge in the end. This implies that the unrighteousness of the world does not have the last word, not even by being wiped out indifferently in a universal act of grace; on the contrary, there is a last court of appeal which preserves justice, in order thus to be able to perfect love.' Cf. *Eschatology: Death and Eternal Life* (Washington: Catholic University of America Press, 1988), p. 215.

[132] 2 Clement 1:1ff cited in Ratzinger, *Introduction to Christianity*, p. 250.

[133] Ratzinger, *Introduction to Christianity*, p. 251.

Ecclesiology and the Second Vatican Council

The discussion so far has sought to showcase the fundamentally conservative or traditional nature of Ratzinger's theology. The argument has been made that even though he was creative, if not daring, in his use of theological sources, there was little doubt that his ultimate convictions were consonant with orthodox belief. One question thus remains with regard to the nature of his early theology. If Ratzinger had always been essentially conservative, why is it that he underwent such a fundamental sea change in outlook in the late 1960s? To address that question we must acquaint ourselves with the reformist Ratzinger who was so strongly identified with the push for renewal and change at Vatican II.

Fortunately, we are uniquely placed to assess Ratzinger's theological stance during and after Vatican II as he was both a significant player in the events that unfolded during the years 1962- 65[134] , as well as a seasoned commentator who wrote extensively on the Council. The following picture emerges as we consider his writings at the time along with his more mature reflections contained in his autobiography.

Ratzinger's later judgment that his reformist tendencies were in reaction to a stultifying neo-scholasticism seems borne out by what he writes about the Council in his 1966 work, *Theological Highlights of Vatican II*. In a discussion regarding the use of Latin, which I will return to later, he makes very clear his dissatisfaction with the path taken by Catholic theology over the previous two to three centuries.

> For it can hardly be denied that the sterility to which Catholic theology and philosophy had in many ways been doomed since the Enlightenment was due not least to a language in which the living choices of the human spirit no longer found a place.[135]

---

[134] Allen, *Cardinal Ratzinger*, p. 55. Allen cites auxiliary bishop of Vienna, Helmut Kratzl's memoir, *Im Sprung Gehemmt: Was mir nach dem Konzil noch alles fehlt* (Mödling: St. Gabriel, 1998), which describes life as a seminarian in Rome at the time of the Council. The future bishop notes the pivotal role of Cardinal Frings and his peritus Ratzinger in helping to shape the Council. To future German-speaking priests Ratzinger was a man of immense stature who 'inserted himself energetically for a renewed vision of the church.' Summarising Kratzl's picture of Ratzinger at Vatican II Allen writes, 'Though Ratzinger's official role was as an advisor to Frings, he was not simply a behind-the-scenes man in the sense that others at the council did not know who he was or what he was doing. Although Ratzinger could not speak on the council floor, he was a public figure in every other way. He gave lectures on council topics at various spots in Rome and in Germany, he organized briefing sessions for the council fathers, and he published a well-known series of council commentaries.'

[135] Ratzinger, *Theological Highlights of Vatican II*, p. 18.

However, the limitations placed on the theological enterprise by neo-scholasticism and its attachment to Latin were not the sole aspect of his lament. The young Ratzinger was concerned about an attitude of defensiveness which had a debilitating effect on Catholic theology. The towering figure of John XXIII and his famed posture of openness was something which Ratzinger felt had the potential to overcome the forces of negativity operating in the church. Perhaps he saw the sixties as the time when the Catholic Church stepped out from the shadow of conservative paranoia.

> We shall have occasion to show in more detail how the anti-Modernist neurosis which had time and again crippled the Church from the turn of the century here seemed to be approaching a cure. Here there emerged a new awareness of how the Church could conduct a dialogue in fraternal frankness without violating the obedience that belongs to faith. [136]

This daring association of traditional Catholic theology with what he describes as an anti-Modernist neurosis certainly places him in the camp of those seeking a fresh direction for theology. The question it raises, though, is how much that stance reflected dissatisfaction with the substance of Catholic theology as opposed to simply its method. The later thought of Küng and Schillebeeckx would indicate that some of his colleagues were becoming as uneasy with substance as they were with methodology.[137] Are we given any clue in the commentaries of the time as to whether Ratzinger's unease extended beyond simple frustration at what he felt to be a self-limiting approach? The answer that seems to emerge is that whilst disapproving of what he terms anti-Modernist hysteria, the earlier Ratzinger was nevertheless a theologian with an orthodox cast of mind. This seems evident in some comments made about two of the famous Catholic modernists from the beginning of the twentieth century.

> During these years [the reactionary period in the early 1900s] there arose an embittered discussion in such tragic figures as Loisy and Tyrrell, men who thought they could not save the faith without throwing away the inner core as well as the expendable shell.[138]

Ratzinger's distinction here between inner core and expendable shell echo comments made much later in *Milestones* about the purpose of his theology always having been to free up the inner kernel of the faith. As a young theologian with intimate knowledge of church history, the history of dogma and the history of religions, he was profoundly aware that the reductionist and simplistic approach of the scholastic text books neither did justice to the task of theology nor to the needs of modern people who would be dissatisfied with any posture deemed to be authoritarian. An altogether more open and intellectually

---

[136] Ratzinger, *Theological Highlights of Vatican II*, p. 11.
[137] For a discussion of Küng's movement away from orthodoxy see Leo Scheffczyk, *On Being A Christian: The Hans Küng Debate* (Dublin: Four Courts Press, 1982).
[138] Ratzinger, *Theological Highlights of Vatican II*, p. 21.

rigorous approach was required for the twentieth century. However there seems to be little sense that what he has in mind is a *carte blanche* to fundamentally reinterpret the faith. I will argue that his approach is summed up in those words cited earlier about the church learning to 'conduct a dialogue in fraternal frankness without violating the obedience that belongs to faith.' The early Ratzinger seems to have felt that a greater degree of honest dialogue was required but that there were clear parameters within which such a discussion could take place. 'Not violating the obedience that belongs to faith' suggests certain boundaries of orthodoxy beyond which no Catholic theologian could legitimately go.[139] An interesting corroboration of this view of Ratzinger comes from G.C. Berkouwer, an evangelical who was an official observer at the Council.

> According to Ratzinger the question of whether the narrow anti-modernist spirit will dominate the Church or whether the Church is ready for 'a revitalized encounter with its own origins, with its brothers and with the world' is the question that forms the background to the Vatican Council ... Those of Ratzinger's mind do not have a drop of modernism in their veins, but they do appreciate that the dangers facing the church in our day cannot be met by avoiding the real problems, for if the church avoids these, it will lose its influence, if not now then for the next generation.[140]

However, whilst Ratzinger's leanings were fundamentally orthodox, there is little doubt that some of his pronouncements placed him at odds with his later more conservative persona. The foremost example may be his position vis-à-vis the issue of collegiality. This was an idea that gained prominence at Vatican II and which highlighted the role Bishops played as the successors of the apostles as well as their function of leadership alongside the Pope. It was a notion that was repugnant to Papal maximalists but one to which the young Ratzinger lent his support. In his *Theological Reflections on Vatican II* he is careful to reiterate that the doctrine of collegiality, of which he clearly approves, does not mean a displacement of the role of the Pope.

> The efforts of the Council were aimed at a new and clear-cut validation of this structure of ecclesiastical office (i.e. collegiality). It is true that the Council in no way diminished the special position Peter occupied among the 12, in keeping with the special mission entrusted to him by the Lord, independently of collegiality. But the debate also brought out the fact that Peter remained one of the 12, and that he remained within the community and not outside of it. So no-one even indirectly questioned the pope's

---

[139] This interpretation of Ratzinger's words is supported by comments made in his autobiography that even in the wake of the council he 'continued to think that the fundamental consensus to be expected among Catholic theologians would remain.' Ratzinger, *Milestones*, p. 135.

[140] G.C. Berkouwer. *The Second Vatican Council and the New Catholicism* (Grand Rapids: Eerdmans, 1965), p. 74.

special position as successor of St Peter, as defined at Vatican Council 1 in 1870. But it was now possible to point more clearly to its inner context. Just as Peter belonged to the community of the 12, so the pope belongs to the college of bishops, regardless of the special role he fills, not outside but within the college.[141]

However, in its outworkings, Ratzinger clearly saw scope for a wider expression of collegiality than would have ever been envisaged before Vatican II. In an extensive 1965 article written for Concilium on 'The Pastoral Implications of Episcopal Collegiality'[142], he explored in detail the case for a model of collegiality which stretched back to the patterns of the early church. Most noteworthy from the standpoint of his later statements is his characterization of Bishops' Conferences as having a partially collegial function.

> Let us dwell for a moment on the bishops' conferences, for these seem to offer themselves today as the best means of concrete plurality in unity. They have their prototype in the synodal activity of the regionally different 'colleges' of the ancient church. They are also a legitimate form of the collegiate structure of the church. One not infrequently hears the opinions that the bishops' conferences lack all theological basis and could therefore not act in a way that could be binding on an individual bishop. The concept of collegiality, so it is said, could be applied only to the common action of the entire episcopate. Here again we have a case where a one-sided and unhistorical systematization breaks down, ...We should say rather that the concept of collegiality, besides the office of unity which pertains to the pope, signifies an element of variety and adaptability that belongs to the structure of the Church, but may be actuated in many different ways. The collegiality of the Bishops signifies that there should be in the Church (under and in the unity guaranteed by the primacy) an ordered plurality. The Bishops' Conferences are, then, one of the possible forms of collegiality that is here partially realised but with a view to the totality.[143]

Avery Dulles, summarising the position of the young Ratzinger in that 1965 article, paints a picture of church authority directly at odds with what the older Ratzinger would have been satisfied. He notes that

---

[141] Ratzinger, *Theological Highlights of Vatican II*, p. 51.
[142] Joseph Ratzinger, 'The Pastoral Implications of Episcopal Collegiality'. *Communio International Review* 1965.
[143] It would be unfair to Ratzinger not to complete the quotation as he makes clear that collegiality in this context only really works when there is inter-relationship between different parts of the church under the facilitation of the primacy:
'After what has been said it appears important that the Bishops' Conferences do not exist side by side but in a kind of *perichoresis,* lest the movement toward plurality lead to a splintering. Mutual exchange will be more important the more the individual areas of the Church unfold their particular characteristics. In comparison to the tasks of the former times, the primacy will face quite new tasks in aiding and initiating such exchanges.'

Behind collegiality lies the vision of the Church as made up of relatively autonomous communities under their respective bishops. The rediscovery of the local church makes it clear that multiplicity belongs to the structure of the church. According to the NT, Ratzinger observes, the church is a communion of local churches, mutually joined together through the Body and the Word of the Lord, especially when gathered at the Eucharist. Bishops, as heads of particular churches, must collaborate with one another in a ministry that is essentially communal. Not all initiative has to rest with the Pope alone; he may simply accept what the body of bishops or some portion of it decrees.[144]

We may note that by the mid 1980s and early 1990s the older Ratzinger had substantially altered his position both with regard to the status of Episcopal Conferences and the priority of the local church. With regard to the former, he wrote in 1986 that; 'We must not forget that the Episcopal conferences have no theological basis; they do not belong to the structure of the Church as willed by Christ, that cannot be eliminated; they have only a practical, concrete function.[145]

Likewise, by 1992, Ratzinger favours the ontological and historical priority of the universal church over the particular churches.[146] This was a standpoint which would later produce conflict with his fellow German prelate, Walter Kasper, who defended the relative autonomy of the local churches with similar argumentation to that supplied by the early Ratzinger. Whatever the justification for the volte-face there can be little doubt that Dulles is right in his judgment that the future Pope retracted his earlier positions.

A similar movement in direction is also evident in Ratzinger's views regarding liturgical innovation. His most recent stances with reference to the liturgy, including the re-introduction of the Tridentine Rite Mass[147] and his advocacy of turning the table around again so that the priest no longer faces the people[148], seem at odds with the young peritus whose comments about liturgy show little hint of reservation or unease with change. In *Theological Highlights* he clearly identifies himself with the progressive faction and speaks approvingly of moves to nurture communal participation in the Mass with the priest in a less isolated position; the greater centrality of the Word of God and preaching; Communion offered in both kinds; greater freedom for regional adaptation under the regulation of Bishops' Conferences; and the use of the

---

[144] Avery Cardinal Dulles, 'From Ratzinger to Benedict.' *First Things* (Feb 2006) http://www.firstthings.com/article/2006/02/from-ratzinger-to-benedict (accessed 10 June 2011).
[145] Cited in Dulles, 'From Ratzinger to Benedict.'
[146] Dulles, 'From Ratzinger to Benedict.'
[147] An initiative first mooted in 2006 and realized in July 2007.
[148] His reconsideration of this issue can be found in Joseph Ratzinger, *The Spirit of the Liturgy* (San Francisco: Ignatius Press, 2000)

vernacular.[149] His citation of Melchite Patriarch Maximos Saigh's speech against the use of Latin in the liturgy emphasises his own dissatisfaction with the practice, as do his closing comments on the speech,

> Only if we consider how deeply the meaning of language pervades man's activity – and that language is not merely an external, superficial and accidental thing, but is rather the incarnation of the human spirit which thinks and lives in its very speech – only then can we judge the extent of the change inaugurated in the liturgical debates.[150]

The end result of the liturgical debate, and Ratzinger's own feelings in regard to that matter, underline the distance he must have travelled in order to become a liturgical traditionalist.

> The ...debate ... ended on November 14th 1962, with a vote for the basic adoption of the schema, with the necessary changes left up to the commission. Even the optimists could not have expected the result of the voting – 2,162 in favour, 46 opposed (with 7 invalid votes). And so the adoption was a decision that both looked to the future and showed encouragingly that the forces of renewal were stronger than anyone would have dared hope.[151]

Why should he have changed so dramatically? One possible response is to suggest that it was the natural effect of age and that one becomes more traditional with the advance of years. It is my contention, however, that his change of course, exemplified in regard to both collegiality and liturgy, may be more than anything else the product of disappointment and dismay at the course of future events. One commentator explained Ratzinger's later actions as the outworking of guilt for his part in letting the liberal genie out of the bottle.[152] Disastrous liturgical innovation and profound theological confusion (as he would have viewed it) on the part of various regional churches, left him with little confidence that the kind of checks and balances collegiality that he had originally favoured was possible. The brand of orthodoxy which underlay his own faith and which he presumed undergirded Catholic theology in general, did not exist to the degree that he hoped and thus any loosening of central authority was an invitation to error.

This judgment, which tries to make sense of the substantial movement Ratzinger has made in terms of ecclesiology, finds some backing in the strong Augustinian critique of some of the Council documents, particularly *Gaudium et Spes*. It is clear that Ratzinger, even in the 1960s, is profoundly unhappy with

---

[149] A summary of Ratzinger's position provided by Avery Dulles in the *First Things* article.
[150] Ratzinger, *Theological Highlights of Vatican II*, p. 18.
[151] Ratzinger, *Theological Highlights of Vatican II*, pp. 19-20.
[152] Rupert Shortt, *Benedict XVI: Commander of the Faith* (London: Hodder & Stoughton, 2005), p. 3.

theological wrong turns and is not averse to making that known. As these instincts have relevance to our later discussion about Ratzinger's theology being a bridge between the Catholic and evangelical traditions, I will comment on them elsewhere. It may be sufficient to note at this point that Ratzinger is outspoken rather than reticent when it comes to issues of truth. Thus should he have noted that innovations which were permissible and legitimate in their own terms had led to unsatisfactory and unwelcome outcomes, he may have felt justified in reversing his previous judgments.

Conclusion

What may one conclude about Ratzinger from this brief survey of his theological outlook in the 1960s? Some assessment of his achievement as a theologian during this period would be a fitting preamble to what will be said later about his standing as an interlocutor with Evangelicalism. For it is clear that his major publication, *Introduction to Christianity*, showcases a level of creativity, poetic expression and theological finesse far in advance of the majority of his fellow Catholic theologians. His was a felt theology designed to engage both the mind and the heart of his readers. It is also undeniable that it was adversarial in tone, in that he challenges not only the foundations of liberal biblical scholarship[153] but the prevailing mindset of the secular culture within which he lived. However, he does this, not in a hectoring way, but through a creative cultural engagement with the great movements of thought of the time. Tracey Rowland is probably accurate in her assessment of Ratzinger that his dialogue with modernity 'was fostered by pastoral concerns and not by any Catholic intellectual inferiority complex vis-à-vis fashionable currents of thought in the 1960s.'[154] What becomes very evident as we explore *Introduction to Christianity* is the central place of Christology in his theological vision. This is not an accidental factor on account of the book being an exposition of the Creed, the figure of Christ is presented throughout as the answer to questions about meaning, purpose and immortality. Perhaps what is most striking about this is Ratzinger's unique means of securing Christ this central place. Drawing on the insights of the philosophy of personalism and – according to the Catholic intellectual fashion of the time -plundering the works of Teilhard de Chardin for evolutionary concepts amenable to the faith, he seeks to demonstrate that some of the most powerful currents in modern thought find their true fulfilment in Christ. Here he shares an important

---

[153] It is instructive to note how often Rudolf Bultmann is presented as the classic proponent of the view which he seeks to challenge. His approach to the historical critical method is reminiscent of moderate evangelical scholars who have challenged Bultmannian presuppositions. See George Eldon Ladd, *The New Testament and Criticism* (Grand Rapids: Eerdmans, 1967), pp. 47, 183, 188, 199ff.

[154] Tracey Rowland, *Ratzinger's Faith* (Oxford: Oxford University Press, 2008), p. 144.

commonality with evangelical theology in that spiritual encounter with Christ fulfils personal and theological longing.

Can we affirm that he may be considered a legitimate dialogue partner for the evangelical tradition? The provisional answer to that question must ultimately be in the affirmative. However, in accepting that Ratzinger and Evangelicalism share in a broad orthodoxy, we must be reminded that he developed his theology in a very different academic milieu to most of those associated with the evangelical tradition. We must not expect him to 'sound' like an evangelical. His theological sources were often different as were the rules of dialogue. His goal was never to assure his readers of the orthodoxy of his thought, nor was he inhibited in drawing inspiration from movements of thought that were not always in accord with his own core beliefs.[155] However, even given these significant dissimilarities, an important commonality with Evangelicalism still pertained. This was evident not only in his essential doctrinal orthodoxy but in his theological method as well. Ratzinger believed in the primacy of revelation over autonomous reason and saw Christ as the Logos personified. He was also committed theologically to the view that the inherited credal beliefs of the church were objectively true and immutable. In this respect he was deeply at odds with liberal Catholics who saw truth as open-ended and contingent. Moreover, this orthodoxy of outlook was evident to students who worked under him as well as to the wider university body when it came to a matter of public theological conflict (the Halbfass Affair). Given these considerations, it is easier to comprehend why there should have been substantial agreement with evangelicals on key doctrinal themes, even if Ratzinger defended these ideas with an alien and suspect vocabulary. If the early Ratzinger's theology allowed for that degree of common ground, there is nothing to indicate that a future dialogue with evangelicals would be fruitless or advanced at cross purposes.

Finally, with regard to the change that Ratzinger did undergo in the late sixties, it is impossible to deny that a considerable gulf separates the young reformer from the later Prefect. His enthusiasm for reform was unmistakeable and his later criticisms of the reforming tendency at Vatican II ring somewhat hollow in light of the key role he played in forwarding that agenda. However, his change of course with reference to ecclesiology does not mean that he necessarily 'changed sides' in any other fundamental way. His unease with the Catholicism of his day seems to have been more with the traditionalist neo-scholasticism of the time than with mainstream Catholic orthodoxy. This is demonstrated by the fact that it was in the area of ecclesiology, as opposed to dogma, that his liberal tendencies emerged. If the reform that he helped initiate had stayed within the boundaries of theological orthodoxy, it is unclear to what

---

[155] Ratzinger is famed for his animosity to Marxism but acknowledges that he was willing to draw on certain Marxist themes which he believed were valuable and helpful (see Ratzinger, *Milestones*, p. 137). This freedom with regard to Marxism underscores the wider observation that Ratzinger can borrow from streams of thought which he would not fully endorse.

degree his position on collegiality or liturgy would have actually changed. Indeed, we may have had a very different ecclesiastical figure to the one we have now, though I doubt that we would have had a substantially different dogmatic theologian.[156]

---

[156] This conclusion is echoed in Miroslav Volf's extensive critique of Ratzinger's ecclesiology. See Miroslav Volf, *After Our Likeness: The Church as the Image of the Trinity* (Grand Rapids: Eerdmans, 1998), pp. 31-32 n.14 where he writes: 'There is no question that Ratzinger's theological development took a significant turn a few years after the Second Vatican Council. Some of his colleagues from that period (such as Hans Küng) claim hardly to know him any longer. It seems to me, however, that this turn did not involve fundamental theological positions. Discounting the changes in emphases, his positions have not only remained constant, but were relatively unaffected by the great turn in the Catholic Church itself introduced by the Second Vatican Council. What Ratzinger as the Prefect of the CDF so vigorously defends now largely coincides either with what he wrote as a young theologian or with what was already implied in his statements.

CHAPTER 3

Ratzinger and Augustinianism

Introduction

In this chapter we explore Ratzinger's Augustinianism with a view to establishing its ecumenical significance for the dialogue with Evangelicalism. Not all Augustinian themes vital to Ratzinger will be fully covered here as some are too substantial for analysis in a general chapter.[1] However, our initial treatment of Augustinianism will tell us much about the nature of Ratzinger's own espousal of Augustine as well as Augustinianism's ecumenical potential within Evangelicalism. The chapter opens with a discussion of how Ratzinger's Augustinianism is perceived amongst evangelicals. It is shown that Ratzinger's identity as an Augustinian carries great weight and that in important respects his theological instincts veer closer to those of Reformed Augustinianism than Catholic Augustinianism. This is followed by a consideration of his early doctoral work on Augustine. His treatment of conversion in that context is shown to illuminate aspects of his ecclesiological outlook which have some bearing on his soteriology.

Arguably, it is Ratzinger's critique of the conciliar document *Gaudium et Spes* which most powerfully illustrates his commitment to a decidedly Augustinian theology.[2] However, Tracey Rowland has taken issue with this interpretation and suggested that it was a much milder form of Augustinian Thomism that had spurred his critique.[3] I challenge this view and demonstrate that a thoroughgoing Augustinianism, redolent of Protestantism, better characterises Ratzinger's perspective. Moreover, his reflections on Augustine's doctrine of the love of God hint at a theological and devotional commonality with Evangelicalism. The penultimate section on reason focuses on a classic historical difference between Catholics and evangelicals. Here Ratzinger, contra the Reformers, argues for the validity of reason in the framing of faith. The closing section exploring Augustine's relationship to the evangelical tradition also functions as a general conclusion to the chapter, highlighting the ecumenical possibilities of Augustine's theology.

---

[1] See the subsequent chapters on soteriology and ecclesiology.
[2] See Joseph Ratzinger, 'The Dignity of the Human Person' in Herbert Vorgrimler, *Commentary on the Documents of Vatican II* Volume 5 (London: Burns & Oats, 1966), pp. 115-163.
[3] Tracey Rowland, *Ratzinger's Faith: The Theology of Pope Benedict XVI* (Oxford: Oxford University Press, 2008), pp. 9-16 and 30-47.

Ratzinger's Augustinianism and Evangelical Protestantism

It is undeniable that Joseph Ratzinger's strong identification with the Augustinian theological tradition[4] and the markedly Augustinian stamp to his thought has placed him in a unique relationship to Evangelicalism.[5] That this should be the case is evident in at least two respects. First, it is apparent that evangelical theologians have rarely found a Catholic thinker so congenial to them in terms of theological vision as Ratzinger. Second, as modern Catholicism's most revered Augustinian, he is probably best placed to represent Catholic theology in any dialogue with Evangelicalism.

The first assertion is borne out by the way some representative evangelicals greeted his election as Supreme Pontiff. Timothy George, Executive Editor of *Christianity Today* and an authoritative voice within American Evangelicalism, described his pontificate as being 'one of great moment for the Christian church, not least for evangelicals.'[6] George was impressed by Ratzinger's commitment to the objectivity of truth; his exegetically centred theology which places Scripture at the heart of all theological reflection; his Christocentric message which faithfully upholds credal beliefs dear to evangelicals; and his Augustinian soteriological perspective which George claimed led not only to an appreciation of Martin Luther but enabled him to play a key role in the framing of the *Joint Declaration on the Doctrine of Justification*.[7] In a similarly positive vein, John Witvliet, Director of the Calvin Institute of Christian Worship at Calvin College, celebrated Ratzinger's election highlighting those themes in his published work which he felt would resonate with Protestant Christians. He noted, in particular, Ratzinger's thoughts about 'the person and nature of Jesus, the beauty of God, and the nature of the church as source of healing and mission in the world.'[8] The reference to Benedict's's emphasis on the beauty of God underscores the appeal of Ratzinger's Augustinian outlook to those in the evangelical tradition.

---

[4] He refers to himself as a 'decided Augustinian.' See Joseph Ratzinger, *Salt of the Earth: The Church at the End of the Millennium (An Interview with Peter Seewald)* (San Francisco: Ignatius Press, 1997), p. 17.

[5] The other great theological tradition which claims Augustine as its forerunner.

[6] Timothy George, 'The Promise of Benedict,' in *Christianity Today*, June 2005, Vol. 49, No. 6, p. 49.

[7] George, 'The Promise of Benedict'.

[8] Cited in Edelle Banks, 'Conservative Evangelicals Say New Pope Speaks Their Moral Language.' [Religious News Service (posted 04/20/2005)] at http://www.christianitytoday.com/ct/2005/aprilweb-only/33.0b.html (accessed 10 June, 2009).

Michael Horton, writing from a much more critical perspective[9], was nevertheless to reiterate how agreeable much of Ratzinger's theology is to evangelicals. In an article entitled, 'What Can Protestants Expect From The New Pope?'[10] he wrote expansively about the theological instincts that Ratzinger shares with evangelicals. Quoting from a range of Ratzinger's works, he catalogues a series of themes which would not only be reassuring to evangelicals, but which hark back to the legacy of Augustine. These include a profound emphasis on the doctrine of original sin; wariness of any rapprochement with the world which has the impact of denying the corrosive effects of sin in individual lives; rejection of Karl Rahner's supernatural transcendentalism which collapses experience of the divine into universal human experience; commitment to objective truth with Scripture as a yardstick by which to identify heresy; and the re-embracing of an emphatic Trinitarian theology. Given such emphases, it is not surprising that Horton summed up his comments by acknowledging that 'Ratzinger displays remarkable commitment to the Augustinian theological heritage and recognizes significant areas of agreement with Protestants who share it.'[11]

His unique situation in relation to Evangelicalism is due not only to the common ground that is shared but also to the vital place Ratzinger occupies within Catholic Augustinianism. A survey of his personal history would indicate that his espousal of Augustinianism has made him part of a permanent minority tradition within the Catholicism of his time, no matter what the prevailing trends have been. At the beginning of his seminary experience in post-war Germany, the neo-scholastic hegemony in theology was still intact and the young Ratzinger identified with those in the German faculties who longed for a different approach. Fortuitously, from his standpoint, this was supplied in the writings of de Lubac and other scholars[12] who sought inspiration in the early Fathers, and most particularly, Augustine of Hippo. Ratzinger's embrace of Augustine seems to have been the ideal decision for someone of his temperament in that he found in the African Father's writings 'the passionate, suffering, questioning man is always right there, and one can identify with him.'[13]

---

[9] Horton shares his concerns over any rapprochement with Roman Catholicism in a contribution to John Armstrong (ed), *Roman Catholics and Protestants: What Divides and Unites Us* (Chicago: Moody Press, 1994), pp. 245-268.

[10] Michael S. Horton, 'What Can Protestants Expect From The New Pope' (White Horse Inn: For A Modern Reformation). Posted April 21 2005 http://www.christianitytoday.com/ct/2005/aprilweb-only/33.0b.html (accessed 12 June, 2009).

[11] Horton, 'What Can Protestants Expect From The New Pope'.

[12] The term *La Nouvelle Théologie* is often applied to that movement of scholars who looked to the ancient Fathers of the Church as the main source of renewal for Catholicism.

[13] Ratzinger, *Salt of the Earth*, p. 61.

This rather daring move on his part associated him with a group which came into its own much later in the Second Vatican Council. However, if he had viewed himself as being in the vanguard of a theological movement which would eventually dominate centre stage in the church, he was to prove mistaken, as a similar movement which shared the same objective of renewal, would in the end define post-conciliar Catholicism. Ratzinger, writing in *Principles of Catholic Theology*, mourns the demise of the theology which sought its energy and dynamism from the great Fathers and, in the process, offers a glimpse of his own sense of isolation as one who still saw *ressourcement* as a remedy for the church's ills.

> We need only recall the names of Odel Casel, Hugo Rahner, Henri de Lubac, Jean Danielou to have before our eyes a theology that knew – and knows – that it was close to the Scriptures because it was close to the Fathers. *This situation seems, in the meantime to have ceased to exist.* In the course of a few years a new awareness has arisen that is so filled with the burning importance of the present moment that it regards any recourse to the past as a kind of romanticism that might have been appropriate in less stirring times but has no meaning today. Instead of *ressourcement,* we have *aggiornamento*, a confrontation with today and tomorrow in which the content of theology is to be made current and effective. The Fathers have been pushed far into the background; a vague impression of allegorical exegesis remains behind and leaves a bad taste and, indeed, a feeling of superiority that regards it as progress to keep yesterday as far as possible from today and so seems to promise an even better tomorrow.[14]

This is not to suggest that Ratzinger was entirely alone in his devotion to the Fathers since de Lubac, von Balthasar and other moderate Catholic theologians associated with *Communio* broadly shared his theological vision. What is significant, though, is that with the deaths of de Lubac and von Balthasar, he was to become probably the most prominent living Augustinian, if his theological output and stature within the Catholic Church were anything to go by. Thus whether as the result of theological compatibility with evangelicals on the basis of shared Augustinian emphases, or as the consequence of being the highest ranking Augustinian within the Catholic church, we may confidently state that he is ideally situated as a dialogue partner for a theological conversation.

The Debate about Ratzinger's Augustinianism

Commentators on Joseph Ratzinger unite in their judgment that he is a thoroughgoing Augustinian. There is dispute, nevertheless, over whether his Augustinianism reflects an austere, anti-worldly, defensive style of thinking such as that which some associate with the Reformers. The point at issue is not

---

[14] Joseph Ratzinger, *Principles of Catholic Theology: Building Stones for a Fundamental Theology* (San Francisco: Ignatius Press, 1987), p. 134 (italics mine).

whether Ratzinger has a Protestant theology *per se* (this charge is only made in extremist traditionalist circles)[15] , but whether his Augustinianism bears the stamp of a supposedly Protestant reading of Augustine.

Tracey Rowland[16], in the second major English language study of his thought, sets about the defence of Ratzinger in that regard. Her conclusion is that Ratzinger's style of Augustinianism is significantly at odds with that of the leading Reformers. According to her,

> Ratzinger stands apart from a Reformation reading of Augustine and belongs to a different branch of Augustinianism with people like Jesuit Erich Pryzwara, for whom Augustine, steeped in classical culture, and rejoicing in its achievements, nonetheless recognises the necessity of Christ's Revelation to transcend its limitations and breach its *aporia,* or doubt.[17]

Her contention is that the negative perception of Ratzinger is largely the result of 'hastily prepared editorials'[18] and an anachronistic reading of Augustine which imposes on the Latin Father the foibles of the Reformers. Thus 'Augustinianism' becomes in the popular imagination, and in the way it has been attributed to Ratzinger, a worldview with an 'extremely negative attitude toward human nature [with no time at all] for the achievements of pagan civilisations.' Her riposte is that while this may be the view of Luther (who wanted nothing to do with Platonic notions of beauty or Aristotelian reason), it in no way sums up the mentality of Ratzinger.[19] Later in the book, she goes on to challenge the widely-held view that Ratzinger's strong criticisms of liberal readings of *Gaudium et spes* were themselves the fruit of his Augustinian mindset. Her argument (which will be considered later in this chapter) is that Ratzinger's reservations about the document derive not from a choice he made of Augustine over Aquinas, so much as a choice between different forms of Thomism. In her opinion, he is influenced by the 'Augustinian Thomism' of de Lubac as opposed to the Transcendental Thomism of Karl Rahner. What Rowland intimates is that even when Ratzinger's voice seems at its most shrill, it still bears the accent of Catholicism. This is not the place to explore Rowland's argument in any detail but the observation must be made that by querying the assumption that Ratzinger's Augustinianism determined his response to *Gaudium et spes,* she has rendered suspect one of the strongest grounds for assuming that a strong commonality exists between Ratzinger and Evangelicalism.

---

[15] See articles such as Rev. Francesco Ricossa, 'Ratzinger: 99% Protestant', Articles:Benedict XVI Heresies and Errors, *traditionalmass.org* (1993) http://www.traditionalmass.org/articles/article.php?id=62&catname=15 (accessed 15 June 2009).
[16] Rowland, *Ratzinger's Faith*, p. 10.
[17] Rowland, *Ratzinger's Faith*, p. 10.
[18] Rowland, *Ratzinger's Faith*, p. 8.
[19] Rowland, *Ratzinger's Faith*, p. 9.

Rowland's assertion that Ratzinger had very little in common with the Reformers in his appropriation of Augustine has been brought into question by a number of Catholic studies. A recent example is a work written by an American Jesuit, Thomas P. Rausch. His conclusions about the nature of Ratzinger's Augustinianism belie the impression made in Rowland's book. Rausch comments that,

> Ratzinger's thought remains deeply influenced by the pessimism about the human evident in Augustine. The confidence one finds in Aquinas about the integrity of human knowing and willing is absent in Ratzinger. In many ways, Ratzinger's instinctive attitudes towards human intelligence and thus its achievement in 'modernity' show him to be more like Jean Calvin and the Reformers than like Thomas Aquinas, and, like Luther, he emphasises a *theologia crucis*, a theology of the cross that stresses the priority of grace over human achievement, philosophical reason or ecclesial power.[20]

In support of this judgment, Rausch references an observation made by Avery Dulles when writing about the Extraordinary Synod of Bishops, held in 1985. Commenting on the two schools of thought which were represented at the meeting (Augustinian and Thomist), he noted that the Augustinian one 'led by figures such as the German cardinals Ratzinger and Hoeffner, had a remarkably supernaturalist point of view, tending to depict the church as an island of grace in a world given over to sin.' Moreover, employing an interpretation of Augustinianism that was not far removed from the caricatures allegedly found in editorials written at the time of Ratzinger's election, Dulles labels the defensive stance attributed to Ratzinger as 'neo-Augustinian.'[21]

Another Jesuit theologian, James Corkery, offers a similar reading of Ratzinger, suggesting that a polarised attitude to the world was determined early in that choice of Augustine over Aquinas that the future Pope made when he was a seminarian in Freising.

> This immersion in Augustine was to have a lifelong effect in his writings, in which Augustinian footprints are highly discernible: a preferring of the humility of faith over the pride of philosophy; a defence of the city of God against the 'earthly city', and a recognition of the duality that lies deep within human beings who, even when desiring good, cannot embrace it. From his earliest experiences – and, as a student of Augustine – Ratzinger has been aware of how much humanity depends on the grace of God, and how much human nature, as manifested in its concrete historical incarnations, is in discontinuity with it. So, there are theological roads taken, and roads not taken: and a direction, a sign posted road, emerges for this young theologian's developing mind. His will be a theology less inclined to seek for 'seeds of the Word' or for grace hidden in the human mess of things

---

[20] Thomas P. Rausch, *Pope Benedict XVI: An Introduction to his Theological Vision* (New York: Paulist Press, 2009), pp. 49-50.
[21] Avery Dulles, *The Re-Shaping of Catholicism* (San Francisco: Harper & Row, 1988), p. 191 cited in Rausch, *An Introduction to his Theological Vision*, p. 41.

and more inclined to identify the pollutants that distort and seduce a humanity that is constantly in need of healing and conversion. It will, on the whole, be a theology more attuned to the tensions between what is godly and what is worldly rather than to the harmonies between the two.[22]

Given these contrasting perceptions of Ratzinger's style of Augustinianism, are there any relatively clear-cut judgments that we may be allowed to make about the nature of his theological vision? I would suggest that three commend themselves. The first is that in one key respect at least, Augustine, the Reformers and Ratzinger shared the same theological method. Augustine was a polemical theologian whose developing ideas were worked out amidst a perceived struggle for truth over and against error. This meant there was an urgency and partisanship to his writings which gave a certain tone to his theology. This is replicated both in the Reformation disputes by the likes of Luther and Calvin as well as in much of Ratzinger's own thought. Vincent Twomey observes that the greater part of his writings were written in response to controversies of the time[23], and James Corkery takes that insight a step further by suggesting that a certain combative instinct coloured most of his work.

> [Ratzinger] has an Augustinian heart, an Augustinian sensibility. Augustine wrote with passion – but so often with a passion that *countered*: countered the Manichees, the Pelagians, the Donatists and, in *The City of God*, countered those who blamed Christians and their God for Rome's collapse. Ratzinger writes similarly, and always has. Pick up any text and see how far you need to read before being able to write in the margin: 'enemy sighted'*.[24]

The point of the observation is that Rowland's distancing of Ratzinger from Protestant expressions of Augustinianism does not really hold up in relation to the way they both pursue their theological goals. To be Augustinian is to pursue an adversarial theology with passion and a constant ear for any false note in the claims made by one's opponents. Although this confirms nothing as yet about the precise content of his theology, it raises the question of whether a similarity of method will in the end lead to shared Augustinian conclusions.

Second, that this is occasionally the case (that he both reaches the same theological conclusions as Protestant Augustinians as well as employing the same method), is borne out by an extended interview which he gave to Italian journalist Vittorio Messori in 1985. In the published account of their meeting, Ratzinger is at his most negative, provoking a critical reception from

---

[22] James Corkery, *Joseph Ratzinger's Theological Ideas: Wise Cautions and Legitimate Hopes* (New York: Paulist Press, 2009), pp. 25-26.
[23] D. Vincent Twomey, *Pope Benedict XVI: The Conscience of our Age* (San Francisco: Ignatius Press, 2005), p. 30.
[24] Corkery, *Theological Ideas*, p. 25.

those factions of the church ill at ease with perceived theological pessimism.[25] Although the comments in no way define every aspect of Ratzinger's thought, one may detect that substantial wariness of 'the world' which theologians such as Rowland associate with the theology of the Reformers. Speaking in his official capacity as Prefect of the CDF, Ratzinger advocates a stance towards the wider culture that consciously distances itself from the optimistic spirit of post-conciliar Catholicism.

> Today more than ever the Christian must be aware that he belongs to a minority and that he is in opposition to everything that appears good, obvious, logical to the 'spirit of the world', as the New Testament calls it. Among the most urgent tasks facing Christians is that of regaining the capacity of nonconformism, i.e., the capacity to oppose many developments of the surrounding culture. In other words, today we must revise this euphoric view of the earlier post-conciliar era.[26]

The stimulus for the position which Ratzinger adopts here is disbelief in a certain Teilhardian theology that dismisses the concept of 'original sin' and holds to an entirely optimistic vision of humankind's future in the world.[27] The ultimate failure of such a theology in Ratzinger's eyes is its inability to identify sin as the heart of the human problem. '[A] lucid realistic view of man and of history cannot but stumble on their alienation and discover that there is a rupture in relationships: in man's relationship to himself, to others, to God.' Indeed, the fact that individuals are not able to identify original sin and its consequences in their lives 'is precisely because it exists, because the derangement is ontological, because it unbalances, confuses in us the logic of nature, thus preventing us from understanding how a fault at the origin of history can draw in its wake a situation of common sin.'[28] Taken as a whole, such language echoes the Reformers' emphasis on sin and human depravity and is stronger in tone than the example of the type of Augustinianism which Rowland believes Ratzinger exemplifies. He is saying something more negative about the state of humanity than its need for Christ's Revelation to transcend its limitations and breach its doubt![29] Rowland's underestimate of how far Ratzinger's Augustinianism could be similar in style to the Reformers is perhaps matched by her tendency to paint the Reformers as more at odds with the achievements of human culture than they, in fact, were. The case can be made that Calvin valued the learning of the new humanism and understood

---

[25] See Eamon Duffy, 'I': Urbi, but not Orbi ... the Cardinal, the Church and the World.' *New Blackfriars* 66, 780, (1985): pp. 272-78.
[26] Joseph Ratzinger and Vittorio Messorri, *The Ratzinger Report* (San Francisco: Ignatius Press, 1985), p. 115.
[27] Ratzinger, *The Ratzinger Report*, p. 80.
[28] Ratzinger, *The Ratzinger Report*, p. 81.
[29] Rowlands, *Ratzinger's Faith*, p. 14.

human depravity in a more nuanced fashion than many of his detractors would allow.[30]

Third, having identified two areas in which Ratzinger's theological approach was similar to that of Protestant Augustinians, it is important to acknowledge that the argument Rowland makes for a distinction between the two does still carry some weight. For example, Ratzinger did maintain that reason and the Greek metaphysical worldview had a place within the structure of Christian faith. In that respect he was entirely at odds with the Reformers who regarded scholasticism of any description as a theological wrong turn. The fruit of the Reformers' rejection of the role of philosophy in religion, Ratzinger asserted, was Protestantism's later vulnerability to Kant's separation of faith from metaphysics.[31] I shall explore the argument later in the chapter when we consider Ratzinger's approach to reason. The other marked difference from classical Augustinian Protestantism is Ratzinger's disavowal of the theology of predestination which had been so prevalent in Calvin and Luther. (See the discussion on pp.107-108 of this current chapter). Here he may well have been influenced by de Lubac's own fulsome rejection of Jansenist and Reformation views of predestination.[32]

Ratzinger as an Augustinian Scholar

The influence of St Augustine on Ratzinger's theology was not limited to an application of Augustinian ideas to the many diverse themes that the latter chose to write upon. Both his doctoral thesis and his later *Habilitationschrift* had a specifically Augustinian focus. The former was a study of Augustine's theology of the church and the latter was an engagement with the Augustinian Bonaventure's theology of history. Both theses had a profound impact on his later theology, particularly his treatment of ecclesiology and his interpretation of Liberation Theology.

Given that Augustine was such a prolific writer and had so seminal an impact on western culture by means of the astounding range of his thought, it may be informative to consider why Ratzinger should settle on Augustine's doctrine of the church as the theme for his doctoral thesis. Aidan Nichols suggests it was out of a shared conviction with Romano Guardini that the twentieth century, theologically speaking, was the 'century of the church', that Ratzinger deemed it a timely exercise to scour the writings of the great Church Father for insight about the nature of the church.[33] His particular theme, 'the

---

[30] See John Calvin, *Institutes of the Christian Religion*. 2.3.3. and Alister McGrath, *Christianity's Dangerous Idea: The Protestant Revolution – A History From The Sixteenth Century to the Twenty-First* (San Francisco: Harper One, 2007), p. 356.
[31] Ratzinger discusses this issue in some depth in *Introduction to Christianity*, pp. 30-47.
[32] See de Lubac's discussion in the preface to *Augustinianism and Modern Theology* (New York: The Crossway Publishing Company, 2000), pp. xvii-xxi.
[33] Aidan Nichols O.P., *The Thought of Benedict XVI: An Introduction to the Theology of Joseph Ratzinger* (London: Burns & Oats, 2007), p. 18. This is to my knowledge the

church as the house and people of God' (*Volk und Haus Gottes in Augustins Lehre von der Kirche*)[34] was inspired by previous studies on these subjects by the Lutheran Hermann Reuter (1883)[35] and the Catholic Fritz Hofman (1933).[36] From the perspective of Ratzinger's relationship to Evangelicalism, the most relevant aspect of the dissertation is his treatment of Augustine's conversion and this will be the point of entry for my own analysis. His understanding of conversion here may shed considerable light on how much commonality exists between the two traditions, given that the concept of 'conversion' is fundamental to evangelical thought and identity. As well as drawing on this formative piece of early research, I shall examine his later writings which make reference to the theme of conversion in Augustine.

The issue at stake for Ratzinger at the outset of the dissertation is 'whether Augustine's 386 conversion to the Gospel was simply a conversion to "spirituality" or to the historic Christian faith.'[37] What that question alluded to was a view promoted by Harnack and others that Augustine's conversion in 386 had merely been a conversion to a philosophical system (Neo-Platonism) and that the language in which it was described in *The Confessions* reflected a later stage of Augustine's thinking which he had read back into his account of what had happened in the Milanese garden. It seems certain, however, that Ratzinger was not simply re-hashing Harnack's opinion. This is evidenced in an account of Augustine's 386 conversion written early in Benedict's Pontificate. Speaking of Augustine's call to take up and read the text of Romans, he states,

> He understood that those words in that moment were addressed personally to him; they came from God through the Apostle and indicated to him what he had to do at the time. Thus, he felt the darkness of doubt clearing and he finally found himself free to give himself entirely to Christ: he described it as 'your converting me to yourself' (*Confessions*, VIII, 12, 30) *This was the first and decisive conversion.*[38]

---

only published work in English which engages directly with Ratzinger's original thesis (written in German and never translated into English) on Augustine and the church. As Nichols was able to devote more space to the thesis than this section allows, I am happy on occasion to make reference to his summaries and conclusions.

[34] Joseph Ratzinger, *Volk und Haus Gottes in Augustins Lehre von der Kirche* (Seiten: Eos Verlag, 1992).
[35] Hermann Reuter, *Augustinische Studien* (Gotha, 1887. Reprint Aalen, 1967).
[36] Fritz Hofmann, *Der Kirchenbegriff des hl. Augustinus in seinen Grundlagen und in seiner Entwicklung* (Munich, 1933).
[37] Nichols, *The Thought of Benedict*, p. 20. Here the author makes the further point that Ratzinger viewed the debate surrounding this issue as essentially a discussion about Augustine's concept of the church.
[38] Ratzinger, 'Augustine's Conversion', *L'Osservatore Romano* (English Edition) 5, March 2008, p. 11 (italics mine).

Thus, we can affirm that at this later stage in his career, Ratzinger communicated the substance of Augustine's conversion in much the same way as evangelicals would. Indeed, Augustine's experience, as relayed by Ratzinger, conforms to the traditional evangelical picture of conversion. The issue to be addressed, however, is the manner in which this event was dealt with in the thesis. What can we tell about his theology from the way he integrated the conversion experience into his general understanding of Augustine's thought? Moreover, what commonality is there between Ratzinger and evangelicals in his interpretation of Augustine's doctrine of the church, which is eventually what emerges out of the enquiry into Augustine's conversion?

What is evident from a few of Ratzinger's earlier writings is that he identified something profoundly incomplete in the conversion process that Augustine recounts in *The Confessions*. This is particularly the case with these trenchant words recorded in his best-selling book, *Introduction to Christianity*.

> The programme of the early Augustine, "God and the soul – nothing else" ', is impracticable; and it is also unchristian. In the last analysis there is no religion along the solitary path of the mystic, but only in the community of proclaiming and hearing.[39]

Thus according to Ratzinger, conversion to spirituality *could* be construed as no more than a change in philosophical standpoint, if it is not combined with a genuine embrace of the visible church. But lest we underplay what is meant by 'philosophical standpoint', Nichols reminds us of the unique situation in which Augustine's conversion took place and the vital interplay which existed between philosophy and spirituality. He asserts, '[T]he ultimate arché of all things sought by the philosopher was precisely that which [was] worthy of religious adoration in a human community.'[40] Thus the religious quest was inherently a philosophical quest and its resolution was as much a philosophical outcome as a religious one. Understood in these terms, we may be able to glimpse the actual direction of Ratzinger's thought and understand why he might dismiss an 'individual' search for God as somehow incomplete when it is without reference to the church. The essential criticism being made is that Augustine's early programme for philosophical and spiritual enlightenment was so tied to the Platonic worldview he had embraced, that had his perception of things not developed from there, the experience might have lacked something in Christian character.

We are given a sense of Ratzinger's dissatisfaction with Augustine's solitary project in these much later words spoken by him on the centenary of the death of John Henry Newman.

---

[39] Ratzinger, *Introduction to Christianity*, p. 60.
[40] Nichols, *The Thought of Benedict*, p. 20.

> When Augustine was converted in the garden at Cassiciacum he understood conversion according to the system of the revered master Plotin and Neo-Platonic philosophers. He thought that his past sinful life would now be definitively cast off; from now on the convert would be someone wholly new and different, and his further journey would be a steady climb to the ever purer heights of closeness to God.[41]

The words by themselves suggest that Ratzinger saw even Augustine's Christian conversion experience as being heavily overlaid by philosophical presuppositions drawn not from the deposit of faith, but from a philosophical/spiritual worldview derived from the mystical experience of Plotinus. One might characterise this understanding of conversion and its aftermath as an ever-deepening individual journey into the mystery of God by the enlightened soul.

This intensely individualistic perspective was not to remain with Augustine for long. Ratzinger introduces his readers to what was to be a huge movement in Augustine's thought ('die ungeheuere Entwicklung der Theologie Augustins'[42]) in relation to conversion. To understand how this change came about and what its nature was, we need to grasp something of the classical worldview which at that time was dominated by Neo-Platonism. Within this *Weltanschauung*, there were understood to be two ways or paths to salvation. The first of these was the 'Regal Path' which was the way of the philosopher, and that entailed an intense metaphysical search which was undertaken only by a few. The other alternative (and one which had much less standing) was the so-called 'universal way' for the masses which was mediated via the religious cultus. Ratzinger contrasts the two approaches, highlighting what at the time were the perceived deficiencies of the latter:

> ... the "regal path" of intellectual purging ... which leads to the depths of the Godhead: ...[is a] privilege [which] belongs to the philosophers. All others, who are not party to this, the broad mass of humankind, must content themselves with the "universal path", with a spiritual purging ... which, as the result of magical worship rites, denotes religion now as a form of substitute for philosophy.[43]

---

[41] Ratzinger, *Presentation On the Occasion Of The Centenary Of The Death Of Cardinal John Henry Newman* Rome, 28 April 1990. http://www.vatican.va/roman_curia/congregations/cfaith/documents/rc_con_cfaith_doc_19900428_ratzinger-newman_en.html (accessed 15 July, 2009).

[42] VHG, p. 38. The original German describes Augustine's progression from an interior view of faith to an ecclesial view as 'momentous'.

[43] VHG, pp. 7-8 : '...der "königliche Weg" der purgatio intellectualis offen, einer rein geistigen Reinigung, die bis in die letzten Tiefen der Gottheit führt: Es sind die Philosophen, denen dieses Privileg gehört. Alle anderen, die dazu nicht im Stande sind, die breite Masse der Menschen, muß sich mit der „universalis via" zufriedengeben, mit einer purgatio spiritualis, die als Ergebnis magisch-kultischer Riten die Religion nun als eine Ersatzform der Philosophie kennzeichnet.'

The great movement on Augustine's part was from embrace of the higher path to acceptance of the religious path of the many. Ratzinger speculates that this journey, spurred by his discovery of the church's teaching, would not have been an easy one for him to have undertaken. 'It must have been impressive and at the same time questionable to Augustine that the Christian religion lays claim to be both popular salvation (salus populi) and the regal path.'[44] However, admiration won over skepticism and Augustine, more than any previous figure, was to help shape a theology in which the church mediated a full salvation to the masses which the philosophers presumed would be attained only by the few. The decisive aspect of this change in perspective, according to Ratzinger, was the manner in which Augustine had come to understand the meaning of 'faith.' It no longer referred to an autonomous metaphysical search (a definition that is congenial to some evangelicals) but was an attitude of humility towards authority. The following is his account of how Augustine made this mental transition.

> An initial way in [to such a view of faith] came when he was able to grasp how many essential truths of our lives are taken simply on faith – above all, what we believe through our parents. Thus the mother figures a second time on his journey to conversion. And maternal authority gives him deeper understanding into the place of authority also in the realm of wisdom. Man stands before her as a child who is still learning and not yet mature, not yet capable of being spiritually independent.[45]

The fact that the church should play this maternal role to the soul is partly premised on Augustine's realisation that he cannot sustain a mystical vision of God[46] (the goal of the philosophers) and that what is needed is for God to

---

[44] VHG, 8: 'Es mußte für Augustin imponierend und fragwürdig zugleich sein, daß die christliche Religion zugleich salus populi und via regian zu sein beanspruchte.'

[45] VHG, 8-9: Ein erster Zugang fand sich für ihn, als er begreifen lernte, wieviel unumgängliche Wahrheiten unseres Lebens eben nur geglaubt sind – vor allem, was wir über unsere Eltern glauben. Damit steht ein zweites Mal die Mutter auf seinem Bekehrungsweg. Und die mütterliche Autorität liefert ihm das tiefere Verständnis der auctoritas auch im Raum der Weisheit. Der Mensch steht ihr gegenüber als das lernende und noch unreife Kind da, das noch nicht zu geistigem Selbstand fähig geworden ist.

[46] Nichols, *The Thought of Benedict*, p. 21, reminds us that Ratzinger places particular weight on two sections from Book Seven of *The Confessions* in which Augustine comes to recognize human immaturity in the realm of the spirit (i.e. that a momentary vision of God is insufficient to sustain the human spirit). Interestingly, there is general consensus that this experience was Augustine's so called philosophical conversion as opposed to his Christian conversion which took place in the garden. The former is different in quality and substance from the Christian conversion recounted in Book Eight whose focus was the surrender of his will. It is a moot question whether the limitations of a pre-conversion vision of God could legitimately be employed to justify the essential role of the church in meeting the needs of someone definitively converted to the faith.

communicate knowledge of himself in more mundane terms that Augustine is able to receive.[47] Ratzinger writes, 'In his weakness, Augustine cannot bear the divine 'food' in its pure form. Therefore the divine Word has mingled itself with flesh so that humanity can enjoy it.' [48]

As previously intimated (see footnote 46 above), Ratzinger's original citing of the pre-Christian Augustine to justify the role of the church in the converted Augustine's life may have been somewhat precipitous. What does seem to be clear, though, is that at some juncture the church undoubtedly took on this pre-eminent role within Augustine's thought. Ratzinger seeks to elucidate this as he explores two key motifs associated with the church in Augustine's ecclesiology: the church as the *house* and the *people* of God. He suggests that Augustine's ruminations on the concept of *faith* were pivotal for his sense of the church as the *people* of God. It would not be difficult to comprehend, opines Ratzinger, that the young Augustine who was struggling to find truth, and engaging intensely with the issues of scepticism and authority, would be struck by a notion of 'faith' which incorporated within it a sense of the universal church – a church capable of fulfilling a uniquely magisterial function.[49] This idea of there being a necessary relationship between the idea of 'faith' and the church comes into clear view in two statements of Ratzinger which Nichols conflates:

> This Church is the place where God gives us the Invisible to feed upon in visible form, thus leading us ever more towards the Invisible until we are become adults in his presence. Because of man's wounding through sin, the Church now becomes a necessary stage in the ascent of the soul to Wisdom. All must pass through the triad of *credere, auctoritas, humilitas,* 'have faith, accept authority, practice humility', if they are to see the divine wisdom in its beauty.[50]

A discussion of the church as the *house* of God leads Ratzinger to similar conclusions about the nature of Augustine's ecclesiology. The difference from the previous discussion about the church as the *people* of God is that the dominant motif here is no longer faith, but love. In terms of being able to assess Ratzinger's perspective on an evangelical ecclesiology, it is intriguing to note that when he explores the *house* of God in Augustine's earlier theology, he deems some of what is contained there to be profoundly insufficient. In particular, he cites *De magistro* where Augustine asserts that the temple of the spiritual God (the closest reference that Ratzinger can find to 'house of God') must be man's interiority.[51] The issue of grave concern here is that ideas like

---

[47] Augustine, *The Confessions* chapter VII, section 10,16.
[48] VHG, p. 9 : 'Die „Speise" Gott in ihrer reinen Gestalt kann Augustin in seiner Schwachheit nicht ertragen, deshalb vermischt sich das göttliche Wort selbst mit Fleisch, damit der Mensch es genießen kann.'
[49] VHG, pp. 10-11.
[50] VHG, pp. 9-10 in Nichols, *The Thought of Benedict*, p. 21.
[51] VHG, p. 36 which cites *De magistro* 1,2.

faith (understood in the sense that we have been discussing), church and sacraments are notably absent. This is interpreted as a serious shortcoming on Augustine's part and he holds out the hope that this will be rectified in a later and more genuinely ecclesial notion of God's 'temple.'[52]

The means of such a situation coming to pass (i.e. Augustine achieving such a perspective) is said to lie in the theological significance he gives to the twin ideas love, *dilectio*, and unity, *unitas*. Ratzinger believed that Augustine's awareness of the dominical command to love our neighbour and his acceptance of the Platonic conviction that everything in existence formed a unity of sorts, would, when brought into conversation with the North African Christian tradition, 'be capable of development' in the direction of a theology of the church.[53]

It is on this subsequent engagement with North African theology that Ratzinger focuses as he expounds the thinking of the later Augustine. The grid by which to understand that thought, as it relates to the church as the *house* of God, is his debate with the Donatists. Ratzinger draws attention to the fact that Augustine's fundamental defence of the Catholic church against these regional schismatics was the claim that the true church must be by definition *ecclesia omnium gentium*, 'the church of all nations.' Ratzinger encapsulates many of Augustine's exegetical arguments to that effect in the following brief summary,

> The multitude of nations who inhabit the globe now appear as the one people of Abraham, brought together out of their segregated diversity into an inner unity through the one Seed of Abraham, Jesus Christ.[54]

It is out of this core understanding of the church, as it was developed in controversy with the Donatists, that Augustine was able to make the claim that his opponents' key lack was *caritas*. Thus Ratzinger introduces the idea that he believed was essential to Augustine's understanding of the church as the *house* of God. However, it is the definition of *caritas* which is of greatest significance. Ratzinger's handling of this term in relation to ecclesiology is crucial to an understanding of his whole theology, especially that part of it which seems to lack empathy for the evangelical perspective. While being careful to acknowledge that Augustine's definition of *caritas* extends beyond that which he chooses to focus upon in the dissertation, Ratzinger stresses that *caritas* in the ecclesiastical context is objective charity. It does not refer to a subjective disposition, 'but rather to being part of the Church, and more

---

[52] VHG, p. 38.
[53] VHG, p. 43.
[54] VHG, pp. 133-134: 'Die Vielzahl der Völker, die den Erdkreis bewohnt, erscheint so als das eine Abrahamsvolk, aus der trennenden Vielfalt zusammenverbunden zu innerer Einheit durch den einen Abrahamssamen: Jesus Christus.'

particularly that Church which itself subsists in charity, that is, 'in Eucharistic love-relationship with [other Christians in] the whole world.'[55]

Before exploring this notion further, it is crucial to reiterate that he is aware of other strains in Augustine's understanding of *caritas* which do not sit as easily with the account he has given of it, and which reveal a 'dialectical' understanding of *caritas* which has 'internal tensions' that 'can never be entirely smoothed out.'[56] He refers to Augustine's view that although anyone who belongs to the universal church shares in outward and visible participation in *caritas*, there may be some who in reality belong with the schismatics on account of their nature as 'sinners'. Summarising Augustine's perspective, Ratzinger writes, '... The catholic Church is the true Church of the holy. Sinners are not truly in her, since their membership is that appearance which is actually the *mundus sensibilis* [imitation of a superior reality].'[57]

His emphasis on objective *caritas*, though qualified by the acknowledgment that Augustine's view of *caritas* is perhaps more ambivalent than the one he presents, helps place the church at the very heart of the salvific mystery. Explaining the importance of this emphasis on *caritas*, Ratzinger talks of it as the ministry of the Holy Spirit creating a unity within the body of Christ that is fundamentally characterised by love. This leads him to the conclusion that where salvation had hitherto been measured by intellectual insight, 'it now consists in that being in the church which is simultaneously a being-in-love.'[58] Such a view of things is a new innovative step by Augustine and makes the church integral to salvation in a way that previously it had apparently not been.[59] Nichols helpfully sums up Ratzinger's perspective on the matter.

> Ratzinger points out that, whereas in the Greek East, theology circled around the concepts of God, his Logos and his Spirit, with the Church tacitly omitted from an account of the inner reality of salvation, Augustine makes the Church 'an inner dogmatic affair'. In Augustine's eyes, Donatism is not primarily a heresy because it includes a doctrinal departure from the teaching of the Great Church ... It is heresy, because 'hard-necked persistence in separation from the Church's community', is ... the very kernel of heresy.[60]

---

[55] VHG, p. 138: 'd.h. In der eucharistischen Liebesbeziehung mit dem ganzen Erdkreis steht.'
[56] Nichols, *The Thought of Benedict*, p. 28.
[57] VHG, p. 146: 'Die katholische Kirche ist die wahre Kirche der Heiligen, die Sünder sind nicht wirklich in ihr, denn ihre Gliedschaft ist jener Schein, der dem mundus sensibilis eigentümlich ist.'
[58] Nichols, *The Thought of Benedict*, p. 29.
[59] This is a surprising judgment given the centrality of the liturgy in Eastern Orthodox soteriology.
[60] Nichols, *The Thought of Benedict*, p. 29. It should be noted that what is referred to as 'the church's community' has an even stronger hierarchical sense in the original German text. Ratzinger speaks of 'the legally constituted church community ('kirchlichen Rechtsgemeinschaft') and 'the historic form itself belonging to the essence of the

Is Ratzinger's perspective a misreading of St Augustine in favour of an ecclesial vision of salvation which obfuscates the African Father's plainest intentions? The nineteenth century Protestant theologian, B.B. Warfield, offers a characterisation of Augustine's ecclesiology which bears out much of what Ratzinger sought to affirm of him. Influenced himself by the work of Reuter, Warfield suggests that Augustine so transfigured the inherited form of Christianity he had embraced that it took on a new form in which 'the idea of the Church became the central power in the religious feeling and in ecclesiastical activity...'[61] Indeed, Warfield goes so far as to cast Augustine as the virtual founder of Roman Catholicism. Moreover, he concludes that the distinction (acknowledged in Ratzinger's thesis) between Augustine's conception of the empirical church and the church of the elect was, in practice, largely ignored by the African Father.

> He is, however, not carefully observant of the distinction between the empirical and the ideal church and repeatedly – often quite unconsciously – carries over to the one the predicates which in his fundamental thought, belonged to the other. Thus the hierarchical organised church tends ever with him to take the place of the *congregatio sanctorum*, even when he is speaking of the Kingdom or the city of God in which alone any communion with God is possible here, and through which alone any blessedness is attainable hereafter.[62]

What is perhaps most significant about Warfield's scholarly endeavours is that he remained hospitable to any and every evidence that would vindicate a Protestant reading of Augustine. For this reason, his effective promotion of a view of Augustine's ecclesiology that was in line with the later position adopted by Ratzinger, gives credibility to the latter's reading of Augustine. Thus whilst Warfield is at pains to underline that it was the exigencies of the Donatist controversy that had provoked Augustine into developing this particular form of ecclesiology, his concluding thoughts about Augustine's legacy resonate strongly with Ratzinger's portrayal of ecclesial salvation.

> The main stream of Augustine's influence ... gave the world a Church as the main authoritative organ of divine truth and the miraculous vehicle of saving grace, through which alone the assured knowledge of the revelation of God could be attained, or the effective operations of his redeeming love experienced. Indeed, on this side of his teaching the Roman Catholic Church may well be accounted Augustine's monument.[63]

---

church' ... 'Christendom only being real in the church ('die geschictliche Gestalt gehört selbst zum Wesen.'... 'Christentum ist nur wirklich in der Kirche.')

[61] Reuter, *Augustinische Studien* vii, p. 499 cited in B.B. Warfield, *Calvin and Augustine*. (Philadelphia: Presbyterian and Reformed, 1956), p. 313.

[62] Warfield, *Calvin and Augustine*, pp. 313-314.

[63] Warfield, *lCalvin and Augustine*, pp. 313-314.

What might we conclude about Ratzinger on the basis of this early piece of scholarship on Augustine's doctrine of the Church? It is unquestionably the case that his choice of theme largely determined which face of Augustine he would encounter in his studies. Augustine the proto Protestant is far submerged when Augustine the Bishop confronts schismatics who are endangering the unity of the universal Church. It is not a surprise, therefore, that the description given of Augustine's soteriology in Ratzinger is heavily ecclesial. Indeed, the conviction shared by the majority of scholars that the Augustine of the Donatist controversy pioneered a markedly ecclesiastical brand of salvation would confirm that Ratzinger's assessment of Augustine' ecclesiology was accurate.

Further, his treatment of Augustine's conversion evidences little sympathy towards any interpretation that would seek to validate it as a fitting and complete model for incorporation into the Church. Classical evangelical soteriology, whilst affirming the centrality of the church in mission and also its necessity for the nurture and upbuilding of the faithful, would still place greatest emphasis on the interiority of faith and the soul's personal engagement with God.[64] Indeed, it might even be said that the ministrations of the church are precisely for the strengthening of the individual's journey into the life of the Triune God. However, the young Ratzinger seems at various points to be uncomfortable with such an emphasis and posits 'believing with the Church' as the necessary complement to the interior journey. This perspective reveals itself particularly in Ratzinger's reaction to a work entitled *de Magistro* where the marked absence of any reference to 'faith, church and sacraments' in Augustine leaves him profoundly unsettled and hoping for better things in the later writings. It is also present in his reference to Augustine's acknowledgment of the limitations of the individual philosophical search for the vision of God in Book Seven of *The Confessions*. Was there too easy an equation of Augustine's thoughts at that moment with his mental state after his Christian conversion in 386? Indeed, is Ratzinger making a judgment about the nature of salvation on the basis of a spurious comparison between the lone journey of the philosopher and the act of corporate believing within the church? Are these really the only two options or do the hints Augustine offers of a more personalised and less sacramentalised faith (particularly in *de Magistro*) suggest that a less church-focused approach was present in Augustine and worth investigating? Joseph Ratzinger at this stage in his own intellectual journey is not particularly interested in such questions. He embraces the Catholic Augustine who placed such emphasis on the church as the agent of salvation and is not perturbed by the agonised believer whose doctrine of predestination rendered null and void the ministrations of the sacramental church to the non-elect. One can see that this more radical Augustine found a willing home among Calvinists but was largely ignored by those who embraced his vision of the universal church united in objective caritas.

---

[64] For an example of this viewpoint see Wayne Grudem, *Systematic Theology: An Introduction to Biblical Doctrine* (Leicester: Inter-Varsity Press, 1994), p. 710.

Ratzinger and *'Gaudium et Spes.'*

Whilst Rowland is conspicuous by her disagreement on this matter[65], there seems to be a general consensus among scholars that Ratzinger's more critical comments about aspects of certain Vatican II documents were the fruit of his Augustinian outlook. Although this movement is most chiefly identified with his work on *Gaudium et Spes*, ('the Divine Constitution on the Church and the Modern World'), it should be noted that there is an Augustinian, if not Lutheran edge, to some of his comments on *Dei Verbum*, the document dealing with Revelation. Foreshadowing his reservations about *Gaudium et Spes*, Ratzinger reveals his unease with what Nichols defines as the 'soteriological optimism' of parts of that document. The following extended quotation gives a flavour of the particular concerns which were troubling Ratzinger at this time.

> The text sees the whole of history, on the one hand, under the sign of the Fall, i.e. as fallen history, but, on the other, under the sign of the promise and the care of God, who alone makes possible 'the patience of good works' and thus eternal life. Here we can scarcely suppress the question as to whether the Council did not start from an over-optimistic view in its account of revelation and salvation history, losing sight of the fact that divine salvation comes essentially as a justification of the *sinner*; that grace is given through the judgment of the cross and thus itself always retains the character of judgment; that therefore the *one* word of God appears in the double guise of Law and Gospel – a statement that is still true even if we consider the specifically Lutheran theology of Law and Gospel as too narrow and inadequate. If Rom 2 was quoted as a testimony for the universal possibility of salvation, should not also mention have been made of the terrifying context of this passage of Scripture, that belongs to an invisible line of thought which runs from 1:17-3:20, ending finally, in 3:20, in the statement that is directly contrary to the text quoted (2.6f): 'For no human being will be justified in his sight by the works of the Law…' cf. also 3:23: 'since all have sinned and fall short of the glory of God…' When salvation is being treated should not the mystery of the anger of God also have been mentioned, that weighs so heavily upon these chapters? The whole vast subject of sin, law and the anger of God is gathered together here in the one little word *lapsus (post eorum lapsum…)* and thus is given neither its full weight nor is it taken seriously enough. The pastoral optimism of an age that is concerned with understanding and reconciliation seems to have somewhat blinded the Council to a not immaterial section of the testimony of Scripture.[66]

It would be inappropriate to follow Ratzinger's argument any further at this stage in that some of it has relevance to a later chapter on soteriology. Suffice it

---

[65] See Rowland, *Ratzinger's Faith*, pp. 30-48.

[66] Joseph Ratzinger, 'Revelation Itself' in Herbert Vorgrimler (ed) *Commentary on the Documents of Vatican II* Vol III. (London: Burns & Oats/Herder and Herder, 1966), pp.173-174.

to say that Ratzinger's terminology is redolent of Reformed or Lutheran reflection on these matters and that there is a most definite Augustinian, if not more than Augustinian colour, to his pronouncements here. However, it is his response to *Gaudium et Spes* that has most definitively associated him with the figure of Augustine. Nichols suggests that this was the Vatican document with which he was most disengaged as a commentator because it had failed to either find appropriate content on which to dialogue with the world nor apposite language to convey its most treasured beliefs. The authors had

> ...unfortunately dragged beyond the protecting walls of the theology faculty building just those affirmations which theology shares anyhow with any spiritual-ethical picture of man whatsoever. Whereas what is proper to theology, discourse about Christ and his work, was left behind in a conceptual deep-freeze, and so allowed to appear, in contrast with the understandable part, even more unintelligible and antiquated.[67]

Ratzinger's brief work on the Council, *Theological Highlights of Vatican II*, offers more background on why he was dissatisfied with the document. We note that he was aware of a growing rift at the Council between those with a markedly biblicist approach and those whose agenda was determined by contemporary society. The framers of *Gaudium et Spes*, in his view, were decidedly for *aggiornamento* and the profoundest frustration for him was their lack of awareness of how self-defeating such a project would be if it was detached from the anchors of faith.

> The chief concern of the text was to speak to contemporary man; thus it had tried to express fundamental theological ideas in a modern way, and in doing so got even further away from scriptural language than did its scholastic predecessors. Biblical citations were little more than ornamental. This not only made the text difficult from an ecumenical point of view, but also it made it questionable for modern man. What interest could an outsider find in a theological statement which had largely divorced itself from its own origins.[68]

Ratzinger's dissatisfaction with the theological methodology employed is aggravated by an Augustinian distaste for Pelagian-sounding soteriology. In the brief survey that follows, I shall view this issue particularly in the light of Rowland's claim that his engagement with *Gaudium et Spes* was influenced by an Augustinian-tinged Thomism as opposed to a straight-forward Augustinianism.

Rowland's justification for reaching such a conclusion is based largely on the perceived impact on Ratzinger's thought of two theologians from the *ressourcement* stable. First, she claims that since Ratzinger's style of

---

[67] J. Ratzinger, *Ergebnisse und Probleme der dritten Konzilsperiode* (Cologne 1965) cited in Nichols, *The Thought of Benedict*, p. 69.
[68] Ratzinger, *Theological Highlights of Vatican II*, pp. 219-220.

Augustinianism was most influenced by Henri de Lubac, and this same de Lubac had identified himself as a Thomist in relation to the debate about nature and grace, it was likely that when issues of nature and grace were touched upon in *Gaudium et Spes* it was de Lubac's outlook that most influenced him.[69] This argument is rather more subtle than I have summarised it here because Rowland's claim is that Thomas is less 'Thomist' than some who are influenced by neo-scholasticism would allow. Indeed, in her view it may have been an Augustinian muse who inspired the Angelic Doctor at points. According to her,

> ...when it comes to debates about how *Gaudium et spes* is to be interpreted it is not a macro-level choice between reading it with Augustinian spectacles and reading it with Thomist spectacles. It is more of a micro-level choice between reading it with the mindset of de Lubac or Rahner in relation to the specific issue of the nature and grace relationship, and here it is significant that de Lubac claimed that his position was classically Thomist, notwithstanding the judgments of Garrigou-Lagrange and Labourdette. It is also fact that contemporary non-partisan scholarship favours de Lubac's historical claim that what the pre-conciliar Thomists regarded as a classical Thomist account of the grace and nature relationship was not classically Thomist at all, but a baroque revision.

Alongside the influence of de Lubac, Rowland cites the impact of Hans Urs von Balthasar and his theology of history on Ratzinger's assessment of *Gaudium et Spes*. Whilst acknowledging that her source cannot easily be equated with a Thomist outlook, she suggests that this poses no great difficulty for her thesis in that Augustinians and Thomists share the same theology of history. It is this much more positive perspective on the world that is said to undergird Ratzinger's reflections. According to Rowland,

> The idea that Augustine was hostile to the world and all the achievements of pagan culture is now coming to be regarded as a discredited stereotype that owes much to Protestant and Jansenist spin ... Whether one is an Augustinian or almost any species of Thomist the same theology of history will be operative. For both Augustine and Aquinas the world is essentially good. It is an epiphany of God's love in which there appears vestiges of God's Trinitarian form. It is the theatre in which the drama of human salvation is played and within this drama the nobility of the human person is manifest in man's spiritual and cultural achievements, in accord with the movement of grace.[70]

To what degree is this reading of Ratzinger's theology realistic and to what extent is it special pleading on the part of a scholar who wishes to rescue Ratzinger from the charge of having an Augustinianism that smacks of the Protestant caricature? The closest we come to any form of answer to that

---

[69] Rowland, *Ratzinger's Faith*, pp. 150-151.
[70] Rowland, *Ratzinger's Faith*. p. 151.

question is found in Ratzinger's treatment of Article 13 of *Gaudium et Spes* in the Vorgrimler commentary. Here he examines the document's understanding of sin and opens his remarks with the negative observation that the Ariccia text (not the final text) had virtually succeeded in ignoring this central concept in its biblical doctrine of man. His sense of why this should have happened was that there was a misunderstanding of the optimistic tone of John XXIII"s opening address to the Council on the part of some of the authors[71] as well as a certain Teilhardian optimism about the human project. In addition, he refers to a strong stress on sin, deriving from Luther, being alien to the French authors of the document. Their perspective is characterised as 'Thomistic in tendency' and, while not ignoring sin, laying most emphasis on the knowledge that redemption has already taken place.[72] Ratzinger then juxtaposes this approach with two other theological perspectives that conversely place sin at the centre of the theological edifice: namely Lutheran theology and Catholic Augustinianism since the Reformation. Whilst not specifically criticising the authors of the document for not adopting the position of the Lutheran and Catholic Augustinians, it is clear that he views the latter two groupings as sharing a common outlook which is undeniably Augustinian and which understands sin to be the fundamental theological issue facing humanity. There is no nuanced distinction made between the Catholic version (which he clearly owns) and the one emanating from the Reformation churches. Indeed, his earlier positive reference to Lutheran exegesis of Romans in his commentary on *Dei Verbum*, as well as the strong *contra mundum* stance taken in *The Ratzinger Report*, would all indicate that his Augustinian perspective is of a piece with the Protestant variety and not a unique type mediated by de Lubac. Indeed, we are given a further hint of his sensibilities when he equates the outlook of those who framed this article with that of a revisionist Lutheran scholar who rhapsodised about the Teihardian vision of humanity.[73]

---

[71] Whilst John XXIII was opposing nostalgia about the loss of the Medieval paradigm and encouraging the belief that God is at work in all ages, Ratzinger suggests that this was mistaken for an optimistic view of man and the world. See Ratzinger, 'The Dignity of the Human Person' in Vorgrimler (ed), *Documents of Vatican II* (Volume 5), p. 123.

[72] Ratzinger, 'The Dignity of the Human Person' in Vorgrimler, *Documents of Vatican II* (Volume 5), p. 124.

[73] Ratzinger writes, 'It is worth noting that in discussions since the Council, voices have been raised from the Lutheran camp in precisely the same sense. Thus S.M. Daecke quotes a remark attributed to Teilhard de Chardin, 'You are all hypnotized by evil', and then continues, 'Isn't he right with his sovereign disdain for sin and evil, with his will to see the world as a good creation, to regard it positively and not to overestimate what is negative? In his conviction that evil is not a power opposed to God but something that is always overcome, Teilhard is in agreement with Karl Barth ... Even for the Bible, sin is not the central idea to the extent it is for Teilhard de Chardin's critics. For Paul himself, to whom they appeal, sin has been overcome in Christ and has lost its domination; it belongs to the old aeon which is past.' ('Dignity of the Human Person') in Vorgrimler (ed), *Documents of Vatican II*, (Volume 5), p. 124.

Ratzinger's anti-Pelagianism (another undeniably Augustinian feature of his critique of *Gaudium et Spes*) is most present when he addresses the document's treatment of freedom. In his view, this is one of the least satisfactory themes because of its optimistic assessment of man's moral capability. The fundamental problem identified is that the authors draw on texts influenced by Old Testament wisdom theology which highlight freedom of choice without taking heed of those other texts which subvert that notion. We pick up Ratzinger's exegesis at the point where he is criticising the document's employment of Ecclesiasticus 15:14. In his setting of the matter straight it is difficult not to hear the tones of Augustine, or indeed perhaps, the voice of Martin Luther.

> It should also have been taken into account that Ecclus 15:14 is a moralising and individualistic interpretation of Deut 11:26ff., which in Jeremiah 21:8 undergoes a striking pragmatic modification, and stands at the starting-point of the Jewish ethical doctrine of the two ways. If Jer 21:8 is rooted in the concrete situation of beleaguered Jerusalem, the statement of Deut 11:26 is entirely determined by the theology of the Covenant. The Thou who is addressed is Israel, which in God's offer of the Covenant receives the choice between life and death. Consequently in using such texts the Christian cannot leave out of account the actual history of the Covenant, cannot exclude the fact that Israel – representing mankind – was not in a position to carry out what the Covenant offered, but inevitably experienced the Law as a yoke 'which neither our fathers nor we have been able to bear.' (Acts 15:10) It is impossible to prescind from the fact that the promised life ultimately came not from freedom in fulfilling the Law but from the death of him who allowed himself in accordance with the Law to hang on the tree as a Transgressor of the Law (Gal. 3:12ff).[74]

Ratzinger's exegesis of this material concludes with a damning indictment of *Gaudium et Spes'* doctrine of freedom which he finds wrong-headed at every point.

> The general doctrine of freedom developed in the conciliar text cannot therefore stand up either to theological or philosophical criticism. Philosophically speaking, it by-passes the whole modern discussion of freedom. It simply takes no account of that overshadowing of freedom of which psychology and sociology at the present time informs us in such a disturbing way. Consequently it shuts itself out from the factual situation of man whose freedom only comes into effect through a lattice of determining factors. Theologically speaking, it leaves aside the whole complex of problems which Luther, with polemical one-sidedness, comprised in the term 'servum arbitrium'. The whole text scarcely gives a hint of the discord which runs through man and which is described so dramatically in Romans 7:13-25. It even falls into downright Pelagian terminology when it speaks of

---

[74] Ratzinger in Vorgrimler (ed), *Documents of Vatican II* (Volume 5), pp. 137-138.

man *'sese ab omni passionum captivitate liberans finem suum persequitur et apta subsidia ...procurat.*[75]

The last two extensive quotations give a stronger sense than any summary could of the profoundly Augustinian bent to Ratzinger's thought. Here we find him underlining emphases within Augustine which have been crucial to Protestant readings of his theology. Ratzinger's geographical location and scholarly engagement with Lutheran colleagues such as Beyerhaus and Wickert may not have been insignificant when it comes to the manner in which his soteriological thinking has been formed. If his work on Augustine's doctrine of the church reinforced his Catholic perception of the central place of the church, it seems equally clear that his profound understanding of both Augustine and the Reformers has left him sympathetic to a view of redemption which takes seriously the incapacity of humanity and which writes of salvation in a script familiar and accessible to those outside of the Catholic fold. In a subsequent chapter examining Ratzinger's perspective on justification we may be able to gauge more clearly whether this sensibility to Protestant concerns amounts to a potential theological rapprochement.

The Love of God

Henry Chadwick in the publication *Augustine* talks about the Church Father's profound influence on western Christian mysticism and how this was effected primarily through his reflections on the love of God.[76] In a similar vein, we cannot fully appreciate the nature of Ratzinger's thought without understanding how central that Augustinian theme is to it. It appears not only in his early teaching[77] but was also the subject forty two years later of his first encyclical as Pope, *Deus Caritas Est.*[78] Viewing the material in terms of what significance it might have for the dialogue with Evangelicalism, we should note that love for God, understood as communion with Jesus Christ, is put forward as the remedy or antidote to a religion purely based on adherence to ethical demands. This Augustinian perspective was encapsulated in a funeral eulogy which Ratzinger delivered in 2004 for Luigi Giussani, the founder of *Communione e liberazione*, one of the new ecclesial movements so beloved by his pontifical predecessor, John Paul II. Ratzinger applauds the Italian church activist for recognising that

---

[75] Ratzinger in Vorgrimler (ed), *Documents of Vatican II* (Volume 5, p. 138.
[76] Henry Chadwick, *Augustine: A Very Short Introduction* (Oxford: Oxford University Press, 2001), p. 3.
[77] Advent sermons delivered to students from the University of Münster's Catholic chaplaincy in 1964 culminated in a profound reflection on 1 John and the nature of God as love. These sermons were later published by an American Catholic press. Joseph Ratzinger, *What It Means To Be A Christian.* (San Francisco: Ignatius Press, 2006)
[78] Benedict XVI, *Deus Caritas Est* (London: CTS, 2006)

'Christianity is not an intellectual system, a collection of dogmas, or a moralism. Christianity is instead an encounter, a love story; it is an event.'[79]

In her penetrating study of Ratzinger's theology of love, Tracey Rowland draws on the work of his collaborator and guide, Hans Urs von Balthasar, to illustrate how insights about the history of Catholic religious practice over the past few centuries had affected Ratzinger and other scholars in the *Communio* school as they addressed the theme of love and the related notion of moralism. Many were conscious that the way Catholicism was practiced in the era prior to the Second Vatican Council was hampered by legalism. Moreover, they interpreted the crisis facing the post-conciliar church as not primarily the impact of secularizing influences but rather 'the logical outgrowth of a centuries-long process separating the true and the beautiful from the good.'[80] An explanation of the terminology employed here will indicate how such a situation facilitated a context of moralistic religion.

Von Balthasar believed that a healthy practice of religion involved the creative interplay of all three transcendentals (the true, the beautiful and the good) and that when this partnership or dance was disrupted by the loss of one or more of the partners, a pathological style of religion was created. This state of affairs is said to have existed from the time of the Reformation. Rowland offers an incisive summary of the type of ecclesiastical fall-out created when one or more of the transcendentals collapse. She suggests that,

> Differently defective accounts of human dignity, moral behaviour, and spiritualities have followed according to which transcendental is left standing when the others drop out. We can end up with immoral aesthetes at the end of one spectrum, and unattractive and iconoclastic puritans at the other, as well as people who get 'hooked' on dogma but who are nonetheless not very charitable to their neighbours, and people who are kind hearted but ignorant of the truth, together with numerous other permutations and combinations depending on which transcendental or combination of transcendentals is lacking ... In the absence of a Christian culture in which the relationship of the transcendentals to one another is clearly visible and culturally embodied, the temptation to moralism is strong.[81]

Exploring the issue further in reference to Catholicism in recent centuries, and drawing on other scholars who share von Balthasar and Ratzinger's

---

[79] Ratzinger, 'Homily for Msgr Luigi Giusanni', *Communio:International Catholic Review, 31* (2004), pp. 685-687 cited in Rowland, *Ratzinger's Faith*, p. 67.
[80] Rowland, *Ratzinger's Faith*, p. 67.
[81] Rowland, *Ratzinger's Faith*, p. 67.

perpective[82], Rowland suggests that in a large swathe of Catholic religious life the motivation for moral obedience was obligation towards duty and the hope that such solicitude to the divine commandments would have a meritorious outcome.[83] The proof that this outlook was pathological in nature is said to be demonstrated by the drastic collapse of traditional morality once this approach came under fire from liberal elements in the church in the wake of Vatican II. According to Rowland,

> [Both Ratzinger and von Balthasar] concluded that people in the pre-conciliar era had a tendency to live prescriptively, not because they believed the moral injunctions were life-giving, not because they could see truth, goodness and beauty in the practices themselves, but because of a fear of eternal damnation. Once the fear was eliminated the motivation holding up the practice dissipated.[84]

This interpretation of Catholic religious life became public on Ratzinger's part when he delivered a series of student sermons in Münster and made reference to the prevailing spiritual apathy within the church. He comments,

> What a strange attitude it is that we no longer find Christian service worthwhile if the denarius of salvation [an allusion to Jesus' parable about the workers in the vineyard recorded in Matt 20:1-10] may be obtained even without it.[85]

The cause of such a diminished spirituality he traces back to the pre-conciliar manualist approach to ethics so popular with the neo-Scholastics. Here, rather than stressing the redemption and freedom which should accompany the encounter with Christ, the rationalist theology of the era is said to have centred on the many prohibitions, the many 'no's and lost sight of the great 'Yes' which the actualisation of the commandments were intended to be.[86]

    It is in the striving for a different outlook, the search for an approach to spirituality which allows each of the transcendentals to operate within the individual's relationship to God, that we are to interpret *Deus Caritas Est* and other writings devoted to the theme of love.

---

[82] For example, P. Henrici, 'Modernity and Christianity', *Communio: International Catholic Review, 17* (1990), pp. 140-151
[83] Rowland, *Ratzinger's Faith*, p. 69.
[84] Rowland, *Ratzinger's Faith*, p. 69.
[85] Ratzinger, *What It Means To Be A Christian* (San Francisco: Ignatius Press), p. 49.
[86] Joseph Ratzinger, 'The Renewal of Moral Theology: Perspectives on Vatican II and *Veritatis Splendor, Communio'*: *International Catholic Review*, 32 (2005), pp. 357-369.

Deus Caritas Est

In his first encyclical, Benedict addresses in typically forthright fashion the charge of Nietzsche's that the church's promotion of *agape* has been to the detriment of *eros,* and that indeed, the most valuable thing for human beings has effectively been poisoned by the church's negative and restrictive teaching. Benedict comments,

> Here the German philosopher was expressing a widely-held perception: doesn't the Church, with all her commandments and prohibitions, turn to bitterness the most precious thing in life? Doesn't she blow the whistle just when the joy which is the Creator's gift offers us happiness which is itself a foretaste of the divine.[87]

His response to that criticism is that *eros* and *agape* are not unrelated realities but that there is a symbiotic relationship whereby one only functions in its proper fashion when it is not separated from the other.[88] Rowland, applying that insight to contemporary culture, paints a picture of a desiccated society when the necessary union of the two has been repudiated.

> Unless *agape* fructifies *eros* it simply dies. Experiments with *eros* which deprive the person of his or her dignity, which commodify or otherwise dehumanize the person, which treat a person as a mere means to the achievement of some desire of another without any self-reciprocal self-giving, or which denigrate the body to the status of a mechanical object, cut short the ascent to the divine which is the work of *agape*. In these situations *eros* ultimately becomes sterile and boring.[89]

Benedict draws on the language of the *Song of Songs* (interpreted here as love poems possibly intended for a Jewish wedding feast) to illustrate the manner in which *agape* can transfigure *eros*. He reminds his readers that two words, and not one word, are used to indicate love in the text. The word first used is *dodim* which he claims suggests a love that is 'still insecure, indeterminate and searching.'[90] However, as the book progresses this is replaced by the word *ahabà*, which the Septuagint translates with the similar sounding *agape*, which becomes the characteristic biblical expression for love. He concludes that by contrast to the original word used with its uncertainty and indeterminacy, this new expression conveys 'the experience of a love which involves the real discovery of the other, moving beyond the selfish character that prevailed earlier. Love now becomes care and concern for the other. No longer is it self-

---

[87] Benedict XVI, *Deus Caritas Est*, p. 6.
[88] Joseph Ratzinger, *Images of Hope: Meditations on Major Feasts* (San Francisco: Ignatius, 2006),
p. 88 cited in Rowland, *Ratzinger's Faith*, p. 71.
[89] Rowland, *Ratzinger's Faith*, p. 71.
[90] Benedict XVI, *Deus Caritas Est*, p. 9.

seeking, a sinking in the intoxication of happiness; instead it seeks the good of the beloved: it becomes renunciation and it is ready, and even willing, for sacrifice.'[91]

From this purified notion of love, Benedict expounds the revelation (one which he believes is unprecedented in the history of religions[92]) of a God who loves the world with a personal love. For Geoffrey Wainwright, the most striking theological feature of the encyclical is the claim that the love characterised here is eros as well as agape.[93] Eros because the prophets (most notably Hosea and Ezekiel) used bold erotic images as a way of describing God's passion for Israel and agape because it is 'bestowed in a completely gratuitous manner, without any previous merit, but also because it forgives.'[94] In an arresting turn of phrase, Benedict asserts that God's love is so great, so full of forgiveness, 'that it turns God against himself, his love against his justice.'[95] This is said to be a 'dim prefigurement of the mystery of the Cross' and what would be the ultimate cost of the Incarnation.[96]

In an impressive display of integrated inter-disciplinary theological reflection, Benedict proceeds to show the relationship between the biblical vision just outlined and the world of philosophy. He notes that while we have 'a strictly metaphysical image of God' who is the 'absolute and ultimate source of all being' – this God as he expresses himself as *Logos* is simultaneously a lover with all of the passion which that identity will carry. Thus *eros* is at one and the same time 'ennobled and purified' so that it might become *agape*.[97] Moreover, we are said to be given some understanding as to why the *Song of Songs* should later be seen as not only depicting human love but ultimately saying something about the inter-relationship between man and God. Finally, placing this discussion in the context of the history of religions as well as the biblical story and the world of philosophy, Benedict utilises the historical impact of the *Song of Songs* as a launching pad for his description of what reciprocal divine and human love really consists.

> ...the Song of Songs became, both in Christian and Jewish literature, a source of mystical knowledge and experience, an expression of the essence of biblical faith: that man can indeed enter into union with God – his primordial aspiration. But this union is no mere fusion, a sinking in the

---

[91] Benedict XVI, *Deus Caritas Est*, p. 9.
[92] Benedict XVI, *Deus Caritas Est*, p. 12.
[93] Geoffrey Wainwright, 'Reflections on Pope Benedict XVI's First Encyclical, *Caritas Deus Est*' in
Pro Ecclesia Vol. XV, No.3, p. 264.
[94] Benedict XVI, *Deus Caritas Est*, p. 13.
[95] Benedict XVI, *Deus Caritas Est*, p. 14.
[96] Benedict XVI, *Deus Caritas Est*, p. 14.
[97] Benedict XVI, *Deus Caritas Est*, p. 14.

nameless ocean of the Divine; it is a unity which creates love, a unity in which both God and man remain themselves and yet become fully one.[98]

The culmination of this first part of the encyclical (which is the focus of this section) is the portrayal of Jesus Christ as the embodiment of the love of God. However, the incarnation does not have the quality of an epiphany in which humanity receives a moment of illumination and must then live off this teasing glimpse. On the contrary, Jesus Christ fully enters into the human situation – it is an action of 'unprecedented realism' as Benedict describes it – and comes in search of a humanity which has strayed and lost its way like a lost sheep. Benedict employs the three parables of Luke 15 to illustrate the pastoral nature of the Incarnation and portrays its climax as the event of the cross where, for the sake of love, God turned against himself in order to raise man up and save him.[99] This is love in its ultimate form and it is through the contemplation of the pierced One that we can understand the claim that 'God is love.' This is where any 'definition of love must begin' and the only true starting point from which redeemed human life can move.[100]

Having considered Benedict's theology of the love of God by means of a brief summary of his first encyclical, as well as with reference to some of his other writings, it is clear that what he has to say has much in common with traditional evangelical theology. Even though there may be a more unfamiliar range of thought involved than would be present in some evangelical studies of the same theme, the message remains broadly similar. Few evangelicals would take issue with the conclusion reached at the end of the first section of the encyclical that contemplation of the cross is the best vantage point from which to comprehend the love of God. Nor would they be displeased with Benedict's firm rejection of any interpretation of the Christian life that might diminish its status as a relationship with God. Indeed, his choice of words on the opening page of the document would serve only as an encouragement to evangelicals that, in some respects at least, the Pope Emeritus shares a common vision.

> *We have come to believe in God's love*: in these words the Christian can express the fundamental decision of his life. Being Christian is not the result of an ethical choice or a lofty idea, but the encounter with an event, a person, which gives life a new horizon and a decisive direction. St John's Gospel describes that event in these words: *'God so loved the world that he gave his only Son, that whoever believes in him should ... have eternal life.'* (3:16)[101]

Thus one might conclude at this juncture that the encyclical's elevation of the love of God, and the way in which it emphasises the gratuitous nature of that love, make it more than an unobjectionable document to evangelicals. Indeed,

---

[98] Benedict XVI, *Deus Caritas Est*, p. 14.
[99] Benedict XVI, *Deus Caritas Est*, p. 16.
[100] Benedict XVI, *Deus Caritas Est* p. 16.
[101] Benedict XVI, *Deus Caritas Est*, p. 3.

perhaps one that carries within it the hope of a deeper understanding between the two traditions. However, it may be possible to take that optimism one step further. The earlier references to the paucity of Catholic piety in the intervening centuries between Trent and Vatican II indicate that Ratzinger, von Balthasar, and other like-minded Catholic theologians have identified a definite Pelagian streak in Catholic devotion. One which is pathological in von Balthasar's terms and which has undermined the validity of much religious practice. Ratzinger's emphasis on the love of God is an attempted antidote to such an unwelcome scenario. He recognises the need for individuals to interact with faith in such a manner that their obedience to the laws of God reflect an embrace of the good, the true and the beautiful. To what degree might an evangelical theology of conversion aid the Catholic church in its bid to move individuals from either a prescriptive or a libertarian approach to faith? Might a theological tradition which is strong in facilitating divine encounters in an evangelistic context, even if it is not always so successful in the longer-term deepening of those relationships, have something to say to a Catholic church which faces oblivion in Europe?[102]

Reason

Those who are familiar with the events of Benedict's early pontificate will remember a controversial lecture he gave at the University of Regensburg in 2006 during a Papal visit to Germany. The media's reporting of the incident focused on intemperate words spoken about Mohammed by a fourteenth century Christian Byzantine Emperor which the Pope had the misfortune or bad judgment to cite in his speech. The widespread publicity accorded to the words stirred up indignation within the Muslim world and even resulted in the killing of a Catholic religious.[103] To those not following the episode closely it may have appeared that the speech was primarily concerned with challenging violent tendencies present within contemporary Islam. In reality the speech was much more a condemnation of secular western culture than an attack on Islam *per se*.

The title of the address was 'Faith, Reason and the University'[104] and in it Benedict teased out the link between faith and reason in order to promote

---

[102] See Jan Kerkhofs, (ed), *Europe Without Priests* (London: SCM Press, 2003) for an analysis of the collapse of the pariochial structure in Western Europe.
[103] Italian nun Sr Leonella Sgorbati was murdered by two gunmen in Mogadishu in the aftermath to Pope Benedict's speech. See Michelle Malkin, 'Remembering Sister Leonella'. (2006). http://michellemalkin.com/2006/09/25/remembering-sister-leonella/ (accessed 4 May, 2011).
[104] Benedict XVI, 'Faith, Reason and the University: Memories and Reflections.' Delivered on 12 September 2006 on the occasion of Benedict's Apostolic Journey to Munich, Altötting and Regensburg. http://pontificateofpopebenedictxvi.blogspot.ie/2008/08/regensburg-address-faith-reason-and.html (accessed 6 July, 2009).

the Augustinian conviction that there was a necessary relationship between the two.[105] In this matter he challenged the perspective of Tertullian, the mystics and ultimately the founders of the Protestant Reformation[106] who all saw reason as inherently suspect. At the same time this endorsement of reason was not a justification of the Enlightenment project. His speech took issue with the reductionist, empirical approach to reason associated with rationalism and sought to resurrect that search for ultimate truth and meaning which he believed characterised Greek thought. The latter he presents as the high water mark in intellectual history and one whose intellectual demise has had a debilitating effect on culture as well as on any potential dialogue with those standing outside the Western tradition. His advocacy of reason is thus a plea for a return to the Greek roots of post biblical-theology.

To gain a fuller picture of Benedict's understanding of reason, it will be instructive to highlight those aspects of the Regensburg address which bring his views into greater relief. For example, the speech opens with a contentious reference to the conflicting Christian and Islamic views of reason. Benedict cites a Medieval dialogue that had taken place between the Byzantine emperor Manuel II Paleologus and an educated Persian on the subject of 'Christianity, Islam and truth.' In an extremely forthright attack on the Islamic concept of 'Holy War' (one from whose spirit Benedict distanced himself) the Christian Emperor asserts that conversion by means of violence runs counter to reason and that 'not to act in accordance with reason is contrary to God's nature.'[107] This point is made in such an absolute fashion because, according to Koury[108] (the editor of the dialogue), someone who had been shaped by Greek philosophy in the way the Emperor had been, could not see things in any other way. In contrast to this, the Muslim teaching is said to assert that God is not bound by rationality in the way that the Greeks presumed he was.[109]

Benedict's question is whether the opinion advanced by the Emperor is merely a Greek idea or something that is always and intrinsically true? His response is that the latter is more likely the case as a profound harmony exists between the best of Greek thought and the biblical understanding of God. He cites the Prologue of John's Gospel as the classic proof of this in that the Greek

---

[105] For a helpful treatment of this theme see John Rist, 'Faith and Reason in Augustine' in Eleonore Stump and Norman Kretzman (ed), *The Cambridge Companion to Augustine* (Cambridge: Cambridge University Press, 2001).

[106] In Martin Luther, *Works*, (Erlangen Edition V. 16), pp. 142-148, the Reformer refers to reason as 'the Devil's whore'.

[107] A.T. Khoury, 'Manuel II Paléologue, Entretiens avec un Musulman. 7e Controverse', in *Sources Chrétiennes* n. 115, (Paris 1966) cited in Benedict XVI, 'Faith, Reason and the University.'

[108] Professor at the University of Münster.

[109] Benedict quotes Koury's citation of the French Islamist, R. Arnaldez, who noted that Ibn Hazm went so far as to assert that God is not bound even by his own word, and that nothing would oblige him to reveal the truth to us. R. Arnaldez, *Grammaire et théologie chez Ibn Hazm de Cordoue* (Paris, 1956), p. 13.

understanding of the Logos (incorporating notions of reason, creativity and self-communication) is attributed to the nature of the divine person whom John identifies as 'the Word.' Given that such a close relationship exists between the being of God and the Greek concept of reason, Benedict concludes that the meeting of Greek thought and the biblical message must have been a divine appointment. In a fascinating piece of biblical exegesis he suggests that the vision received by St Paul barring the road to Asia, that was then followed by a dream in which a Macedonian pleaded with him to come to Greece (Acts 16:6-10), was a case of God reinforcing the 'intrinsic necessity of a rapprochement between Biblical faith and Greek inquiry.'[110]

Benedict laments the fact that by the Middle Ages certain influences in theology were beginning to tear asunder this synthesis between Greek and Christian thought. Duns Scotus is portrayed as the major culprit in the matter, as a line of thought beginning with him led later to positions which were similar to the more extreme Islamic ideas referred to earlier in the speech. Benedict comments that,

> In contrast with the so-called intellectualism of Augustine and Thomas, there arose with Duns Scotus a voluntarism which, in its later developments, led to the claim that we can only know God's voluntas ordinata. Beyond this is the realm of God's freedom, in virtue of which he could have done the opposite of everything he has actually done. This gives rise to positions which clearly approach those of Ibn Hazm and might even lead to the image of a capricious God, who is not even bound to truth and goodness. God's transcendence and otherness are so exalted that our reason, our sense of the true and good, are no longer an authentic mirror of God, whose deepest possibilities remain eternally unattainable and hidden behind his actual decisions.[111]

Over time this attack on a 'critically purified Greek heritage [as] an integral part of Christian faith' is said to have intensified. Benedict highlights as an example the Reformers' dismissal of scholasticism as an alien system of thought dependent on philosophy and not scripture. This is a view which he claims involved metaphysics itself being regarded as a premise derived from philosophy and not something intrinsic to the very nature of reality. His point is that whilst the Reformers continued to retain beliefs consistent with a Catholic metaphysical worldview, there was in principle nothing to stop someone like Kant from later divorcing faith from metaphysics and '[anchoring it] exclusively in practical reason'. His suggestion is that the Reformers had inadvertently, through their adoption of *Sola Scriptura*, undermined the relationship between reason and metaphysics in their denial that philosophy had any potential to ascertain truth about God.

For Benedict, this departure from scholasticism was the first phase in a process of dehellenization which continued over the subsequent centuries. The

---

[110] Benedict XVI, 'Faith, Reason and the University.'
[111] Benedict XVI, 'Faith, Reason and the University.'

next important stage was said to be the impact of liberal theology in the nineteenth and twentieth centuries. Von Harnack is singled out here for special notice as he is deemed to be the main protagonist in the matter. It was Harnack who characterized the supernatural aspects of the faith as being merely of Hellenistic origin and therefore in need of being jettisoned so that Jesus' simple humanitarian gospel might be re-discovered. In taking such a stance, he is perceived by Benedict as aligning himself with 'the modern self-limitation of reason, classically expressed in Kant's critiques ... and further radicalized by the impact of the natural sciences.'[112]

This unease with the Greek influence on Christianity is said to have given rise to two principles that were highly destructive to faith. First, the view that certainty could only be defined in terms that would pass muster empirically or mathematically. Second, the 'knock-on' effect of this outlook that the question of God is excluded from rational purview because it can only be understood as a pre-scientific or unscientific datum. Benedict laments such a situation and highlights both the theological and human cost. In terms of theology as a discipline, it has meant that any attempt to bolster it 'scientifically' would only result in it becoming a shadow of its former self. More disturbingly, though, human beings would themselves be reduced when truth was defined solely by the empirical method. This was the case because the uniquely human questions about humanity's origin and destiny – the questions inspired by religion and ethics – would have no tenure in modern rational discourse. Rather, they are demoted to the sphere of the private where peoples' experiences and the subjective 'conscience' define what is right or true. The outcome of that situation, claims Benedict, is that 'ethics and religion lose their ability to create community' and what is left as an alternative means to that goal is simply inadequate to the task.[113]

Before drawing his final conclusions he alludes briefly to the third stage of dehellenization, cultural pluralism, and challenges its assumption that Christianity's synthesis with Hellenism was a type of inculturation that need not have been passed on to other cultures. The fact that the New Testament was written in Greek, that it has the imprint of the Greek spirit, and that Greek thought had already impacted the Septuagint, point for him to the irrevocable relationship between Greek thought and its embrace of human reason and the Christian faith itself.

Benedict is at pains, however, to show that his critique of modern reason has nothing to do with repudiating the gains of the Enlightenment and modern thought. It is more a challenge to broaden the definition of reason as well as peoples' sense of how it might be applied. While acknowledging that the new possibilities now opened up to human beings are to be celebrated, he is also aware that they bring with them their own dangers. It is his conviction that these will only be overcome if reason and faith combine in a new way and the

---

[112] Benedict XVI, 'Faith, Reason and the University.'

[113] He instances efforts at constructing an ethic from the rules of evolution or from psychology or sociology.

self-imposed limitations of the empirical method are left behind in favour of a grander vision of rationality. Theology itself can be used to great effect with regard to the achievement of that goal within the context of the university. Moreover, this combination of reason and faith is the only means of actually creating that much needed dialogue of religions and cultures. Those parts of the world which do not accept modern western philosophy see the exclusion of the divine from rational discourse as an affront to their own convictions. It would be impossible, argues Benedict, to have a genuine dialogue with them should the West continue to employ a reason which is deaf to the divine.

The speech closes with commentary on words spoken by Socrates to Phaedo which sum up the Pontiff's elevation of the concept of reason.

> Here I am reminded of something Socrates said to Phaedo. In their earlier conversations, many false philosophical opinions had been raised, and so Socrates says: "It would be easily understandable if someone became so annoyed at all these false notions that for the rest of his life he despised and mocked all talk about being - but in this way he would be deprived of the truth of existence and would suffer a great loss".[13] The West has long been endangered by this aversion to the questions which underlie its rationality, and can only suffer great harm thereby. The courage to engage the whole breadth of reason, and not the denial of its grandeur - this is the programme with which a theology grounded in Biblical faith enters into the debates of our time.[114]

While this section has functioned largely as a summary of Benedict's views on reason, it is clear that his vision of a 'purified reason' shedding light on the central themes of faith challenges certain aspects of Reformation thinking. The rejection of scholasticism, root and branch, is understood as the opening of the door to a style of thinking which would ultimately undermine metaphysics and the Christian worldview. In a similar vein, his questioning of a view of God which presents the actions of the Deity as beyond our scrutiny, might be seen as implicitly undermining certain expressions of Calvinism that would seem to justify God acting in a way that confounds our moral categories. But notwithstanding these points of difference with the Reformed tradition, Benedict's Catholic position on the place of reason in faith is rooted not so much in simple adherence to tradition but an argument which he derives from Scripture itself. This would suggest that evangelicals must engage with that argument on these terms and not see it as self-defeating because it reflects Roman Catholic tradition. Moreover the recent rehabilitation of Aquinas in evangelical thought (see the work of Norman Geisler[115]) would indicate that Benedict's plea for a synthesis of reason and faith might not fall on entirely deaf ears.

---

[114] Benedict XVI, 'Faith, Reason and the University.'

[115] Norman Geisler, *Thomas Aquinas: An Evangelical Appraisal* (Eugene: Widf & Stock Publishers, 2003).

Augustine and the Evangelical Tradition

The argument that a significant relationship exists between the theology of Joseph Ratzinger and mainstream evangelical theology is premised on the Augustinian heritage which they share. The aim of this final section will be to explore the nature of that heritage in the Protestant tradition and to ask what significance it might have for future relations with Roman Catholicism. The more profound the Augustinian influence is in Protestantism - both in terms of its general impact on the tradition as well as its capacity to be a bridge to Catholicism - the more we may be hopeful that Ratzinger's embrace of Augustinianism is ecumenically significant.

The discussion will be framed around two central issues: the doctrinal content of so-called Protestant Augustinianism within the churches of the Reformation; and the potential ecumenical possibilities of Augustine's theology. There will not be a separate treatment of Augustine's influence on the magisterial Reformers, Luther and Calvin, as his pivotal role in the development of early Reformation thought is widely acknowledged and requires little vindication.[116]

Protestant Augustinianism

The above allusions to Augustine's early influence on the magisterial Reformers raises the question of what precisely constitutes the Protestant Augustinian legacy. To what degree was the Latin Father responsible for the particular shape of Protestantism and which of its doctrines correspond most to his original thought?[117] Diarmaid MacCullough in his magisterial study of the Reformation suggests that it is impossible to explain the event or the issues surrounding the rupture of the medieval church without reference to Augustine's doctrine of salvation.[118] In reaching this judgment he rejects the view that the success of the Reformation lay with the weakness and instability of the old church. With Eamon Duffy[119], he is convinced that the pre-Reformation Catholic church was immensely strong. Indeed, in his view only

---

[116] For insight into the impact of Augustine on Luther and Calvin see Manfred Schulze, 'Martin Luther and the Church Fathers' in Irena Backus (ed), *The Reception of the Church Fathers in the West: From the Carolingians to the Maurists* Volume 2 (Leiden/Boston: Brill Academic, 2001), p. 577 and Francois Wendell, *Calvin*, (London: Collins, 1976), p. 124.

[117] This is an impossibly large question and in the brief space available I can offer only a provisional answer.

[118] Diarmaid MacCullough, *Reformation: Europe's House Divided* (London: Penguin, 2004), p.110.

[119] Eamon Duffy, *The Stripping of the Altars: Traditional Religion in England 1400-1580* (London: Yale University Press, 1992).

the power of an explosive idea could have undermined such a secure foundation. Thus it was a new statement of Augustine's ideas on salvation which tore the heart out of the Medieval theological synthesis.

MacCullough is not entirely approving of the Augustinian outlook which he believes motivated the Reformers. He argues that more than anything else it was Augustine's theology of grace, founded on the absolute incapacity of the human will to obey God, which struck the strongest chord in them. This view is reiterated by Smits who, in his summary of Augustinian influence on Calvin, casts human depravity as the predominant theme.

> Calvin shows a real preoccupation to cover himself with the authority of Augustine in the questions of predestination, sacraments and original sin. His reasons for this are, first, the veneration which his adversaries, be they Catholic or Protestant, felt for the Bishop of Hippo, and then the fact that he himself had discovered in Augustine's writings the fundamental principle of the Reformation, namely, the corruption of the human heart.[120]

B.B. Warfield's classic study on Augustine and Calvin seems to concur with the conclusions of MacCullough and Smits that human inability and the absolute need for grace were the core ideas that drove the Reformation. In the quintessential statement of Augustinian influence on Protestantism, Warfield writes,

> ... it is Augustine who gave us the Reformation. For the Reformation, inwardly considered, was just the ultimate triumph of Augustine's doctrine of grace over Augustine's doctrine of the Church. This doctrine of grace came from Augustine's hands in its positive outline completely formulated: sinful man depends, for his recovery to the good and to God, entirely on the free grace of God; this grace therefore is indispensable, prevenient, irresistible, indefectible; and, being thus the free grace of God, must have lain, in all the details of its conference and working, in the intention of God from all eternity.[121]

The elements present in Warfield's depiction of grace highlight for us the strong emphasis on predestination that not only characterized much of Augustine's later theology but also determined the outlook of the magisterial Reformers themselves. Thus while it cannot be gainsaid that some form of predestination is present in the New Testament[122], it is Augustine himself who offers the most systematic treatment of the theme and this undoubtedly influenced works such as Luther's *Bondage of the Will* as well as Calvin's

---

[120] L. Smits, 'The Augustinian Roots of Calvin's Eucharistic Thought', *Augustinian Studies* 7 (1976) translated by Joseph Fitzer and cited in Thomas F. Martin, *Our Restless Heart: The Augustinian Tradition* (London: DLT, 2003), pp.129-130.

[121] Warfield, *Calvin and Augustine*, p. 223.

[122] For example, Paul's discussion of the fate of Israel in Romans 9-11 and the stress on election that may be detected within Luke's writings .

teaching on predestination. That this appropriation of Augustine's views on predestination was not an entirely Protestant preoccupation is evidenced by the strong Jansenist influence on seventeenth century French Catholicism. Cornelius Jansen, the Bishop of Ypres, had read the anti-Pelagian works of Augustine no fewer than thirty times and arrived at a doctrine of salvation which had the same element of apparent capriciousness as the Reformed one. The movement was eventually declared heretical and with its demise came the end of what we might term full-blooded Augustinianism in the Catholic Church. As Warfield put it in a discussion of events in the wake of the Jansenist controversy, '...the irresistibility of ... prevenient grace was put under the ban, and there remained no place for a complete 'Augustinianism' within the Church, as Gottschalk and Jansen were fully to discover.'[123]

Two notable absences from this brief consideration of Protestant Augustinianism are the themes of 'justification' and 'faith' in Augustine's theology. As stated earlier, I have reserved detailed comment for the concluding chapters of the monograph which specifically address the subjects of justification and faith respectively. There I will explore how Ratzinger's soteriological perspective has been influenced by Augustine and ask whether there may be any rapprochement with Evangelicalism on the basis of Ratzinger's own formulations.

Conclusion: The Ecumenical Possibilities of Augustine's Theology

Some of those scholars who identify most ecumenical potential in Augustine's theology do so because of its so-called paradoxical nature. This word 'paradox' is used advisedly because these authors would deny that Augustine is inconsistent in any straightforward kind of way.[124] Indeed, according to some, Augustine's theological vision is so rich that it has the potential to unite Protestant and Catholic thought in a higher synthesis that transcends the old divisions. Mark Ellingsen cites nineteenth century church historian, Philip Schaff, to this effect.

> In great men, and only in great men, great opposites and apparently antagonistic truths live together. Small minds cannot hold them ... Such a personage as Augustine, still holding a mediating place between the two great divisions of Christendom, revered alike by both, and of equal influence with both is furthermore a welcome pledge of the elevating prospect of a future reconciliation of Catholicism and Protestantism in a higher unity,

---

[123] Warfield, *Calvin and Augustine*, p. 323.

[124] A charge which was levelled against Augustine by Warfield who believed, that given more time, the African Father would have recognized the inconsistencies in his thought and followed the logic of his later writings towards a more thoroughly evangelical theology.

conserving all the truths, losing all the errors, forgiving all the sins, forgetting all the enmities of both.[125]

What gives Augustine such an elevated place within Catholicism is not only that he is seen as belonging to the tradition, but that he stands above and beyond it as its chief architect. Schaff acknowledges the pivotal place occupied by Augustine in the Catholic firmament when he states,

> Augustine is…the principal theological creator of the *Latin-Catholic* system as distinct from Greek Catholicism on the one hand, and from evangelical Protestantism on the other. He ruled the entire theology of the middle age, and became the father of scholasticism in virtue of his dialectic mind, and the father of mysticism in virtue of his devout heart, without being responsible for the excesses of either system.[126]

It is precisely this unparalleled role within Catholic theology which should encourage reflection about aspects of Augustine's teaching that have touched profoundly other traditions. Might there not be hidden riches in insights brought by Augustine that have nurtured Protestants over the centuries? Schaff instances Augustine's anti-Pelagian works as a case in point. He notes that Catholicism has at least marginally benefited from these already as they have exercised a restraining influence on pelagianizing tendencies within the hierarchical church, even if they have 'never passed into its blood and marrow.'[127] This revealing turn of phrase on the part of a writer of a much earlier vintage hints of further possibilities for the Catholic church should Augustine's teachings about the futility of works and the primacy of grace be fully imbibed within the life of the institution.

In a similar vein, Schaff speaks of Augustine's piety as something which militates against the faith being viewed primarily as a matter of outward practice rather than inward conviction and experience. He presents Augustine as paving the way for the Reformation and the evolution of a new approach to faith.

> [Augustine] was sufficiently catholic for the principle of church authority, and yet at the same time so free and evangelical that he modified its hierarchical and sacramental character, reacted against its tendencies to outward, mechanical ritualism, and kept alive a deep consciousness of sin and grace, and a spirit of fervent and truly Christian piety, until that spirit grew strong enough to break the shell of hierarchical tutelage, and enter a new stage of its development.[128]

---

[125] Philip Schaff, 'Prolegemena: St Augustine's Life and Work' (1886), *NPNF* 1:19ff cited in Mark Ellingsen, *The Richness of Augustine: His Context and Pastoral Theology* (Louisville: Westminster John Knox Press), p. 143.
[126] Schaff, 'Prolegomena', p. 19.
[127] Schaff, 'Prolegomena', p. 22.
[128] Schaff, 'Prolegomena', p. 24.

The question-mark arising from this quotation is whether those aspects of Augustinian theology that have been thought to fuel Protestant piety might have a similarly energising impact on the practice of Catholic spirituality. Schaff's hope is that this might be the case and that a reconciliation of both traditions could be realised in the embrace of a heartfelt Augustinian faith.

It is significant that it is precisely around the themes highlighted by Schaff (anti-Pelagianism and the interior engagement with God) that Ratzinger's own Augustinian theology seems to turn. He is perhaps more wedded to the sacramental system than is Augustine as he is presented in Schaff, but there is an Augustinian core to his faith which leads him to lament the presence of Pelagianism within the church. Moreover, his lifelong engagement with Augustine had spurred him to promote the possibility of an intimate experience of the love of God. While only an in-depth analysis of his position on justification will offer a fuller picture of his understanding of grace, there is much in what already is known to indicate that he is open to key elements in evangelical Augustinianism.

This generally positive assessment of the ecumenical possibilities within Augustinian theology must be balanced by two significant caveats lest a false impression be given. The first is that whilst there is a current Augustinian legacy in all streams of Evangelicalism (as discussed above), this is an Augustinianism of a generally modified variety. Only the Calvinist stream of that tradition has embraced wholeheartedly the doctrines of grace enunciated by Augustine. For the majority of evangelicals, it is not the doctrine of predestination but the general anti-Pelagianism of the African Father which lies at the root of their theology. Indeed, it is this rediscovery of Augustinian teaching, mediated through Luther, that continues to animate evangelical Protestantism and retain pride of place within it.[129] This core and ecumenically viable Augustinianism was well summed up by Catholic scholar, Michael J. Scanlon, in his eirenic piece, 'Martin Luther: the Separated Son of Augustine.'[130] Not only does Scanlon speak here of Luther as 'a religious genius ... deserving of consideration as a doctor of the Church universal,' but he acknowledges his theology of grace as being 'a valid complement' to Roman Catholic and 'other traditional formulations.' The context for his words is his historical re-counting of Luther's epoch-making discovery.

> [In] his lectures on St Paul's Epistle to the Romans (1515-16), Luther breaks through to the Pauline-Johannine-Augustinian assertion that the fallen person is a slave of sin, for grace alone can save us from egoistic self-love.

---

[129] Note the impact of Luther's 1522 Preface to Romans on Wesley's own conversion. Here we may detect the more distant but nonetheless significant influence of Augustine's anti-Pelagian theology on the birth of Methodism.

[130] Michael J. Scanlon, 'All Things Augustine.' *Villanova Magazine* Winter 1999 http://www.heritage.villanova.edu/vu/heritage/allthings/1999Wa.htm (accessed 10 September, 2010).

> Without grace, one's natural powers avail only for sin. Indeed Christians sin insofar as they do not act out of faith in Christ. Without faith, the fallen cannot avoid sin by natural powers alone.[131]

This admission of the modified nature of evangelical Augustinianism must be balanced by a critical piece of information regarding Ratzinger's own outlook. In common with many evangelicals, his brand of Augustinianism exhibits little sympathy for the thoroughgoing version of the system advocated by the Reformers and the Jansenists. The resolute rejection of any form of soteriological determinism is present in a handful of paragraphs spanning a period of three decades. His repudiation of predestination first surfaces in a 1972 article written for *Communio* entitled 'The Unity of the Church – the Unity of Mankind'[132] wherein he clearly distances himself from the doctrine. This view is reiterated in the devotional publication, *God Is Near Us*, in which he writes 'Jesus died, not just for a part of mankind, but for everyone ... [God] does not make any distinction between people he dislikes, people he does not want to be saved, and others whom he prefers, ...'[133] His most recent reference to the subject came in the second of his collaborations with journalist, Peter Seewald, entitled *God and the World*.[134] Here he responds to a question concerning the Islamic concept Maktub which he loosely designates as predestination. In a surprisingly unequivocal way, given the major figures within the Catholic tradition who have espoused some form of predestination, Ratzinger asserts that there is a 'clear distinction' between Islam and Christianity on the matter. This is the case even though predestination as an idea was also taken forward within the Church. He writes,

> In Christianity, too, the so-called teaching on predestination was developed. According to this teaching, it is already settled that those for whom it is planned will go to hell, and the others to heaven; it has been decided from all eternity. The faith of the Church has always rejected this. For the idea that as an individual I can do nothing one way or the other – that if I am bound for hell, then I just am, and if I am going to heaven, then that's the way it is – is certainly not consistent with the faith.[135]

Thus we are left with a modified version of Augustinianism, congenial perhaps to the majority in both the Catholic and the evangelical tradition, determining Ratzinger's theological vision and making him an unparalleled Roman Catholic dialogue partner with conservative Protestantism. However, as already intimated, it will require a more detailed critique of his thought with regard to

---

[131] Scanlon, *Villanova Magazine*.

[132] Joseph Ratzinger, 'The Unity of the Church – the Unity of Mankind.' *Communio International Review* 1, (1972): pp. 53-57.

[133] Joseph Ratzinger, *God Is Near Us: The Eucharist, the Heart of Life* (San Francisco: Ignatius Press, 2003), p. 35.

[134] Joseph Ratzinger, *God and the World* (San Francisco: Ignatius Press, 2002).

[135] Ratzinger, *God and the World*, pp. 57-58.

justification, faith, church and sacraments before we shall be in a position to judge whether and to what degree there is a genuine meeting point between the two traditions.

CHAPTER 4

Ratzinger and Soteriology

Introduction

Any assessment of whether Joseph Ratzinger's theology is an effective bridge to the evangelical tradition must take into account the issue of soteriology and the contentious doctrine of justification by faith alone. Historically, this was the main issue of division between the two traditions and the presenting cause of the Reformation. So central has the notion been to Protestant identity that Martin Luther called it, 'The doctrine by which the church stands or falls'[1], whilst John Calvin speaks of it as the 'hinge' of the Reformation.[2] Naturally, Ratzinger's stance on justification will be a major indicator as to how much ecumenical potential is truly present in his theology. However, even as I state the matter in these terms, I must address the disparity that exists between what might be termed the caricature of Ratzinger and the reality. For many critics, the former Prefect of the CDF is so intransigent ecumenically that it is not possible for him to act as a model for ecumenical engagement. I shall suggest to the contrary that rather than being a rigid and uncompromising Roman maximalist (as the critics of *Dominus Iesus* have alleged), he is, in fact, a nuanced and fundamentally open theologian who is willing to take risks for the sake of legitimate ecumenism.[3] Moreover, I shall argue that this mindset is probably more evident in his engagement with the doctrine of 'justification' than anywhere else.

Tracey Rowland highlights Ratzinger's ecumenical significance in a recent publication entitled, *Benedict XVI: A Guide for the Perplexed*. It is her opinion that his 'most significant ecumenical achievement as a Cardinal was to be instrumental in saving the *Joint Declaration on the Doctrine of Justification*

---

[1] For an expression of this sentiment see *Luther's Works* (Volume 26): 'Lectures on Galatians 1535'. (St. Louis: Concordia Publishing, 1963), p. 10.
[2] John Calvin, *Institutes of the Christian Religion*, ed. John T McNeill, trans. Ford Lewis Battles, Library of Christian Classics (Philadelphia: Westminster, 1960), 3.11.1, p. 726.
[3] See leading evangelical Timothy George's positive response to *Dominus Iesus* in 'Symposium on the Declaration *Dominus Iesus*' in *Pro Ecclesia* Vol. X No.1 (2001), p. 8. George states, 'It is unfortunate that the media blitz over the document has obscured its primary thrust as a corrective to various relativistic theories used to justify religious pluralism in large sectors of contemporary theology ... In no way does it backtrack on the kind of ecumenical openness that has become more and more central in Catholic life since Vatican II. True enough, much misunderstanding could perhaps have been avoided simply by relating this important admonition to the very positive ecumenical initiative set forth by the Holy Father in *Ut Unum Sint*. I do not see this document as undermining or qualifying *Ut Unum Sint*, but rather as supporting or undergirding it.'

with the Lutheran World Federation.'[4] Citing the head of the Evangelical Lutheran Church of America, Bishop George Anderson, she confirms that it was 'Ratzinger who untied the knots' and made a joint declaration possible when representatives of the Pontifical Council for the Promotion of Christian Unity were in danger of scuttling any potential progress. Ratzinger's personal investment in the project was underscored by the fact that he organised a private meeting with the Lutheran leaders at his brother Georg's home in a bid to bring some resolution to the difficulties. Moreover, he made three significant concessions to the Lutherans which effectively secured the joint agreement: he conceded that the aim of the ecumenical process is unity in diversity as opposed to re-assimilation into the Church of Rome; he acknowledged that the Lutheran World Federation had the right or authority to reach an agreement with the Vatican in the name of world Lutheranism (according to Rowland, this was precisely the sticking point in the eyes of the Pontifical Council for Christian Unity); and thirdly, and most significantly from the standpoint of this publication, he agreed with the Lutherans that justification was entirely by grace. Indeed, this view was enshrined in what Rowland believes to be the key statement of the agreement: 'By grace alone, in faith in Christ's saving work and not because of any merit on our own part, we are accepted by God and receive the Holy Spirit, who renews our hearts while equipping us and calling us to do good works.'[5]

This brief excursion into recent ecclesiastical history cannot but cast Ratzinger in a more positive ecumenical light. However, it does not immediately resolve the question of whether or not his Augustinianism establishes a bridge to Evangelicalism in the matter of justification. The fact that he has engaged generously with Lutheran theology and accepts the priority of grace in salvation does not provide a complete answer to the issue being addressed in this chapter. Further considerations must also be borne in mind before one is in a position to draw definitive conclusions about the significance of Ratzinger's soteriological outlook.

The first concerns Augustine's understanding of justification and whether this has been correctly interpreted by the Reformation. Whilst this question sheds no immediate light on Ratzinger's own perspective, it provides a better vantage point for assessing Augustine's ecumenical potential in relation to the doctrine of justification. The second crucial factor will be Ratzinger's explicit writings on justification. Although these are tantalizingly brief in contrast to some of his more detailed work on other theological themes[6], I shall argue that there is enough substance in these reflections to furnish a clear understanding of where he stands in relation to the historic debate on justification.

---

[4] Tracey Rowland, *Benedict XVI: A Guide for the Perplexed* (London: Continuum, 2010), p. 139.

[5] See Rowland's discussion in *Benedict XVI: A Guide for the Perplexed*, p. 139.

[6] Themes such as ecclesiology and the eucharist have had more prominence in Ratzinger's published writings than subjects related to the Reformation disputes.

The Dispute Over the True Nature of Augustine's Soteriology

It is perhaps nowhere more present than in the claim to be the legitimate heirs of his soteriology that evangelicals assert their commonality with St Augustine. Are they justified (no pun intended) in claiming his mantel and has Catholicism fundamentally misunderstood its most revered Church Father? These fundamental questions form the entry point for this brief study of Augustine and justification. To begin addressing them we need first to explore a claim which made its literary debut in the polemical works of Philip Melanchthon and continues today in certain Protestant theological circles.[7] This is the assertion that over the course of history the apostolic teaching was preserved within the church by a faithful Augustinian remnant and that the Reformation was the catalyst for bringing this message back to the forefront of the church's consciousness. Nineteenth century Scottish Reformed scholar, James Buchanan, offers a classic statement of this view in a major study entitled *The Doctrine of Justification*.

> It is of special importance that the precise object and reason of any appeal to the Fathers on the subject of justification should be distinctly understood. It is simply to prove a matter of FACT, in opposition to an erroneous assertion – the fact, namely, that the Protestant doctrine of justification was not a novelty introduced for the first time by Luther and Calvin – that it was held and taught, more or less explicitly, by some writers in every successive stage – and that there is no truth in the allegation that it had been unknown for 1,400 years before the Reformation.[8]

The motivation for making such a strong claim in relation to the teaching of Luther and Calvin is plain when we consider the implications of the two magisterial Reformers having promoted a truly novel doctrine of redemption. Alister McGrath, in an article for the *Harvard Theological Review*, articulates why there has been such a sustained search for precedents on the part of some defenders of the Reformation. The following judgment is made with particular reference to the works of Melanchthon but has a much wider application.

> It can be shown without difficulty that it was the desire to demonstrate the catholicity of the Lutheran Reformation which led to the search for such Forerunners in the first instance. This question is of particular importance in connection with the doctrines of justification associated with the Reformers, and which are generally considered to be the fulcrum about which the Reformation turned. If it can be shown that the chief teaching of the

---

[7] See Thomas C. Oden, *The Justification Reader* (Grand Rapids: Eerdmans, 2002), pp. 20-21. Oden asserts an Augustinian provenance for Reformation notions about justification and disputes claims made by evangelicals that Luther was at odds with Augustine.

[8] James Buchanan *The Doctrine of Justification* Edinburgh 1867, reprinted 1997, (Edinburgh: Banner of Truth Trust, 1997), p. 80.

Reformation, the *articulus stantis aut cadentis ecclesiae*, constitutes a theological novum, unknown to the previous fifteen centuries of Christian thought, it will be clear that any Protestant claim to catholicity is seriously prejudiced.[9]

McGrath in that same article goes on to challenge the view that a Reformation-style soteriology maintained itself within the Augustinian tradition during the intervening centuries of church history. Such a stance is unexpected given the writer's strong identification with the evangelical tradition and requires some explanation. The question to be addressed is why a scholar of his convictions would be dubious about attempts to demonstrate that a Protestant doctrine of justification subsisted within the historic church? The answer lies with the interpretation he places on certain early disputes about justification which occurred within Lutheranism. McGrath in no way rejects the notion that there was a strong theology of grace (understood as a rejection of the doctrine of salvation by works) present in each generation of the church from the time of Augustine onwards. What he observes, however, is that the most profound focus of the Reformation soteriology lay not with anti-Pelagianism *per se* but with a particular doctrine of imputed or alien righteous. That is, the notion that salvation depends on Christ's righteousness being applied to the believer rather than on any form of righteousness which might be inherent in the individual, even should that righteousness be understood as entirely the fruit of grace.

Early in the Reformation this emerging consensus was brought into question by the work of Osiander who proposed a mediating view of justification that allowed for some form of inherent righteousness rooted in the presence of Christ within the believer. The main body of Lutheranism roundly condemned this notion but what is more significant is that the idea itself was deemed 'Popish' even though it was thoroughly grounded in an anti-Pelagian soteriology. It is from his observation of such disputes that McGrath felt it legitimate to question whether a distinctly Protestant soteriology ever existed prior to the new insights developed by Luther and the other Reformers. He comments,

> Compared with this, [meaning the uncompromising stance on forensic righteousness] the basically anti-Pelagian character of Protestant doctrines of justification must be considered an inadequate criterion of whether a given doctrine of justification can be considered Protestant or not. As the Osiandrist controversy made abundantly clear, an anti-Pelagian doctrine of justification could still be branded as 'Romanist' if its position on the question of the nature of justifying righteousness was incorrect. The history of the Reformation itself, particularly as it concerns Latomus and Osiander, shows that the criterion employed at the time to determine whether a

---

[9] Alister E. McGrath, 'Forerunners of the Reformation? A Critical Examination of the Evidence for Precursors of the Reformation Doctrines of Justification.' *Harvard Theological Review* 75:2 (1982), pp. 219-220.

particular doctrine of justification was Protestant was *whether justifying righteousness was conceived extrinsically.*[10]

Before proceeding to explore the precise nature of Augustine's view on justification it may be helpful to note the degree to which Luther and Calvin subscribe to Melanchthon's thesis that the Reformation doctrine is simply the theology of Augustine re-visited. Whilst neither Reformer wishes to repudiate the connection between their own thought and Augustine's on this matter, both seem to show some unease with the way the Church Father formulates his ideas on justification, and view what has been stated as incomplete to say the least. According to Luther, whilst Augustine understood the concept of righteousness in the same way as himself (i.e. as God's gracious action in salvation) '… his statement of this is still open to criticism, and he is neither clear nor comprehensive in the matter of imputation.'[11] Similarly Calvin, with a subtle note of censure in his voice, comments that, 'The sentiment of Augustine, or at least his way of expressing it, cannot be wholly approved of.'[12] What was it in the theology of Augustine which made the two pre-eminent Reformers less than sanguine about its merits? The answer must lie in the extent to which Augustine's outlook could be understood as being detrimental to the position adopted by them.

Augustine's Theology of Grace and his Teaching on Justification

The following synopsis draws heavily on the most extensive study of the doctrine of justification undertaken in recent times. This is Alister McGrath's *Magnum opus, Iustitia Dei.*[13] However, to preserve some balance, I have taken into consideration the work of the Catholic scholar Hans Küng, as well as the concerns of James Buchanan who spies the face of a more Protestant Augustine staring at us out of the mists of time.

The origins of Augustine's theology of grace, out of which springs his doctrine of justification, may be traced to a change of theological perspective that occurred circa 396/397 when he wrote the first of two books dedicated to his interlocutor, Simplicianus.[14] In this he outlined a doctrine of divine predestination which had recently superseded his previous belief in the absolute freedom of the human will. The change of perspective is often identified with Augustine's dispute with Pelagius but the reality is that Simplicianus' passionate espousal of a certain interpretation of Romans 9:10-29 was the

---

[10] McGrath, 'Forerunners of the Reformation?', pp. 227-228.

[11] (*WA* LVI. 186.19-20) cited in McGrath, 'Forerunners of the Reformation?', p. 231.

[12] Calvin, *Institutes of the Christian Religion*, 3.11.11 cited in McGrath, 'Forerunners of the Reformation?', p. 232.

[13] Alister E. McGrath, *Iustitia Dei: A History of the Doctrine of Justification* (Cambridge: Cambridge University Press, 2005).

[14] *De praedestinatione sanctorum iv*, 8, PL 44.966A cited in McGrath, *Iustitia Dei*, p. 39.

decisive influence on him.[15] Thus while the later controversy with Pelagius sharpened Augustine's thinking, it is important to note that a framework of thought had already been set in place as a result of these earlier conversations.

McGrath highlights three cardinal beliefs from that early period which provide the foundation for Augustine's subsequent thought on justification in works such as *The Letter and the Spirit*.[16] It is clear from the strong emphasis on predestination that his thought has much in common with classical Calvinism, at least in regard to the role of the divine will in salvation. Augustine will state unequivocally that humanity's ultimate destiny depends upon God's eternal decree of predestination[17]; that even the response of faith is a gift from God and not a matter of human initiative[18]; and that the human will is so compromised by sin that it is incapable of being open to the process of justification without being liberated by grace.[19] However, when it comes to the more specific references to the doctrine of justification by faith, that follow later, Augustine's approach appears to take on a more Catholic hue. According to McGrath, the defining concept of his thinking around justification is *fides quae per dilectionem opertur*, 'faith working through love.' The understanding of 'faith' in this construct is distinct from what the Reformers understood by the term. It is drawn primarily from Augustine's interpretation of 'faith' in a section of *De Trinitate* in which he grapples with Paul's ruling in 1 Cor. 13:1-3 that faith without love is useless. On the basis of Paul's reasoning there he draws a distinction between what one might term a purely mental or cognitive faith and true justifying faith which is 'accompanied by love.' Paul's apposite words in Galatians 5:16 about the only thing of value in the Christian life being 'faith that works through love' thus becomes the summary of Augustine's thought on justification.

McGrath is correct that this emphasis on love cannot easily be construed in a Pelagian sense. Augustine himself makes clear that both faith and love are to be understood as gifts from God and not the outworking of any natural capability or endowment.[20] Indeed, faith defined in this more limited way must be supplemented by love of God and neighbour in order for it not to be a dead faith.[21] One might say that the formula justification by faith and love, or indeed justification by love, comes closer to telling us something of

---

[15] McGrath, *Iustitia Dei*, p. 39.
[16] 'The Spirit and the Letter' in *Library of Christian Classics* Volume VIII, Augustine: Later Works. (London: SCM Press, 1955).
[17] Augustine, *Ad Simplicianum* 1, ii. 6 cited in McGrath, *Iustitia Dei*, p. 40.
[18] Augustine, *Ad Simplicianum*, 1, ii, 12, 40.
[19] Augustine, *Ad Simplicianum*, 1, ii. 21, 40.
[20] McGrath, *Iustitia Dei*, p. 46.
[21] McGrath, *Iustitia Dei*, p.46.

Augustine's actual stance on this matter than any simple identification of him with the slogan 'justification by faith.'[22]

The idea that McGrath and similar commentators are correct in distancing Augustine from a 'Protestant' understanding of justification is confirmed when we consider Augustine's view of justifying righteousness. Indeed, if one were to measure Augustine's words by the same standard as was applied at the Reformation to 'deviant' Lutheran theologians such as Osiander, there is little likelihood his approach would pass muster as sound theology. This is the case because for Augustine the crucial verb 'to justify' had the meaning of 'to make righteous' as opposed to the more forensic 'to declare to be righteous.' This interpretation is evident in *The Spirit and the Letter* when he states, 'What does 'justified' mean other than 'made righteous', just as 'he justifies the ungodly' means 'he makes a righteous person out of an ungodly person'?[23]

Augustine is able to speak of the matter in such terms because he was never acquainted with the later Reformation distinction between justification and sanctification and saw the two as innately one. Justification, in his terms, was an all-embracing concept which included both the event by which it was initiated (something achieved through operative grace in baptism) and the process by which it was completed (achieved through co-operative grace in the individual). Viewed in this light, humanity's righteousness before God is ultimately not an alien righteousness which is always extrinsic to him but is rather a part of his very being due to the operation of grace.[24]

Augustine's standpoint is reflected both in his sermons and also in his borrowing of the Eastern church's concept of deification to explain the work of inner transformation. In a homily based on Romans 8, for example, he speaks both of the moment of justification and the growth of righteousness in the forgiven sinner.

> We have been justified; but this justice increases, as we make advance. And how it increases I will say, and so to confer with you, that each of you already established in that justification, having received to wit the remission of sins by the laver of regeneration (= baptism), having received the Holy

---

[22] McGrath, *Iustitia Dei*, p. 46. McGrath whilst not promoting the notion of turning Augustine's theory of justification into a slogan, acknowledges that if one were to do so the formulations involving love would be truer to his thought.

[23] Augustine, *De Spiritu et littera* xxxvi, p. 45 cited in McGrath, *Iustitia Dei*, p. 47.

[24] See McGrath's discussion in 'Justification – 'Making Just' or 'Declaring Just', *Churchman*, Vol. 96, No.1 (1982), p. 45. Note also his words in *Iustitia Dei*, p. 48 where he reiterates the anti-Pelagian nature of Augustine's ideas but also their incompatibility with Protestantism, 'A concept of 'imputed righteousness' in the later Protestant sense of the term, is quite redundant within Augustine's doctrine of justification, in that humans are *'made righteous'* in justification. The righteousness which they thus receive, although originating from God, is nevertheless located within human beings, and can be said to be *theirs*, part of their being and intrinsic to their person.'

Ghost, making advancement from day to day, may see where he is, may go on, advance, and grow, till he be consummated, not so as to come to an end, but to perfection.[25]

These same notions are evident in Augustine's later writings on this theme wherein the language of deification and adoptive filiation is often used to characterize what is happening in justification. The upshot of such action on the part of God, according to Augustine, is that the individual grows in his or her likeness to Christ becoming righteous in reality, and not merely being someone whom God *treats* as if they are righteous.[26] This view of Augustine's soteriology finds support amongst other evangelical scholars who also view the Latin Father's perspective as essentially Catholic. Peter Toon concludes his reflection on Augustine with words which echo McGrath but also highlight how difficult it would have been for Augustine to have articulated a 'Protestant' position in the first place.

> It will be seen that while Augustine teaches the non-imputation of sin (= forgiveness from God) he does not teach the imputation of righteousness, as did Luther and Protestantism after him. Protestant writers from the sixteenth to the twentieth century have tried to find in Augustine the same doctrine of justification as is found in the Protestant confessions of the Reformation period. It has to be admitted that the great theologian of grace does not teach a 'Protestant' doctrine of justification. In fact, Augustine never had more than a minimal knowledge of the Greek language and was therefore unable seriously to face the question of what *dikaioō* meant for St Paul. Thus his legacy to the Latin West, which is still to be found in the Roman Catholic Church, is the interpretation of justification as both an event and a process of making the unrighteous man into a righteous man.[27]

Before juxtaposing Ratzinger's outlook with that of Augustine, it is important to register briefly Hans Küng's opinion on the extent to which forensic righteousness was a 'pre-Reformation' doctrine. This will be complemented by a brief analysis of the classic Reformed arguments deployed by Buchanan. In the case of Hans Küng, there seems to be virtual agreement with McGrath that a forensic doctrine of justification was absent within pre-Reformation Catholic thought. He cites Ritschl to the effect that only a few, if any, forerunners of the dogma existed amongst the pre-Reformation divines.[28] Intriguingly, Küng leaves the impression of having to give an account for why such a doctrine is

---

[25] Augustine, *Sermons*, Vol. 2, sermon 108, p.781, in *A Library of Fathers*, (1883) cited in Peter Toon, *Justification and Sanctification* (London: Marshall, Morgan and Scott, 1983), p. 48.
[26] McGrath, *Iustitia Dei*, p. 47.
[27] Toon, *Justification and Sanctification*, p. 50.
[28] A Ritschl, *Rechtfertigung und Versöhnung*, 1, pp. 105-109; pp. 129-135 cited in Hans Küng, *Justification: The Doctrine of Karl Barth and a Catholic Reflection* (London: Burns & Oats, 1981), p. 216.

relatively unknown in this period.[29] A scholar who is thus sympathetic to the idea of forerunners but unable to locate them hardly bolsters the view that the pre-Reformation tradition (or at least a recognisable remnant within it) was propelled by Augustine into a forensic view of justification.

Buchanan succeeds no more than Küng has in convincing the reader that a belief in forensic righteousness existed within the early or Medieval church. However, in contrast to Küng, there seems to be little admission on his part of the paucity of reference to the subject in Augustine or his peers. Indeed, the polemical tone in which Buchanan advances his opinion leaves the present writer unconvinced that less partisan scholars have somehow failed to note the obvious in the writings of Augustine and other church luminaries. The following two observations hint at some of the shortcomings in Buchanan's approach. Whilst these do not amount to a full-scale refutation of his work, they demonstrate the distance that may exist between assertion and fact in some of his claims. Most significantly, one must note the assumption that the only choice open to commentators is to interpret Augustine as teaching forensic justification or else some form of works righteousness. He states,

> [I]t would be strange, if it were true, that he who did so much to establish the doctrine of free grace, in opposition to free will, in the matter of our Sanctification, should have said anything to undermine the doctrine of free grace, in opposition to self-righteousness, in the matter of our justification.[30]

Apart from the fact that he is stressing a distinction in Augustine's thinking between justification and sanctification which never existed, Buchanan commits the more serious error of suggesting that any intended association between inherent righteousness and justification is an undermining of the principle of grace. A move of which he would have been deemed Augustine incapable. However, is this 'association' not precisely what Augustine had in mind in his teaching on justification? Indeed, might it not be argued that his emphasis on faith expressing itself through love is another way of conveying the notion of an imparted righteousness which is itself the product of grace? Buchanan seems to be at fault here for not taking serious account of Augustine's marriage of faith and love.

---

[29] Küng, *Justification*, pp. 215-16. Küng writes, 'To avoid dealing unfairly with whole theological epochs, we must remember that not all the truths of faith need to be grasped with equal force in every age. Differences will prevail, especially with regard to justification, and such differences are very noticeable even in scripture itself ... In the captivity and pastoral letters the idea of a declaration of justice is certainly not forgotten, but who would insist that this is among the vitally significant central themes in those later letters? And who would reproach Paul on that account. How unfair it is, on the other hand, to disparage patristic and medieval theology for not expressly stressing the idea of a forensic declaration of justice.'

[30] Buchanan, *The Doctrine of Justification*, p. 102.

A second difficulty lies with the manner in which he adduces the testimony of the Church Fathers to substantiate his claims about forensic righteousness. Toon captured the heart of modern objections to this perspective when making these comments about the work of Buchanan and another nineteenth century evangelical scholar called Faber.

> A careful study of the quotations supplied by Faber and Buchanan proves only one thing – the early Fathers believed that salvation is by grace. The Victorians claimed too much and read back into an earlier period the structure of thought which belonged to a later period.[31]

Buchanan's citation of the theology of St Basil of Caesarea is a good example of the manner in which the idea of salvation by grace can be read anachronistically as the promotion of forensic justification. The whole thrust of Basil's argument turns on the contrast between self-righteousness and dependence on grace for one's salvation rather than any explicit notion of alien righteousness. Basil writes,

> This is the true and perfect glorying in God when a man is not lifted up on account of his own righteousness, but has known himself to be wanting in true righteousness, and to be justified by faith alone in Christ. And Paul glories, in that he despises his own righteousness, and seeks the righteousness which is from God by faith ... Thou hast not known God through righteousness on thy part, but God hath known thee on account of his goodness; thou hast not apprehended Christ through thy virtue, but Christ hath apprehended thee through His coming.[32]

In justice to that earlier Reformed scholarship, it should be acknowledged that Augustine's kinship with Calvinism in his theology of predestination as well as his adamant anti-Pelagianism, might easily have led scholars to assume that he implicitly embraced the rest of their system.[33] What is clear, though, is that in the matter of justification Augustine not only affirmed the Catholic doctrine but contributed some of its major features. The question that will be of interest, therefore, is the degree to which Ratzinger conformed his own thought to Augustine and the extent to which he is open to Reformation insights.

---

[31] Toon, *Justification and Sanctification*, pp. 45-46.
[32] Buchanan, *Doctrine of Justification*, p. 108.
[33] This is a point acknowledged by David F. Wright who suggests that the Reformers' misleading impression that they shared a common doctrine of justification with Augustine was fuelled by the latter's unequivocal anti-Pelagianism and 'uncompromising doctrine of election.' See David F. Wright, 'Justification in Augustine' in Bruce L. McCormack (ed.), *Justification in Perspective* (Grand Rapids: Baker Academic and Rutherford House, 2006), p. 71.

Ratzinger and Justification

One cannot address Ratzinger's thoughts on justification without reference to the positive manner in which he has engaged with other dogmatic disputes. It is clear that he has always been open to a rapprochement between Catholicism and Protestantism in areas of theology where there had hitherto been largely division and stalemate. An example of this is his early attitude to Mariology. In *Theological Highlights of Vatican II*, he shares his aspiration that the Council's decision to integrate Mariology into the wider doctrine of the church (via *Lumen Gentium*) might '... have brought us nearer to the time when it will again be conceivable that Christians of different denominations will understand one another on this particularly divisive issue'.[34] Allowing for the fact that this statement begs the question of whether there has ever been a time in which it was conceivable that different denominations might understand one another on the question of Mary, it does indicate that Ratzinger's early instincts were towards convergence in matters of theological deadlock. That this attitude was not confined to the earliest phase of his career is confirmed by an article published during his tenure as Prefect of the CDF. In 'Luther and the Unity of the Churches'[35] he expresses the hope that modern exegetes might unravel some of the theological knots pertaining to long-standing doctrinal controversies and help the denominations genuinely transcend old differences. However, it should be noted that this statement is sandwiched between warnings about the dangers of exegesis becoming too distanced from the church and degenerating into an academic exercise.[36] Notwithstanding these necessary caveats, Ratzinger is hopeful that new and unexpected ways forward may be discovered.

> Nevertheless, it is true that agreement among exegetes is capable of surmounting antiquated contradictions and of revealing their secondary character. It can create new avenues of dialogue for all the great themes of intra-Christian controversy: Scripture, tradition, magisterium, the papacy, the eucharist, and so on. It is in this sense that there is, indeed, hope even for a church which undergoes the afore-mentioned turmoil [i.e. the Reformation rupture].[37]

---

[34] Joseph Ratzinger, *Theological Highlights of Vatican II* (New York: Paulist Press, 1979), p. 96.
[35] Joseph Ratzinger, 'Luther and the Unity of the Churches.' *Communio: International Catholic Review* 11 (1984) cf. Joseph Ratzinger, 'Luther and the Unity of the Churches' with Postscript, pp. 99-134, in *Church, Ecumenism and Politics: New Essays in Ecclesiology* (Slough: St Paul Publications, 1988)
[36] Ratzinger, 'Luther and the Unity of the Churches', *Communio* 11, pp. 215-216.
[37] Ratzinger, 'Luther and the Unity of the Churches', *Communio* 11, pp. 215-216.

Ratzinger and Küng

The ecumenically hopeful attitude captured in the preceding quotation was to some extent to characterise Ratzinger's first written engagement with the theme of justification. In a 1958 review of Hans Küng's epoch-making publication, *Justification*, he holds out the hope that final theological agreement on this theme between Catholics and Protestants may be achievable. What is also noteworthy, however, is that there is uncertainty as to whether Küng had completely succeeded in his attempt at reconciling the two positions.

> With this, I have arrived at the final and decisive question: Must we reject as false Küng's basic thesis that Barth's doctrine of justification is essentially congruent with the teaching of the Catholic church correctly understood? I believe that to make such a statement would constitute a premature judgment. One would have to concede, however, that Küng's argument for congruence is not convincing at every point. Several fundamental differences have been too easily glossed over and this has compromised the final conclusion. *This does not exclude the possibility, though, that a more in-depth discussion might advance towards a final unity.*[38]

Ratzinger's reservations lie mainly with the way that the Tridentine doctrine has been represented by Küng. He remains unconvinced that the differences between the two traditions can be reduced to a simple misunderstanding over terminology. The area of unresolved difficulty is that whilst man's being put right with God depends entirely upon an external factor in Karl Barth's thought (i.e. forensic or alien righteousness), it is inextricably associated with the internal transformation of the person in Catholic thought.

> I ask myself: is it really only a terminological difference, when Barth speaks of 'justification' where we would talk of 'salvation' and calls 'salvation' that which we refer to as 'justification.' I believe that more is at issue here. There exists on both sides a shared understanding of the term 'justification' which is precisely this event through which God receives and accepts the sinner as righteous. According to Barth this event is perfected or achieved in Christ alone and merely accepted as an accomplished fact by the sinner – the justificatio in its own sense takes place entirely 'extra nos' (outside of us);

---

[38] Joseph Ratzinger, 'Hans Küngs *Rechfertigung.* Jahrgang 54, 1958 *Theologische Review* Nr.1, 34, 1958 (italics mine).
'Damit komme ich zu der abschließenden Entsscheidungsfrage: Muß demnach die Grundthese Küngs, - daß Barths Rechtfertigunslehre sachlich mit der recht verstandenen Lehre der katholischen Kirche übereinstimmt, als falsch abgelehnt werden? Ich glaube, daß dies zu behaupten dennoch ein übereiltes Urteil wäre. Zugeben wird man aber müssen, daß der Erweis der Übereinstimmt bei Küng noch nicht durchwegs überzeugend gelungen ist, sondern daß einzelne grundlegende Gegensätze doch vorschnell geglättet sind und dadurch gerade der letzte Austrag verhindert wird. Das schließt nicht aus, daß eine noch tiefer gehende Diskussion möglicherweise dennoch zu einer letzten Einheit vorstößt.'

Catholic teaching holds that the transformation of man by justification from being a sinner to being righteous is a central aspect of justification, which puts special emphasis on the 'intra nos' (within us).[39]

As those words indicate, the crux of Ratzinger's unease with Küng's position is that the latter has assumed that Barth's emphasis on the existential transformation of the sinner (i.e. sanctification) functions as the exact counterpart to what is being taught in Catholicism about 'justification.' However, this seems not to have been the case when the teaching of Trent is compared to the message of the *Church Dogmatics*. According to Ratzinger,

> What happens in man and through man has no part in a justification which has been worked out solely through the cross of Christ. Precisely this differentiation between justification and sanctification is alien to the Tridentine and Catholic tradition, which holds that what happens in us is truly salvational and the good works to be done by the justified sinner participate in this salvational function – even though it entirely depends, of course, on the preceding, accompanying and on-going power of the grace of Christ.[40]

Ratzinger emphasizes this point when he notes that, according to the Council of Trent, the status of justification is lost through the commission of mortal sin and only subsequently regained by means of penance. He believes that such a perspective is only possible if justification is *intra nos* in distinction to Barth's *extra nos*. Moreover, the sacramental element to justification serves to highlight the degree to which Barth's deviation from Catholic teaching on the sacraments has been the natural fruit of an extrinsic view of justification.

---

[39] 'Ich frage mich: ist es wirklich nur ein terminologischer Unterschied, wenn Barth da von 'Rechtfertigung' spricht, wo wir von 'Erlösung' reden, und da 'Heiligung' sagt, wo es bei uns 'Rechtfertigung' heißt? Ich glaube, hier geht es doch um die Sache selbst. Denn es gibt sehr wohl auf beiden Seiten einen gemeinsamen Sinn des Wortes 'Rechtfertigung' die eben jenes Geschehen ist, durch welches Gott den Sünder wieder als Gerechten annimmt. Nach Barth vollendet sich dieses Geschehen in Christus allein und wird vom Sünder lediglich zur Kenntnis genommen – die iustificatio vollzieht sich als solche und ganze extra nos; nach katholischer Lehre gehört die den Menschen umwandelnde Einformung der Gerechtigkeit in den Sünder noch wesentlich zur iustificatio selbst, der gerade das 'intra nos' wesentlich ist.

[40] Das, was im Menschen und durch den Menschen geschieht, ist nicht mehr Teil der Rechtfertigung, die vielmehr allein im Kreuz Christi vollzogen ist (Barth IV 1, 113 bei Kung 87). Gerade diese Unterscheidung von Rechtfertigung und Heiligung ist aber dem Tridentinum und der katholischen Überlieferung fremd, für sie ist das, was in uns geschiet, wahrhaft heilsbegründend, und das vom Gerechtfertigten zu tuende gute Werk nimmt an dieser heilsbegründenden Funktion teil – auch wenn es selbstverständlich ganz an der vorangehenden, geleitenden und nachfolgenden Kraft der Gnade Christi hängt (Denz 809).

How could you otherwise explain the loss of the status of justification through serious sin and its restoration by means of the sacrament of penance? Barth's rejection of the distinction between serious and venial sin does not appear now as a trivial matter in that the weight he gives to the sacraments (in clear deviation from the Catholic view) takes its root here. The value Catholicism attributes to the sacraments is grounded in the internal nature of justification just as Barth's reduction of the effectiveness of the sacraments is rooted in his extrinsic notion of justification. Insofar [as these issues are concerned] it would have been good not to exclude the sacramental question but rather to include it as a critical reverse test to measure the correctness of the results achieved.[41]

It is Ratzinger's conclusion that if the investigation had remained focused on the distinction between the Barthian *intra nos* and the Catholic *intra nos* the reconciliation of the two viewpoints achieved by Küng would be brought into serious question. This is demonstrated by what Ratzinger characterises as the 'somewhat laboured concordance' in the sola fide and the place given to merit. In the case of the Catholic *sola fide* the readers are reminded that Küng employs the *fides caritas* formula which Luther himself, in the commentary on Galatians, rejected with great fury and passion.

> '... : there is certainly a Catholic sola fide, which however refers – as Küng correctly states – to the fides caritas formula of which Luther once said: 'therefore one must be aware of the fides caritas formula which is a quite devilish and hellish poison ... as long as we are dealing with justification in this article, we are rejecting and condemning works and cutting short any discussion of law or works of the law.'[42]

It is Ratzinger's opinion that Barth explicitly adopts this Lutheran position himself in the *Dogmatics* and that this is in full harmony with the consistent

---

[41] 'Wie sollte man auch sonst den Verlust des Rechtfertigungsstandes in der schweren Sünde und seine Wiedergewinnung im Bußsakrament erklären? Daß Barth die Unterscheidung von schwerer und leichter Sünde ablehnt, erscheint nun doch nicht so beiläufig, wie denn auch die vom Katholizismus deutlich abweichende Wertung der Sakramente hier ihre Wurzel hat: Das Gewicht, das die katholische Auffasung den Sakramenten beilegt, gründet in der Idee der Innerlichkeit der Rechtfertigung, wie Barths Reduktion der sakramentalen Wirksamkeit in seinem extrinsezistischen Rechtfertigungsbegriff wurzelt. Insofern wäre es wohl doch gut gewesen, die Sakramentenfrage nicht auszuklammern, sondern als kritische Rückprobe für die Richtigkeit der erzielten Ergebnisse einzubeziehen.'

[42] 'Gewiß gibt es ein katholisches sola fide, das sich aber – wie Küng richtig sagt – auf die fides caritate formata bezieht, zu der Luther einmal bemerkt: 'Darum soll man sich auch für der 'fides formata caritate' hüten und vorsehen, als für einem recht teuflischen und höllischen Gifte ... Solange wir in diesem Artikel von der Rechtfertigung zu tun haben, verwerfen und verdammen wir die Werke und schneiden in dieser Sache alle Gesetze und Gesetzeswerke kurz ab.'

separation he has made between justification and sanctification. Seen in this light there is a fundamental conflict between the two perspectives which cannot be resolved by reducing the difference to mere semantic confusion. In a closing thrust he puts paid to Küng's precarious defence of merit by drawing what appears to him to be an obvious conclusion, given the rest of the discussion. He avers that the notion of merit (at least that understanding of merit which is employed by the Council of Trent) carries with it the sense of human participation in the achievement of salvation. Whilst Ratzinger is careful to acknowledge that even this mode of co-operation in salvation ultimately rests on the prior action/grace of God, he is equally clear that such a way of construing salvation would be unimaginable to Barth.

> It appears to me that Barth has expressly adopted this position. It is also concordant with his separation of justification and sanctification which emerges again as *the* [italics mine] core difference (and this not only in the sense of terminology!). So a final point becomes obvious: the notion of merit in the Tridentine sense necessarily involves the inclusion of some form of human participation in the salvation process that has its origin in God. This is something which Barth would find unthinkable.[43]

What can this early foray into the justification debate tell us about Ratzinger's initial position on justification? What seems to be abundantly clear is that he was less sanguine about Küng's ecumenical achievement than the majority of other Catholic scholars of the time.[44] Moreover, he appears to have been deeply committed to the *fides caritas* formula of St Augustine which he presents as fundamentally at odds with the forensic view of justification affirmed by Protestant theology. Viewed from a purely dispassionate standpoint, I would suggest that this fairly strict Catholic line taken by Ratzinger (at least when contrasted with the positive stance of scholars such as J.L. Witte[45]) may be read as an example of honest and frank ecumenism. We have in Ratzinger's review

---

[43] 'Barth hat sich, wie mir scheint, zu dieser Position ausdrücklich bekannt (IV 1, 699; Küng 84); sie entspricht auch durchaus seiner Trennung von Rechtferigung und Heiligung, die damit erneut als der eigenliche Kern der Unterscheidung (und dies eben nicht bloß im terminologischen Sinn!) erscheint. So wird ein Letztes deutlich: der Begriff des meitum im tridentinischen Sinn besagt ein gewisses Eingehen des menschlichen Mitwirkens in die von Gott kommende Heilskausalität, was widerum bei Barth undenkbar ware.'[43]

[44] Anthony N.S. Lane in his detailed study of justification notes that not only did most of Küng's fellow Catholic scholars accept his thesis but that no objections were raised by Rome. See *Justification by Faith in Catholic-Protestant Dialogue: An Evangelical Assessment* (London: T & T Clark, 2002), p. 89.

[45] Küng, *Justification*, p. xii, cites Witte to the effect that 'an express Catholic consensus has become apparent insofar as all Catholic reviews, with all their criticism of details, are agreed that the elements of the doctrine of justification as developed in the second part of this book do present *a* theological interpretation which is, at least, a possible one in the Catholic Church.'

of *Justification* an honest treatment of the historic Catholic position. It is certainly not insignificant that both Karl Barth and Alister McGrath are similarly unconvinced that Küng's account of the Tridentine teaching was historically accurate.[46] Indeed, Lane acknowledges as much although he suggests that Catholic teaching is less defined by what was taught 500 years ago than the current stance of the *Magisterium*.[47] However, this acknowledgment of Ratzinger's uncompromising frankness with regard to justification must be balanced by the hope expressed in his review of Küng's work that reconciliation on the matter of justification would be attained, an attitude which was demonstrated in his unwillingness to outrightly judge Küng's thesis a failure.

Justification in Ratzinger's Reflections on Vatican II

The next significant, albeit oblique, engagement with the theme of justification is found in Ratzinger's contributions to the series of commentaries on Vatican II edited by Herbert Vorgrimler. Whilst the majority of the relevant citations have been referenced in the previous chapter, there is scope at this point for a more focused exploration of what import Ratzinger's words might have for our understanding of his view of justification. The first point to observe is that in his discussion of *Dei Verbum* (the document on Divine Revelation) he manages to combine suspicion of the document's Pelagian undertones with a soteriological vocabulary more akin to Reformation discourse than anything one might associate with Catholicism.

> Here we can scarcely suppress the question as to whether the Council did not start from an over-optimistic view in its account of revelation and salvation history, losing sight of the fact that divine salvation comes essentially as a justification of the *sinner*; that grace is given through the judgment of the cross and thus itself always retains the character of judgment; that therefore the *one* word of God appears in the double guise of Law and Gospel – a statement that is still true even if we consider the specifically Lutheran theology of Law and Gospel as too narrow and inadequate.[48]

Ratzinger's most significant concession here is that to some extent the Lutheran theology of Law and Gospel captures the essence of the divine revelation. This is the case even though the articulation of the dialectic is too narrow and inadequate to be entirely acceptable. In a later article which I will make reference to presently, 'Luther and the unity of the churches', Ratzinger again

---

[46] Alister McGrath, 'Justification: Barth, Trent and Küng' in *Scottish Journal of Theology* 34 (1981).
[47] Lane, *Justification by Faith*, p. 90.
[48] Joseph Ratzinger, 'Revelation Itself' in Herbert Vorgrimler (ed), *Commentary on the Documents of Vatican II*, Volume III (London: Burns & Oats/Herder and Herder, 1966), pp. 173-174.

voices dissatisfaction with Luther's particular framing of the relationship between Law and Gospel whilst at the same time conceding that the Law/Gospel distinction is fundamental to the way we are to understand salvation. Ratzinger writes, 'To be sure, one has to view justification as radical and deep as he did, that is, as a reduction of the entire anthropology and thus also of all other matters of doctrine to the dialectic of Law and Gospel.'[49]

What might such an admission amount to in concrete terms? His discussion of *Dei Verbum* furnishes at least a partial answer to that question. Ratzinger expresses a concern here that the optimistic anthropology, captured in the document's citation of Romans 2:6, has somehow misunderstood the fundamentally opposing message that Paul was seeking to communicate in his over all discourse.

> If Rom 2 was quoted as a testimony for the universal possibility of salvation, should not also mention have been made of the terrifying context of this passage of Scripture, that belongs to an invisible line of thought which runs from 1:17-3:20, ending finally, in 3:20, in the statement that is directly contrary to the text quoted (2.6f): 'For no human being will be justified in his sight by the works of the Law...' cf. also 3:23: 'since all have sinned and fall short of the glory of God...' When salvation is being treated should not the mystery of the anger of God also have been mentioned, that weighs so heavily upon these chapters? The whole vast subject of sin, law and the anger of God is gathered together here in the one little word *lapsus (post eorum lapsum...)* and thus is given neither its full weight nor is it taken seriously enough.[50]

His argument is that Paul's soteriology rests on the presumption of humanity's inability to find justification on the basis of works of the law. Such a strong affirmation of the Law's redundancy in these terms cannot be taken as anything other than evidence that a dialectic between Law and Gospel was reasonably central to Ratzinger's own thought. Indeed, the weight given to the anger or wrath of God and the obvious displeasure at *Dei Verbum*'s failure to take significant cognizance of that element in Paul's soteriology, emphasises the degree to which the cross was key to Ratzinger's whole theological outlook.

However, it is in his response to *Gaudium et Spes*[51] that we are given perhaps the fullest corroberation of his embrace of the Law/Gospel dialectic. In this contribution to the Vorgrimler series Ratzinger questions the notion of human freedom which he suspects the framers of the document were in danger of promulgating. As was the case with *Dei Verbum*, his concerns were triggered by an apparent pelagianising scriptural exegesis which had failed to keep in view the over all thrust of the biblical text.

---

[49] Ratzinger, 'Luther and the Unity of the Churches', p. 220.

[50] Ratzinger, 'Revelation Itself' in Vorgrimler (ed), *Documents of Vatican II* (Volume 3), p. 174.

[51] Joseph Ratzinger, 'The Dignity of the Human Person' in Vorgrimler (ed) *Commentary on the Documents of Vatican II* (Volume 5).

> It should also have been taken into account that Ecclus 15:14 is a moralising and individualistic interpretation of Deut 11:26ff., which in Jeremiah 21:8 undergoes a striking pragmatic modification, and stands at the starting-point of the Jewish ethical doctrine of the two ways. If Jer 21:8 is rooted in the concrete situation of beleaguered Jerusalem, the statement of Deut 11:26 is entirely determined by the theology of the Covenant. The Thou who is addressed is Israel, which in God's offer of the Covenant receives the choice between life and death. Consequently in using such texts the Christian cannot leave out of account the actual history of the Covenant, cannot exclude the fact that Israel – representing mankind – was not in a position to carry out what the Covenant offered, but inevitably experienced the Law as a yoke 'which neither our fathers nor we have been able to bear.' (Acts 15:10) It is impossible to prescind from the fact that the promised life ultimately came not from freedom in fulfilling the Law but from the death of him who allowed himself in accordance with the Law to hang on the tree as a Transgressor of the Law. (Gal. 3:12ff.)[52]

The essence of Ratzinger's objections to the line taken by the theologians behind *Gaudium et Spes* is that they begin with a biblical text (in this case from the deutero-canonical book of Ecclesiasticus) which ostensibly promoted a fairly optimistic view of human freedom, and built an entire doctrine of freedom from that isolated text. Whilst acknowledging that a similar notion of freedom permeates the theology of the Covenant as it is developed in Deuteronomy, Ratzinger pleads the succeeding history of the covenant people as evidence of the inability of Israel (and *ipso facto* humanity in general) to fulfil the obligations of that covenant and experience its benefits. Indeed, rather than being a pathway to life, the Law was ultimately to be experienced as bondage. Freedom in the end, according to Ratzinger, is found not in the fulfilment of the law but in the death of the one who bore the curse of the law on the tree. The Pauline and even Lutheran tone of Ratzinger's discourse highlights the absolute failure of the Law as a means to life or justification. It is in this sense that I would suggest that the clear separation between Law and Gospel becomes apparent in Ratzinger's thought.

In a final rebuttal of the Pelagianism lurking within *Gaudium et Spes*, Ratzinger goes on to challenge the short-sightedness of the authors in their failure to take into account the discoveries of the social sciences about the restricted nature of human freedom as well as the insights of Martin Luther regarding the bondage of the human will. Once again, in this reference to Luther, we have a strange ambivalence in Ratzinger whereby he both affirms the Reformer's theology but also accuses it of lacking balance.

> The general doctrine of freedom developed in the conciliar text cannot therefore stand up either to theological or philosophical criticism. Philosophically speaking, it by-passes the whole modern discussion of

---

[52] Ratzinger, 'The Dignity of the Human Person' in Vorgrimler, *Documents of Vatican II* (Volume 5), pp. 137-138.

freedom. It simply takes no account of that overshadowing of freedom of which psychology and sociology at the present time informs us in such a disturbing way. Consequently it shuts itself out from the factual situation of man whose freedom only comes into effect through a lattice of determining factors. Theologically speaking, it leaves aside the whole complex of problems which Luther, with polemical one-sidedness, comprised in the term 'servum arbitrium'. The whole text scarcely gives a hint of the discord which runs through man and which is described so dramatically in Romans 7:13-25. It even falls into downright Pelagian terminology when it speaks of man *'sese ab omni passionum captivitate liberans finem suum persequitur et apta subsidia ... procurat.*[53]

Ratzinger's Critique of Luther

The reference to the lop-sidedness of Luther's theology was to pre-empt Ratzinger's next chronological engagement with the theology of justification which was an interview published in *Communio* entitled 'Luther and the unity of the churches.' There is a sense in which this subject matter trespasses on to territory properly relevant to the concluding chapter of the thesis. It was in this publication that Ratzinger highlighted his objections to the type of individualism which he thought undergirded Luther's understanding of justification. Here we have the important distinction between believing 'with the church' and believing in a radically individualised manner. This question will obviously have most significance when I explore how Ratzinger's theology of church and sacraments might detract from his capacity to be a bridge to the evangelical tradition. Nevertheless a brief orientation to the issues raised by Ratzinger in this article will not only give us a sense of his thinking on justification at this juncture in his career but also anticipate the deeper questions relating to the relationship between soteriology and ecclesiology that will dominate the concluding chapter of the publication.

Ratzinger's comments on justification arise in response to the question, 'Are there still any serious differences between the Catholic Church and the Reformed Churches and, if so, what are they?' After enumerating a number of acknowledged areas of controversy (Scripture and tradition, Scripture and magisterium, the papal office, the sacrificial nature of the eucharist, etc), Ratzinger turns his attention to Luther's own characterization of what most fundamentally divided the emerging 'Evangelische Kirche' from Rome. Unsurprisingly, this was the matter of justification and Ratzinger speculates in a highly creative and original way why only an idea that is deeply anchored in religious experience, as this one was, could have the capacity to create such a fundamental breach with all that had gone before.

> It seems to me that the decisive cause of the breach cannot be found solely in changes in the constellation of ideas and in the concomitant shifts in

---

[53] Ratzinger, 'The Dignity of the Human Person' in Vorgrimler, *Documents of Vatican II* (Volume 5), p. 138.

theological theory, no matter how important these elements are. For there is no denying the truth that a new religious movement can be generated only by a new relgous experience which is, perhaps, aided by the total configuration of an epoch and which incorporates its resources but is itself not consumed by them. It seems to me that the basic feature is the fear of God by which Luther's very existence was struck down, torn between God's calling and the realization of his own sinfulness, so much so that God appears to him sub contrario, as the opposite of Himself, i.e., as the Devil who wants to destroy man. To break free of this fear of God becomes the real issue of redemption. Redemption is realized the moment faith appears as the rescue from the demands of self-justification, that is, as a personal certainty of salvation. This "axis" of the concept of faith is explained very clearly in Luther's Little Catechism: "I believe that God created me. . . . I believe that Jesus Christ . . . is my Lord who saved me . . . in order that I may be His . . . and serve Him forever in justice and innocence forever." Faith assures, above all, the certainty of one's own salvation.[54]

Ratzinger goes on to intimate that this emphasis on the personal certainty of salvation led to the re-configuring of the relationship between the divine virtues of faith, hope and love. Within the Catholic model of faith these were said to be essentially united and did not exist outside of relationship with each other. They also had distinct meanings. Luther, however, is said to have re-defined their content and divorced love from faith in such a manner that love was no longer seen as having a bearing on the issue of salvation.[55] The following extended quotation gives a fuller sense of Ratzinger's critique of this understanding of faith.

> The personal certainty of redemption becomes the center of Luther's ideas. Without it, there would be no salvation. Thus, the importance of the three divine virtues, faith, hope, and love, to a Christian formula of existence undergoes a significant change: the certainties of hope and faith, though hitherto essentially different, become identical. To the Catholic, the certainty of faith refers to that which God worked and which the church witnesses. The certainty of hope refers to the salvation of individuals and, among them, of one self. Yet, to Luther, the latter represented the crux without which nothing else really mattered. That is why love, which lies at the center of the Catholic faith, is dropped from the concept of faith, all the way to the polemic formulations of the large commentary on St. Paul's Epistle to the Galatians: *maledicta sit caritas,* down with love![56]

Ratzinger's concluding comments on justification feature the three major concerns he has with the view of faith articulated by Luther. First, Luther's 'sola fide' is said to make love 'profane' in that it is now identified with what has been negatively categorised as 'works.' This negation of the *fides caritas*

---

[54] Ratzinger, 'Luther and the Unity of the Churches'.
[55] 'Luther's insistence on "by faith alone" clearly and exactly excludes love from the question of salvation.' Ratzinger, 'Luther and the Unity of the Churches', pp. 218-219.
[56] Ratzinger, 'Luther and the Unity of the Churches', p. 218.

formula is said to place love in a context to which it does not belong. Second, an unhealthy dialectic at the heart of Luther's faith is said to pit certain things against each other that ought never to have been in tension. In his analysis of this dysfunctional dialectic we are introduced to what he has referred to elsewhere as the Reformer's one-sided dialectic of Law and Gospel. What Luther is accused of doing is having a dialectical view of God which has somehow had a detrimental effect on his portrayal of the life of faith. Thus to Luther God always appears in two guises and the exercise of faith is associated with the choice one makes about which image of God to accept or embrace. Speaking of this dynamic, Ratzinger characterises Luther's view of the Christian life as one in which the believer clings to the merciful God while at the same time knowing that God is not entirely defined by that gracious mode in which he is perceived. 'At the same time, man has to depend time and again on the forgiving God against a demanding and judgmental God, that is, Christ, who appears *sub contrario* (as Devil).'[57] Ratzinger further claims that this dialectical view of God naturally gave birth to a dialectical view of Scripture. Luther is said to portray the believer as being plunged into crisis by the weight of condemnation communicated by the message of Scripture as a whole, while at the same time offered miraculous release through the gospel as it emerges in St Paul's letters. It is this negative identification of the majority of Scripture with Law that constitutes what Ratzinger defined as the one-sided dialectic of Law and Gospel in Luther's theology.[58]

> In some respects this incorporates the point of departure for the entire movement; for it was exactly the unity of Scripture – the Old and the New Testament, the gospels, the epistles of St. Paul, and the Catholic letters – on the basis of which Luther felt confronted with a Devil-God whom he felt compelled to resist and whom he resisted with the assistance of the divine God which he discovered in St. Paul. The unity of Scripture which had hitherto been interpreted as a unity of steps toward salvation, as a unity of analogy, is now replaced with the dialectic of Law and Gospel.[59]

The final concern voiced by Ratzinger centres on the deeply individualistic understanding of faith that emerges in Luther. He defines this as 'a radical personalization of the act of faith which consists in an exciting and, in some sense exclusive 'eye for eye' relationship between God and man.'[60] This is viewed as not an entirely healthy development because Luther's highly individualised view of faith combined with his dialectic view of God are said to have had an effect on how 'faith' itself was understood. What follows is a contrast which Ratzinger draws between the more corporate Catholic understanding of faith and the individualistic faith of Luther, characterised as it was, by a radical diminution of the role of the church. Ratzinger writes,

---

[57] Ratzinger,'Luther and the Unity of the Churches', p. 218.
[58] Ratzinger, 'Luther and the Unity of the Churches', p. 219.
[59] Ratzinger, 'Luther and the Unity of the Churches', p. 219.
[60] Ratzinger, 'Luther and the Unity of the Churches', p. 219.

> This "personalism" and this "dialectic," together to a lesser or greater degree with an anthropology, have also altered the remaining structure of his teachings. For this basic assessment signifies that, according to Luther, faith is no longer, as to the Catholic, essentially the communal belief of the entire church. In any case, according to Luther, the church can neither assume the certain guarantee for personal salvation nor decide definitely and compellingly on matters (that is, the content) of faith. On the other hand, to the Catholic, the church is central to the act of faith itself: only by communal belief do I partake of the certainty on which I can base my life. This corresponds to the Catholic view that church and Scripture are inseparable while, in Luther, Scripture becomes an independent measure of church and tradition.[61]

In this brief quotation we are given hints of a very fundamental difference between Ratzinger and those who might seek to champion the individualistic view of faith attributed to Luther. The final chapter will afford us the opportunity to engage more deeply with Ratzinger's concept of churchly faith and address the question of whether this idea can be accommodated to the more traditional evangelical conception of personal faith. For the present, we shall examine Ratzinger's most explicit teaching on justification which, significantly, includes comments on the nature and meaning of faith as this is articulated in the writings of St Paul. The level of vocabulary used by Ratzinger is somewhat less complex than the language of his academic articles. This is the case because the publication, *St Paul*, is a collection of addresses delivered to pilgrims at the Vatican during the Wednesday papal audiences.[62] Thus while the content is not deeply scholarly, it may have the advantage of being an attempt to make the complexities of the issue of justification clearer for those who are non-expert.

Papal Addresses on Justification

The Benedict of these papal homilies emerges much more as a pastor than a systematic theologian. The tone of the material is exhortatory and the content is almost exclusively biblical. Indeed, the primary medium of communication is straightforward exegesis of the scriptural text. On a cursory reading, the Pope Emeritus' language and thought forms are more reminiscent of Protestantism than of material one might normally associate with a papal address. *St Paul* is composed of twenty chapters in all though the four that are most relevant to our theme have a markedly soteriological focus: 'The Importance of Christology: The Theology of the Cross'; 'The Doctrine of Justification: From Works to Faith'; 'The Doctrine of Justification: The Apostle's Teaching on Faith and Works'; and 'Theology of the Sacraments.' I shall attempt to demonstrate that

---

[61] Ratzinger, 'Luther and the Unity of the Churches', p. 219.
[62] Pope Benedict XVI, *Saint Paul* (San Francisco: Ignatius Press, 2009). This publication contains papal homilies on the theology of St Paul delivered between 2 July 2008 and 4 February 2009.

Benedict's presentation of Pauline teaching does at points highlight precisely those elements of it which evangelicals tend to regard as most significant. As well as identifying the areas of commonality with Protestants, I will explore those points where his understanding of justification reflects his Catholic and Augustinian background. Finally, I shall argue that his exegetically-driven theology causes him to use language that does not sit easily with certain Catholic soteriological assumptions. Indeed, I shall suggest that there *appears* to be a certain ambivalence in Benedict's theology when he is attempting to marry Pauline soteriology with the viewpoint of the tradition and the magisterium. Thus, the tension between evangelical and Catholic displays itself not only in the dialogue *between* Ratzinger and Protestantism, but also *within* the thought processes of someone who is an outstanding Catholic exegetical theologian.

The most recurrent theme in the featured addresses is the impossibility of salvation on the basis of good works or self effort. This Pauline idea so prevalent in evangelical soteriology is driven home by Benedict with thoroughgoing rigour on a number of occasions. In the address on Paul's teaching on faith and works he goes so far as to assert that the 'centrality of justification without works' was 'the primary object of Paul's preaching.'[63] Earlier in the sermon series he traces the gratuitous nature of salvation to the work of Jesus on the cross. Speaking of Paul's own encounter with Christ, he writes,

> Day after day, in his new life, he experienced that salvation was 'grace', that everything derived from the death of Christ and not from his own merit which did not exist. The 'Gospel of grace' thus became for him the only way of understanding the Cross, not only the criterion of his new existence but also his response to those who questioned him. *First and foremost among these were the Jews who put their hope in deeds and from these hoped for salvation...*[64]

Whilst the reference to the futility of works for salvation appeared *en passant* in Benedict's reflections on the cross, it takes centre stage in his first specific treatment of justification. Framing his comments in light of the Reformation controversy, Benedict presents Paul's Damascus road experience as a catalyst which overturned the apostle's value system and helped him see the redundancy of any human merit.

> The illumination of Damascus radically changed his life; he began to consider all merits acquired in an impeccable religious career as 'refuse', in comparison with the sublimity of knowing Jesus Christ (cf. Phil 3:8) The Letter to the Philippians offers us a moving testimony of Paul's transition from a justice founded on the Law and acquired by his observance of the required actions to a justice based on faith in Christ. He had understood that

---

[63] Benedict XVI, *Saint Paul*, p. 86.
[64] Benedict XVI, *Saint Paul*, p. 62 (italics mine).

what until then had seemed to him to be gain, before God was, a loss; and thus he had decided to stake his whole existence on Jesus Christ (cf. Phil. 3:7) The treasure hidden in the field and the precious pearl for whose purchase all was to be invested were no longer the works of the Law, but Jesus Christ, his Lord.[65]

Undergirding the marked anti-Pelagianism of this discourse is a profound christocentric devotion which merits comment on its own terms. This may be best developed later when we look at Benedict's ambivalent response to the notion of a highly individualized faith in Christ. It will suffice for now to note that he happily portrays experiential knowledge of Christ as the factor which facilitated such a revolution in Paul's thought.

> It is precisely because of this personal experience of relationship with Jesus Christ that Paul henceforth places at the center of his Gospel an irreducible opposition between the two alternative paths to justice: one built on the works of the Law, the other founded on the grace of faith in Christ.[66]

Benedict's litany of texts used to illustrate this dialectic in Paul's thought (eg. Gal. 2:15-16, Rom. 3:23-24) lead him to ponder Luther's translation of Romans 3:28, 'we hold that a man is justified by faith *alone* apart from works of the law.' Returning to that subject at the end of the catechesis, after having given an impressively comprehensive account of the Law in all its many facets, Benedict proceeds to acknowledge the rightness of Luther's *sola fide* translation providing it is not affirmed at the cost of love. He writes, 'For this reason[67] Luther's phrase *'faith alone'* is true, if it is not opposed to faith in charity, in love.' This sentiment reveals his lifelong attachment to the Augustinian *fides caritas* formula which is the Catholic version of justification through faith alone. Whether this may be regarded as Benedict smuggling in the necessity of works for salvation by the back door will be explored in detail when we look at where he differs from a mainstream evangelical reading of Paul.

His pronounced rejection of human works as a means to salvation continues in the third of the four featured addresses which is also the last one to specifically treat the matter of justification. A programmatic statement at the outset gives much food for thought.

> In the Catechesis last Wednesday I spoke of how man is justified before God. Following Saint Paul, we have seen that man is unable to 'justify' himself with his own actions, but can only truly become 'just' before God because God confers his 'justice' upon him, uniting him to Christ his Son.

---

[65] Benedict XVI, *Saint Paul*, pp. 78-79.
[66] Benedict XVI, *Saint Paul*, p. 79.
[67] Benedict XVI, *Saint Paul*, p.82. A reference to the previous statement in which he affirms, 'Being just simply means being with Christ and in Christ. And this suffices.'

> And man obtains this union through faith. In this sense, Paul tells us: not our deeds, but rather faith renders us 'just'.[68]

Benedict, whilst reiterating the anti-Pelagian nature of Christianity, proceeds from this point onwards to delineate the meaning of the Catholic *sola fide*. This is thus the appropriate juncture to consider where he differs most significantly from the traditional evangelical view of justification. However, in anticipation of this it may be helpful to gauge whether Benedict's theology of justification allows for the possibility of any kind of forensic or alien righteousness. Arguably, there is an indirect reference to this within the quotation cited above where it is said that 'man' 'can only truly become "just" before God because God confers his "justice" upon him, uniting him to Christ his Son.' The language is clearly capable of being read in a forensic sense, though Benedict does not expound this idea any further during the address. The closest he comes to making any clarifying statement about the issue is found in the second volume of *Jesus of Nazareth* where he discusses the *sola fide*. Whilst again starkly repudiating a Pelagian view of salvation, Benedict is also careful to reject the traditional Protestant notion of imputed righteousness as a perpetually alien righteousness. He writes,

> If ... we should acknowledge that Paul in no way yields to moralism in this exhortation [i.e. to be a holy and living sacrifice] or in any sense belies his doctrine of justification through faith and not through works, *it is equally clear that this doctrine of justification does not condemn man to passivity – he does not become a purely passive recipient of a divine righteousness that always remains external to him.*[69]

What is undeniable here is that Benedict views righteousness as being imparted to the sinner and not merely existing as an external status given by God on account of Christ's passion. The phrase 'does not become a purely passive recipient of a divine righteousness that *always*[70] remains external to him' might hint that he is in agreement with Küng's view that justification is both a declaratory act as well as the internal transformation of the individual.[71] This understanding is possible if we view God's justifying decree as having performative effect. However, even if this should be the view taken by Ratzinger it would not make rapprochement possible with that brand of Evangelicalism which views cognitive adherence to 'imputed righteousness' as the absolute essence of the gospel.[72]

---

[68] Benedict XVI, *Saint Paul*, p. 84.
[69] Joseph Ratzinger, *Jesus of Nazareth: Holy Week* (San Francisco: Ignatius Press, 2011), p. 237.
[70] Italics mine
[71] Küng, *Justification*, p. 215.
[72] R.C. Sproul, *Faith Alone: The Evangelical Doctrine of Justification* (Grand Rapids: Baker, 1995).

It is my view that Benedict's long-standing opposition to Pelagian theology is a heartfelt position which accords with historic Augustinianism. Indeed, his embrace of the *fides caritas* formula is in conscious emulation of his mentor's teaching in documents such as *de Trinitate*[73] and there would seem to be little basis for demurring from McGrath's judgment that such an outlook does not compromise the gratuitous nature of the gospel. What remains to be seen, and what will be of critical importance for evangelical/Catholic dialogue, is the manner in which Benedict defends *fides caritas* as a biblically mandated first principle.

Benedict's starting point, unsurprisingly, is the theology of Paul, which is said to have two elements within it that have historically prompted confusion and disagreement within Christianity. Although many will not question their individual validity or appropriateness as theological ideas, difficulties have arisen when their relationship to each other has been considered. It is precisely how these two elements are configured that has been the catalyst for debate within the church. Benedict introduces the point at issue in his final address on justification.

> ... in our last Catechesis, we discovered two levels; that of the insignificance of our actions and of our deeds to achieve salvation and that of 'justification' through faith which produces the fruit of the Spirit. The confusion of these two levels has caused a few misunderstandings in Christianity over the course of centuries.[74]

Historically, the Reformed churches have rejected the idea of the fruit of the Spirit having any direct bearing on justification as this is perceived as reintroducing the concept of salvation by works. 'Down with love' as Luther put it, in his polemical commentary on Galatians. Benedict, however, advocates a virtually symbiotic relationship between the two which does not allow for the strict demarcation demanded by Lutheranism. He traces the provenance of this idea to the thought of St Paul himself.

> In this context [i.e. Benedict's prior discussion of the historical misunderstandings surrounding this question] it is important that St Paul, in the same Letter to the Galatians, radically accentuates, on the one hand, the freely given nature of justification that is not dependent on our works, but which at the same time also emphasizes the relationship between faith and charity, between faith and works.[75]

Thus Galatians 5:16, so often read as a winsome exhortation to kindly living by evangelicals, may also be taken as Pauline shorthand for certain fundamentals of the faith if we take the symbiotic idea seriously. 'In Christ Jesus neither

---

[73] See Benedict's discussion of Paul's paeon to love in the address, 'The Apostles Teaching on Faith and Works' in *Saint Paul*, p. 86.

[74] Benedict XVI, *Saint Paul*, pp. 84-85.

[75] Benedict XVI, *Saint Paul*, p. 85.

circumcision nor uncircumcision counts for anything, but only faith working through love.' It is important to stress that Benedict, in his depiction of love, detaches it from any impression of it being a human striving when he characterises it as the action of the Holy Spirit on the believing subject. Referring to the fruit of the Spirit in Galatians 5:22-23, he explains the unique interplay between love, the Triune God and the believer.

> These are the fruits of the Spirit that blossom from faith ... *Agape*, love, is cited at the beginning of this list of virtues and self-control at the conclusion. In fact, the Spirit who is the love of the Father and the Son pours out his first gift, *agape*, into our hearts (cf. Rm 5:5); and to be fully expressed, *agape*, love, requires self-control. In my first Encyclical, *Deus Caritas Est*, I also treated of the love of the Father and the Son which reaches us and profoundly transforms our existence. Believers know that reciprocal love is embodied in the love of God and of Christ, through the Spirit.[76]

It is from this locating of love as the expression of the dynamic of faith that Benedict relates the Catholic *sola fide* (*fides caritas*) to those texts which are most problematic from the standpoint of Luther's *sola fide*. He claims that the gift of justification means effectively being called to live in the love of Christ for the sake of neighbour *because* it is on that criterion that individuals will be judged at the end of their lives.[77] Whilst somewhat dubiously attributing that sentiment to Paul ('In reality Paul only repeats what Jesus himself said and which is proposed to us anew by last Sunday's Gospel, in the parable of the Last Judgment[78]), he does seem to be on firmer ground with the allusion to the story of the sheep and the goats (Matt 25:31-46). This pericope, at least viewed from the standpoint of our discussion on righteousness, hints that eschatological salvation may be worked out on the basis of imparted righteousness! Benedict also has the added advantage that this, along with other difficult texts, may be integrated into the Catholic *sola fide* whereas Luther must risk dismembering the canon by questioning the view of justification articulated by James. Benedict's brief vindication of *fides caritas* towards the close of his discussion is a model of succinct theological reasoning.

> Seen in this perspective, the centrality of justification without works, the primary object of Paul's preaching, does not clash with faith that works through love; indeed, it demands that our faith itself be expressed in a life in accordance with the Spirit. Often there is seen an unfounded opposition between Paul's theology and that of St James, who writes in his Letter: 'as the body apart from the spirit is dead, so faith apart from works is dead' (2:26). In reality, while Paul is primarily concerned to show that faith in Christ is necessary and sufficient, James accentuates the consequential relations between faith and works (cf. James 2:24). Therefore, for both Paul

---

[76] Benedict XVI, *Saint Paul*, p. 85.
[77] Benedict XVI, *Saint Paul*, p. 85.
[78] Benedict XVI, *Saint Paul*, p. 86.

and James, faith that is active in love testifies to the freely given gift of justification in Christ.[79]

Ratzinger's acceptance of the *fides caritas* formula may not place him at such an absolute distance from evangelicals as may be thought. Some contemporary scholars are optimistic that the historic rapprochement on justification achieved at Regensburg in 1541 offer hope for future Catholic/evangelical dialogue.[80]

---

[79] Benedict XVI, *Saint Paul*, p. 86.

[80] See Lane, *Justification by Faith* and Matthew C. Heckel, 'Is R.C. Sproul Wrong About Martin Luther? An Analysis of R.C. Sproul's *Faith Alone: The Evangelical Doctrine of Justification* With Respect to Augustine, Luther, Calvin and Catholic Luther Scholarship' in *JETS* 47/1 (March 2004) pp. 89-120. This historic conversation between Catholic and Reformed theologians preceded the formal declarations of Trent (where views were set in stone) and thus both sides had more room for manoeuvre on the disputed matter of justification. Significantly, some of the Catholic participants (most notably Contarini) had considerable sympathy with the Protestant position and a remarkable degree of convergence between the two perspectives was achieved. The Regensburg Colloquy ultimately ran aground, not on account of its consensus on justification, but the failure to agree on a host of other accompanying issues. Scholars have debated whether the agreement was theologically coherent and there seems to be no clear consensus of opinion. (E.g. A.E. McGrath, *Iustitia Dei Second Edition* (Cambridge: Cambridge University Press, 1998), pp. 247-248 suggests that it was 'a scissors and paste job' in which opposing views were juxtaposed rather than integrated, whereas P. Matheson, *Cardinal Contarini at Regensburg* (Oxford: Oxford University Press, 1972), p. 181 speaks of it as '… no mere mediatorial formula, offering a crumb of theological comfort to every grouping. [Rather,] [i]t takes up a clear line, and it is because of this uncomfortable clarity, not because of an alleged ambiguity, that it was later rejected by Catholic and Protestant confessionalists'). Notwithstanding this uncertainty, Lane is adamant that on the matter of the *fides caritas* formula there was a remarkable concession made on the Catholic side. He avers in relation to Article 5, '…[T]he statement that justifying faith is effectual through love is immediately followed by the affirmation that this faith justifies by appropriating mercy and imputed righteousness and that this righteousness is not imputed on account of any imparted worthiness or perfection (Lane, *Justification by Faith*, p. 59) This is deemed to be highly significant and to underscore this both Lane and Heckel cite the surprisingly positive response of Calvin, who was in Regensburg as an observer of these discussions. Calvin states, 'The debate in controversy was more keen upon the doctrine of justification. At length, a formula was drawn up, which, on receiving certain corrections was accepted on both sides. You will be astonished, I am sure, that our opponents have yielded so much … Our friends have thus retained all the substance of the true doctrine, so that nothing can be comprehended within it which is not to be found in our writings; you will desire, I know, a more distinct explication and statement of doctrine, and in that respect, you shall find me in complete agreement… However, if you consider with what kind of men we have to agree upon this doctrine, you will acknowledge that much has been accomplished.' (Cited in Heckel, 118, Letter to Farel of 11 May, 1541, *Corpus Reformatorum* 39.215. *Letters of Calvin*, Vol. 1. Translated by David Constable, 1871,

The final paragraph in the address indirectly anticipates the sort of objection to which the *fides caritas* formula might give rise. Benedict asserts that the ethics put forward by Paul to believers will not degenerate into legalism providing their starting point is 'the personal and communal relationship with Christ.'[81] With his usual gift for pithy summary (at least within this medium of communication) he writes, 'This is essential: the Christian ethic is not born from a system of commandments but is a consequence of our friendship with Christ. This friendship influences life; if it is true, it incarnates and fulfils itself in love for neighbour.'[82] His intimation is that the depth of personal relationship with Christ will help create a sense of security or ease that will militate against any moralistic striving on the part of believers. Using the same exhortatory and pastoral tone that has characterised so many of these addresses, Benedict ends with a plea to his listeners that they allow themselves to be impacted by this great redeeming relationship that has been made possible for them.

> Therefore let us allow ourselves to be touched by reconciliation, which God has given us in Christ, by God's 'foolish' love for us; nothing and no one can ever separate us from his love. (cf. Rm 8:39) *We live in this certainty. It is this certainty that gives us the strength to live concretely the faith that works in love.*[83]

The intensely pietistic language cited above hints at an anomaly which I suggest may be present in Benedict's theology. Whilst he has placed major emphasis on the corporate nature of belief and the appropriateness of believing 'with the church', there is another side to his thought, expressed in a minor key, which is more redolent of Evangelicalism than traditional Catholicism. This 'minority report', if one might call it that, occurs especially in the context of exegesis and/or preaching. Here he will sometimes employ language which, on the face of it, jars with Catholic soteriological assumptions. The earliest example of this alien strain in Ratzinger's theology is found in *Introduction to Christianity* where he questions the assumption that the bulk of those living during the Middle Ages were *bona fide* believers.[84] Indeed, his language states unequivocally that there was a great majority of Catholics from that time who - though exposed to the sacraments and living under the sacred canopy, so to speak - had never embraced faith in any 'interior' sense. What is even more suggestive is that the wider context for these comments is a discussion of the nature of belief where Ratzinger portrays the activity as a deeply personal and

---

p. 260. Now available as an E-Book at http://books.google.co.uk/books/about/Letters_of_John_Calvin.html?id=iGEwAQAAM AAJ&redir_esc=y

[81] Benedict XVI, *Saint Paul*, p. 88.
[82] Benedict XVI, *ISaint Paul*, p. 88.
[83] Benedict XVI, *Saint Paul*, p. 88 (italics mine).
[84] Ratzinger, *Introduction to Christianity*, p. 23. This was initially drawn attention to in chapter two of the publication.

'all-or-nothing' engagement with God in the person of Jesus Christ. Moreover, his description of faith, though couched in the language of personalism, would be in no way inimical to the way evangelicals might define the phenomenon.

> Thus faith is the finding of a 'You' that bears me up and amid all the unfulfilled – and in the last resort unfulfillable – hope of human encounters, gives me the promise of an indestructible love which not only longs for eternity but guarantees it. Christian faith lives on the discovery that not only is there such a thing as objective meaning, but this meaning knows me and loves me, I can *entrust myself to it like a child that knows all its questions answered in the 'You' of its mother. Thus in the last analysis believing, trusting and loving are one, and all the theses around which belief revolves are only concrete expressions of the all-embracing about-turn, of the assertion 'I believe in You' – of the discovery of God in the countenance of the man Jesus of Nazareth.*[85]

This radical personalising of faith, expressed originally in a lecture context awash with agnostics and unbelievers (the material in *Introduction to Christianity* was based on a course of lectures offered to the generality of students at Tübingen), was also replicated in his papal homilies on justification. Here the definition of faith takes on a particularly strong Protestant hue when he defines it as 'looking at Christ, entrusting oneself to Christ, being united to Christ...'[86] I would hazard the opinion that such language would be misleading if it were not describing a fairly definitive action similar to the one he has already described in *Introduction to Christianity*. However, there is no requirement to rely on that earlier work to prove such a conclusion when we consider the impassioned closure to the first papal address on justification. I shall argue that straightforward exegesis of this final appeal would suggest that the Pope Emeritus, at least momentarily, is bringing certain Catholic assumptions about the nature of salvation into question. He states,

> At the end, we can only pray the Lord that he help us to believe; really believe. Believing thus becomes life, unity with Christ, the transformation of our life. And thus, transformed by his love, by the love of God and neighbour, we can truly be just in God's eyes.[87]

The call to 'believe, really believe' suggests a quality of response to God which may not yet have been attained on the part of all of his listeners but is yet indispensable to the Christian life. Moreover, the activity called upon seems not to involve the ministrations of the church *per se*, but engagement with what we might characterise as an 'unmediated Christ.' The Christ, as Benedict puts it, to whom I look, to whom I entrust myself, and ultimately, to whom I become united. It is this radical entering into the interiority of belief which results in the

---

[85] Ratzinger, *Introduction to Christianity*, p. 48 (italics mine).
[86] Benedict XVI, *Saint Paul*, p. 82.
[87] Benedict XVI, *Saint Paul*, p. 83.

transformative impact of justification. Essentially, Pope Benedict XVI seems to be inviting his listeners to be justified by faith.

As has already been stated, the somewhat alien language employed by Benedict highlights a tension between straightforward and sympathetic exegesis of Pauline soteriology (which has been the goal of these addresses) and the viewpoint of the magisterium. The seeming dissonance between the two becomes more apparent in his homily on the theology of the sacraments. Here the context for the sermon is his portrayal of history as having a new beginning in the incarnation of Christ. As an Augustinian he deems this new start necessary on account of the pollution of human nature by the misuse of freedom.

> [W]e have learned from St Paul that a new beginning exists *in* history and *of* history in Jesus Christ, the one who is man and God. With Jesus, who comes from God, a new history begins that is shaped by his 'yes' to the Father and is therefore not founded on the pride of a false emancipation but on love and truth.[88]

However the fundamental question he sees requiring address is how individuals can enter into the new beginning and be set free from their original history? In other words, '... how is new birth achieved in order to enter into the new humanity? How does Jesus come into my life, into my being?'[89]

His initial answer is that that which begins in biology in the first instance, now starts with the creative action of the Holy Spirit. It is the Spirit's ministry, so to speak, which allows Jesus to enter into the lives of individuals. But 'how can this Spirit of Christ, the Holy Spirit, become my Spirit?' enquires Benedict.[90] In addressing that question he gives the appearance of fluctuating between the plain sense of the Pauline texts and allegiance to the tradition. His original explanation of incorporation into Christ is that it 'happens in three ways which are closely interconnected.'[91] The first of these is the Spirit of Christ knocking on the door of the individual's heart and moving them from within.[92] It would be difficult not to identify in these words at least some reference to a conscious subject coming under the influence of the Spirit. Thus Benedict at this point in the address seems to acknowledge that the Spirit's regenerating work is not achieved entirely without regard to the response of the individual. However, a new line of thought is immediately introduced which will have significant ramifications for his doctrine of salvation. Drawing heavily on the theology of Henri de Lubac (which will be explored in the closing chapter), he sows the seeds of a more corporate and sacramental

---

[88] Benedict XVI, *Saint Paul*, p. 95.
[89] Benedict XVI, *Saint Paul*, p. 96.
[90] Benedict XVI, *Saint Paul*, p. 96.
[91] Benedict XVI, *Saint Paul*, p. 96.
[92] Benedict XVI, *Saint Paul*, p. 96.

understanding of the Spirit's ministry which seems to jar with his initial thoughts on the matter.

> ... the Spirit knocks at the door of my heart, moves me from within. *However, since* the new humanity must be a true body, since the Spirit must gather us together and really create a community, since overcoming divisions and creating a gathering of the dispersed is characteristic of the new beginning, this Spirit of Christ uses two elements visibly aggregated: the Word of the proclamation and the sacraments ...[93]

Benedict here suggests that God's pre-eminent intention of unity for the human race requires that faith be received in a corporate context and that the Spirit's ministry will involve the nurturing of this corporate dimension. With this end in view the two-pronged agency of the Spirit in regeneration is said to be the Word of the Proclamation and the sacraments. His employment of certain Pauline texts in the wake of this statement seem to corroborate the view already implied that responsive human agents participate in the process of incorporation into Christ. For example, he says of Romans 10:9 that confession of Jesus' Lordship and heartfelt belief in his resurrection will be the means of entering into 'a new history, a history of life and not of death.'[94] Here we have what appears to be an identification of new birth with a faith response to the proclamation. The other Pauline reference utilised equally serves to bolster the notion that the Spirit's regenerating ministry occurs (at least partially) in the context of human encounter with the proclamation. Drawing on Pauline language about the need for the message to be heard or received in order to have effect (cf. Romans 10:14-15,17), Benedict asserts that,

> Faith is not a product of our thought or our reflection; it is something new that we cannot invent but only receive as a gift, as a new thing produced by God. Moreover, faith does not come from reading but from listening. It is not only something interior but also a relationship with Someone. It implies an encounter with the proclamation; it implies the existence of the Other, whom it proclaims, and creates communion.[95]

By this stage in the development of the homily two of the three ways in which Benedict believes the new birth becomes reality have already been treated and neither seem to entail the inactivity or passive reception of the human subject. Indeed, the language used makes most sense in the context of engagement or encounter. However, it is when the third element in Christian initiation (the sacraments) is introduced that Benedict, at least on the face of it, seems to be guilty of inserting a *non sequitur*.

---

[93] Benedict XVI, *Saint Paul*, p. 96 (italics mine).
[94] Benedict XVI, *Saint Paul*, p. 96.
[95] Benedict XVI, *Saint Paul*, p. 97.

> The new fabric of history takes shape in this structure of missions [i.e. the sending of the Son by the Father, and the sending of the apostles and their successors by the Son] in which we ultimately hear God himself speaking; his personal Word, the Son speaks with us, reaches us. The Word was made flesh, Jesus, in order to really create a new humanity. *The word of the proclamation thus becomes a sacrament in Baptism, which is rebirth from water and the Spirit, as Saint John was to say.*[96]

This abrupt change of theme is followed by a brief exposition of Paul's teaching on baptism in Romans 6. The unexpected weight just given to the importance of sacramental baptism (at least unexpected in terms of the lines of thought followed earlier in the homily) seems also to colour the language used by Benedict to describe Paul's conception of baptism in Romans. We are thus left with a picture of Christian initiation which seems at odds with what has been outlined at the opening of the homily.

> ... 'we have been baptized' is in the passive. No one can baptize himself, he needs the other. No one can become Christian on his own. Becoming Christian is a passive process. Only by another can we be made Christians, and this 'other' who makes us Christians, who gives us the gift of faith, is in the first instance the community of believers, the Church. From the Church we receive faith, Baptism.[97]

From the standpoint of a non-Catholic reading of this material it is difficult to defend the idea that Benedict's position is fully coherent. The threefold way in which he describes individuals receiving the life of Jesus *appears* to collapse into a straightforward sacramentalist understanding of salvation when the context of regeneration is moved from encounter with the Other who is Christ to passive reception of the ministrations of the 'other' which is the church. Moreover, the identification of faith with baptism seems to be at odds with his previous definition of the term whereby it is a 'looking to' and an 'entrusting of oneself' to Christ. The question which now faces any commentator seeking to establish a bridge between Evangelicalism and Catholicism is how to read the apparent anomalies in Benedict's theology.[98] Is it most telling that he seems to revert to a classical sacramentalist understanding of soteriology at the close of his homily, or is there a complexity within Ratzinger's thought which cannot be captured adequately in a brief homiletical summary. I would suggest that we

---

[96] Benedict XVI, *Saint Paul*, p. 97 (italics mine).
[97] Benedict XVI, *Saint Paul*, p. 98.
[98] It should be clear that methodologically, I have sought to understand Benedict's thought as it would appear to a public audience untutored in the complexities of Catholic soteriological discourse. As the closing paragraphs of this chapter illustrate, however, that approach will not render a definitive understanding of Ratzinger's content and intentions. A detailed study of his understanding of faith and its mediation will be required for that.

will not satisfactorily answer this question until we explore in detail his view of church and sacraments. Only after a thorough engagement with these apparent roadblocks to unity shall we be in a position to draw final conclusions regarding the ecumenical value of Joseph Ratzinger's theology.

CHAPTER 5

Obstacles to Rapprochement

Introduction

The concern of the publication thus far has been to engage sympathetically but not uncritically with the theology of Joseph Ratzinger in order to measure its ecumenical potential. Previous chapters have confirmed that undoubted convergences exist between Ratzinger and the evangelical tradition, and that his theology is orientated towards Scripture and the early church in a way that some conservative Protestants would applaud. However, we have reached that stage in our investigation where the focus must change and the spotlight be placed on those elements of his thought which are most likely to constitute a barrier to ecumenical rapprochement. The inevitability of such an exercise makes sense in the light of Schleiermacher's classic antithesis between the two traditions. In *The Christian Faith*, Schleirermacher observes that while Protestantism has made 'the individual's relationship to the Church dependent on his relation to Christ,' Catholicism has embraced the opposite path of making 'the individual's relation to Christ dependent on his relation to the church'.[1] Those familiar with Ratzinger's approach to ecclesiology would not debate the accuracy of Schleiermacher's characterization of the Catholic mindset.

Nevertheless, as the previous chapter intimated, there is also a tension present in Ratzinger's theology. While his language usually reflects his concern to place the Church at the centre of the soteriological enterprise, his exegetical work on Pauline soteriology *seems* to tacitly accept the 'Protestant' emphasis on the importance of the individual's relation to Christ. This apparent ambivalence appears in a homily on the sacraments featured in the previous chapter in which Ratzinger speaks of a believing subject whose regeneration is partially effected by the internal promptings of the Spirit and his response to the gospel proclamation, but who is also characterised as being made regenerate through the power of the sacramental act.[2] Indeed, the emphasis on the sacramental aspect of regeneration is so marked at the close of the homily that the process of becoming a Christian seems reduced to one in which the individual's role is essentially a passive one. He states,

> No one can baptize himself, he needs the other. No one can become a Christian on his own. Becoming Christian is a passive process. Only by another can we be made Christians, and this 'other' who makes us

---

[1] Friedrich Schleiermacher, *The Christian Faith* (Edinburgh: T & T Clark, 1999), §24, p. 103.
[2] 'Theology of the Sacraments' in Benedict XVI, *Saint Paul* (San Francisco: Ignatius Press, 2009), p. 98.

Christians, who gives us the gift of faith, is in the first instance the community of believers, the Church. From the Church, we receive faith, Baptism.³

How are we to make sense of such seemingly contradictory language? A useful starting point will be a more thorough grasp of Ratzinger's ecclesiology, as this will shed light on the complex interplay between the individual and the church in the mediation of salvation. To understand the trajectory of his thought and identify its core elements we must begin with the work of French Jesuit, Henri de Lubac, whose publication *Catholicism*⁴ was to prove pivotal for Ratzinger's own understanding of ecclesial salvation.⁵ Of course, Ratzinger is not entirely defined by the insights of de Lubac and the bulk of the next section of the chapter will focus on his own published works which most clearly articulate his theology of the Church in relation to soteriology.

Following on from an account of this aspect of Ratzinger's ecclesiology, I will attempt to gauge whether the approach adopted by him can in any way be accommodated by Evangelicalism. This move returns us to the issues of how Evangelicalism is defined and how Ratzinger's ecclesiology might be critiqued from an evangelical standpoint. As stated in the Introduction, I deem it prudent in relation to these matters to anchor the discussion in Bebbington's widely accepted characterization of Evangelicalism as conversionist, activist, biblicist and crucicentric.⁶ The first and third (conversionist and biblicist) perhaps hold most relevance for this chapter as they reflect the fundamental evangelical concerns about ecclesiology. Conversionism highlights what evangelicals believe about the nature of faith and the manner in which salvation is mediated⁷, whilst biblicism speaks to the issue of authority and the role that Scripture plays in the formation of a doctrine of the church. Both of these defining features of Evangelicalism will inform and to a large degree shape the critique of Ratzinger. In this regard, particular

---

³ Benedict XVI, *St Paul*, p.98.
⁴ Henri de Lubac, *Catholicism: Christ and the Common Destiny of Man* (San Francisco: Ignatius Press, 1988).
⁵ John Webster commends de Lubac's *Catholicism* as one of the magisterial ecclesiological texts of the last century. See John Webster, 'The Church and the Perfection of God,' in Mark Husbands and Daniel J. Treier, *The Community of the Word: Toward an Evangelical Ecclesiology* (Leicester: Apollos, 2005), p. 93.
⁶ David W. Bebbington, *Evangelicalism in Modern Britain: A History from the 1730s to the 1990s* (Grand Rapids: Baker House, 1992), p. 3. For the rationale behind the decision to employ Bebbington's definition of evangelicalism see the Introduction and Methodology.
⁷ Bebbington, *Evangelicalism in Modern Britain*, p. 9. Bebbington, while acknowledging that some evangelicals view conversion as being either gradual or sudden, is clear that the majority perceive conversion as the point at which one becomes a Christian.

attention will be paid to the work of Miroslav Volf[8], John Webster and Leonardo De Chirico[9] whose recent publications constitute a high water mark in informed evangelical engagement with Catholic ecclesiology. In the penultimate section of the chapter, which will involve a closer examination of what is meant by the mediation of faith, I will argue controversially that Ratzinger is not fully consistent in his presentation of Catholic soteriology and that this equivocation allows scope to explore both the uncertainties and the possibilities within Ratzinger's own theology for rapprochement with evangelical Christianity. The suggestion will be made that the mining of these ambivalences may offer a way forward for ecumenical dialogue. Perhaps in the realm of ecclesiology there exists not only the materials which make for an impasse between the two traditions but also the germ of a new understanding.

The concluding section of the chapter widens the discussion and examines two areas of Roman Catholic dogma and practice which have perennially posed problems for evangelicals and caused some to rule out the possibility of any genuine convergence with Catholic theology. The doctrines in question are Purgatory and Mariology and my task will be to follow Ratzinger's own theological method[10] and apply a critical reverse test whereby I measure his teaching on Purgatory and Mariology against his stated positions on the primacy of grace and the centrality of Christ. My aim will be to demonstrate that in these unpromising areas of doctrinal stalemate, Ratzinger's Catholic formulation of these ideas can be reconciled to *Sola gratia* and *Solus Christus* and are therefore of great ecumenical significance.

The Contours of Ratzinger's Soteriological Ecclesiology

One gains a sense of how determining Henri de Lubac's theological vision is for Ratzinger in the Foreword which the latter contributed to the 1988 edition of de Lubac's most famous work, *Catholicism*. Here the insights of the Jesuit theologian were heralded not only as a hermeneutical key to all the issues of theology but as a major stimulus for his own thought. He writes,

> For me, the encounter with [*Catholicism*] became an essential milestone on my theological journey. For in it de Lubac does not treat merely isolated questions. He makes visible to us in a new way the fundamental intuition of the Christian Faith so that from this inner core all the particular elements appear in a new light. He shows how the idea of community and universality, rooted in the Trinitarian concept of God, permeates and shapes all the individual elements of Faith's content. *The idea of the Catholic, the*

---

[8] Miroslav Volf, *After Our Likeness: The Church as the Image of the Trinity* (Grand Rapids: Eerdmans, 1998).
[9] Leonardo De Chirico, *Evangelical Theological Perspectives on post-Vatican II Roman Catholicism* (Bern: Peter Lang, 2003).
[10] In Ratzinger's review of Hans Küng's *Justification*, he suggests that any significant ecumenical proposal should be explored in the light of other traditional teachings which are deemed to be at odds with the new view that is being promoted.

> *all-embracing, the inner unity of I and Thou and We does not constitute one chapter of theology among others. It is the key that opens the door to a proper understanding of the whole.*[11]

Ratzinger's confidence in de Lubac must rest partly on the extensive patristic evidence marshalled in favour of the ecclesiological vision undergirding the book. However, what was to give *Catholicism* added significance was that it was written as a counterbalance to an unattractive and self-serving individualism that both de Lubac and Ratzinger believed to be prevalent in the Catholic Church.[12] The core insight of de Lubac is that the Christian faith possesses an essential social dimension which determines its entire character. We are given a flavour of what this means in de Lubac's depiction of the unity of the church when viewed in its mystical dimension.

> Thus the unity of the Mystical Body of Christ, a supernatural unity, supposes a previous natural unity, the unity of the human race. So the Fathers of the Church, in their treatment of grace and salvation, kept constantly before them this Body of Christ, and in dealing with the creation were not content only to mention the formation of individuals, the first man and the first woman, but delighted to contemplate God creating humanity as a whole. "God," says Iranaeus, for example, "in the beginning of time plants the vine of the human race; he loved this human race and purposed to pour out his Spirit upon it and to give it the adoption of sons."[13]

This mysterious unity that de Lubac finds everywhere acknowledged amongst the Fathers has a particular consequence with regard to the Incarnation itself. In becoming human, Christ was to both participate in human nature and ultimately incorporate it into himself.

> For the Word did not merely take a human body; his humanity was not a simple *corporatio*, but, as Hilary says, a *concorporatio*. He incorporated himself in our humanity, and incorporated it in himself. *Universitatis nostrae caro est factus* (he became the flesh of our humanity). In taking a human nature, it is *human nature* that he united to himself, and it is the latter, whole and entire, that in some sort he uses as a body. Whole and entire ... he will save it. Christ the Redeemer does not offer salvation merely to each one; he affects it, he is himself the salvation of the whole, and for each one salvation consists in a personal ramification of his original belonging to Christ, so that he be not cast out, cut off from this whole.[14]

Whilst the majority of de Lubac's evidence is patristic, he is in no doubt that the Fathers were faithfully expounding the theology of St John and St Paul.[15]

---

[11] Foreword to De Lubac, *Catholicism*, p. 11 (italics mine).
[12] De Lubac, *Catholicism*, pp. 12, 13-15.
[13] De Lubac, *Catholicism*, p. 25.
[14] De Lubac, *Catholicism*, p. 25.
[15] De Lubac, *Catholicism*, p. 44.

The metaphor of the vine is drawn from Jesus' final discourse in John 15 and the even more potent image of the body is drawn from Paul's own musings on the nature of the church. Indeed, de Lubac's sense of the communion existing within the church is fundamentally derived from a notion of corporate personality which he believes underlies Paul's thought. He comments,

> If for St John the bond uniting the faithful to each other and to their Saviour seems to emerge as the expression of an exceedingly close and mutual relationship, for St Paul, on the other hand, it is Christ who appears as a centre, an atmosphere, a whole world even, in which man and God, man and man, are in communion and achieve union.[16]

We are drawn closer to Ratzinger's own nomenclature at the point where de Lubac refers to another Pauline metaphor which the Fathers take up and employ in their discussion of the church. The metaphor in question is that of 'the new man' in Christ and the language used by some of these early patristic commentators anticipates what Ratzinger himself will say later. De Lubac cites Clement of Alexandria who speaks of 'The whole Christ', 'the total Christ'[17] (a favourite phrase of Ratzinger's) though it is Cyril of Alexandria whose words most clearly serve as a preview of what will come later. De Lubac comments,

> But it is in Cyril of Alexandria beyond all others that this thought [i.e. the total Christ] appears almost as an obsession ... Christ, he remarks, not only threw down the old dividing wall, but has made of himself the cornerstone of the building; indeed, through his agency not a single but a threefold wall of division was thrown down ... God cannot be worshipped save in one edifice, and his straying children can only find the way to the Father if they are gathered together in one Body, the new Man whose head is our Redeemer.[18]

De Lubac further notes that this inexpressible mystical unity between Christ and the church is deemed by the Fathers to be realised in the Eucharist. Once again he cites Cyril of Alexandria whose language and structure of thought most nearly approximates that of Ratzinger:

> We are all of us, by nature, separately confined in our own individualities, but in another way, all of us are united together. Divided as it were into distinct personalities by which one is Peter or John or Thomas or Matthew, we are, so to say, molded into one sole body in Christ, feeding on one flesh alone. One Spirit singles us out for unity, and as Christ is one and indivisible

---

[16] De Lubac, *Catholicism*, p. 45.

[17] It is significant that the notion of the *Totus Christus* has a firm foundation in the thought of St Augustine. See Tarsicius Jan van Bavel, 'The "Totus Christus" Idea: A Forgotten Aspect to Augustine's Spirituality' in Thomas Finan and Vincent Twomey (eds) *Studies in Patristic Christology* (Dublin: Four Courts Press, 1998), pp. 84-94.

[18] De Lubac, *Catholicism*, pp. 46-47.

we are all no more but one in him. So did he say to his heavenly Father, "That they may be one, as we are one."[19]

De Lubac's deployment of patristic evidence underscores the profound mystical unity which the Church Fathers believed existed between Christ and the Church. However, Ratzinger's use of their ecclesiology as a launching pad for his own has been fuelled by other concerns and cannot be viewed merely as homage to earlier patristic thought. Volf, for example, highlights Ratzinger's antagonism to the modern concept of the individual which took shape at the Enlightenment.[20] This view is explicit in a 1967 publication, *The Sacramental Nature of Christian Existence* [21], in which Ratzinger suggests that the current wariness of the sacraments stems from a deep-seated anthropological error that has permeated European thought. This error is rooted in Idealism which is said to reduce human personhood to 'autonomous mind' and views human beings as being entirely the product of their own individual choices. In the ecclesiastical realm it is liberal Protestantism rather than Evangelicalism *per se* which bears the brunt of Ratzinger's criticism. He suggests that Bultmann's repudiation of the sacramental principle was born largely out of this 'naïve conception of human beings' mental autonomy'.[22] However, Idealism – and more particularly Fichte – ought not to be viewed as the total explanation for this cultural wrong turn. Christian metaphysics itself has suffered an 'excessive dose of Greek idealism' and was already well on the way to perceiving the human soul as 'substantially atomised'. This anthropological misapprehension is said to ultimately raise questions about the sacramental vision of reality that are unanswerable given the false presuppositions already in place. Ratzinger comments,

> And then one can indeed really ask oneself why God, as mind, does not choose an easier way to encounter the mind of man, and to accord him his mercy or grace. If it were only the solitary soul, as individual, being addressed by its God and receiving mercy, then indeed it would be impossible to see what, in this highly intimate, totally internal and spiritual process, the intervention of the Church and the material media of the sacraments could actually mean.[23]

Of course, it is Ratzinger's contention that this anthropology is false to the nature of reality and that we must envisage the human encounter with God in

---

[19] Cyril of Alexandria, *In* Joannen, 11, 11 (Patrologia Graeca 59, 260) cited in de Lubac, *Catholicism*, p. 91.
[20] Volf, *After Our Likeness*, p. 30.
[21] Joseph Ratzinger, *Die sakramentale Begründgung christlicher Existenz* (Meitingen: Kyrios-Verlag, 1966).
[22] 'The Sacramental Nature of Existence' in Lieven Boeve and Gerard Mannion (eds), *The Ratzinger Reader: Mapping a Theological Journey* (London: T&T Clark, 2010), p. 76.
[23] Boeve and Mannion (eds), *The Ratzinger Reader*, pp. 76-77.

terms that reflect the true state of things. For this reason he sets down in cursory form the essential argument in favour of sacramental and ecclesial salvation. It should be noted in passing that what he contrasts it with is a profoundly Idealist view of reality which many evangelicals would take issue with themselves.[24] However, set in contrast to this extreme form of individualism, the Catholic worldview as articulated by Ratzinger is persuasive, at least in general terms. He states,

> If, however, there is no such thing as the autonomy of the human mind, if it is not a relationshipless mental atom [*Geistatom*], but rather, as a human being, lives only in an incarnated and historical way, with other human beings, then the question poses itself in a fundamentally different way. Then, his relationship to God, if it should be a human relationship to God, must be just as the human being is: incarnate, historical, with other human beings. Otherwise there is no relationship. The error of the anti-sacramental [*sakramentsfeindlichen*: literally sacrament-hostile] idealism is that it wants to make man a pure mind before God. Instead of a human being, only a phantom remains here, a phantom that does not exist, and a religiosity that would build on such foundations, builds on treacherous sand.[25]

The ultimate source of Ratzinger's ecclesiology is Augustinian Trinitarian theology and a particular understanding of personhood. However, in advance of being introduced to that key facet of Ratzinger's thought it may be helpful to trace the steps which allow him to locate the church as the essential element in an individual's reception of faith. Volf's synopsis of an early section from *Principles of Catholic Theology* offers a useful orientation to Ratzinger's Trinitarian-inspired ecclesiology:

> The God in whom one believes is the triune God, and thus not a self-enclosed unity, but rather a community of the three divine persons. Believing in this God – surrendering one's existence to this God – necessarily means entering into the divine community. Because the triune God is not a private deity, one cannot create a private fellowship with this God. Fellowship with the triune God *is* therefore at once also fellowship with all other human beings who in faith have surrendered their existence to the same God. Trinitarian faith accordingly means community.[26]

Writing in another context, Ratzinger confirms that Christology naturally carries with it the same soteriological implications as the doctrine of the

---

[24] Mirosalv Volf is a prime example of an evangelical in search of a more communal view of faith. See further his ' "The Trinity is our Social Program": The Doctrine of the Trinity and the Shape of Social Engagement.' *Modern Theology* Volume 14, Issue 3, pp. 403-423, July 1998.
[25] Boeve and Mannion (eds), *The Ratzinger Reader*, p. 77.
[26] Volf, *After Our Likeness*, p. 33, summarizing Ratzinger's discussion in *Theologische Prinzipienlehre: Bausteine zur Fundamentaltheologie* (Munich: Erich Wewel, 1982), pp. 22-23.

Trinity.[27] One cannot build a private relationship with Christ any more than one can build a private relationship with the Triune God. Christ is not 'a solitary, self-enclosed individual' (Volf) but a corporate personality who embodies the entire church. As an outcome of this, relationship with Christ will involve a *necessary* relation with the Church. The logic of this position is set out in his discussion of Christ as 'the Last Man' in the Christology section of *Introduction to Christianity*. The designation 'Man' or 'Adam' is understood as indicating one 'who [has] overstep[ped] the bounds of humanity' by functioning at a new and transcendent level. This new way of being is characterized by a movement away from the self and a being taken up by 'the other'.[28] Ratzinger writes, 'For man is the more himself the more he is with 'the other'. He only comes *to* himself by moving away *from* himself. Only through 'the other' and through 'being' with 'the other' does he come to himself.'

This 'other' is not a universal construct in *Introduction to Christianity* but rather the God with whom Jesus is in relationship. Whilst little hermeneutical or theological justification is offered for the view that Jesus transcended the perceived boundaries of individuality, Ratzinger's unfolding of this notion anticipates much of what he has to say about the Trinitarian life. He states,

> Man is finally intended for *the* other, the truly other, for God; he is all the more himself the more he is with the *quite* other, with God. Accordingly, he is completely himself when he has ceased to stand in himself, to shut himself off in himself and to assert himself, when in fact he is pure openness to God.[29]

The 'overstepping of the boundaries' in the case of Jesus implies 'the abolition of yet another frontier' with regard to humanity. Here we are confronted with the very crux of Ratzinger's proposal. If Jesus is truly the exemplary human, this extension of his being beyond the confines of individuality must have implications for the rest of humanity and, indeed, for Jesus' own relationship to humanity. According to Ratzinger,

> His existence concerns all mankind. The New Testament makes this perceptible by calling him an "Adam"; in the Bible this word expresses the unity of the whole creature 'man', so that one can speak of the biblical idea of a "corporate personality." So if Jesus is called 'Adam' this implies that he is intended to gather the whole creature "Adam" in himself. But this

---

[27] Ratzinger, *Introduction to Christianity*, pp. 175 ff.
[28] Interestingly, Moltmann traces this understanding of personhood as a movement towards 'the other' to the thought of Hegel. '[According to Hegel] [i]t is the nature of the person to give himself entirely to the counterpart, and to find himself in the other most of all. The person only comes to himself by expressing and expending himself in others.' G.W.F. Hegel, *Philosophie der Religion*, PhB 63, 61 and pp. 71ff. in Jürgen Moltmann, *The Trinity and the Kingdom of God* (London: SCM Press, 1981), p. 174.
[29] Ratzinger, *Introduction to Christianity*, p. 175.

means that the reality which Paul calls, in a way that is largely incomprehensible to us today, the "body of Christ" is an intrinsic postulate of this existence, which cannot remain an exception but must "draw to itself" the whole of mankind (cf. John 12:32)[30]

Although the case is more speculative and philosophical than exegetical (see later critique), Ratzinger does anchor his position in a small number of Pauline texts which he utilizes to make extensive claims about the nature of the church. Thus when Paul describes the Christian life as one in which, 'it is no longer I who live, but Christ who lives in me,' his intention is said to be to show that the believer has ceased to function as a 'self-contained subject' but has been 'inserted into a new subject.' [31] The specific ramifications of this transference come to light in Ratzinger's exegesis of Galatians 3:28. To give a fuller sense of Ratzinger's argument, we shall return to the discussion in *Introduction to Christianity* at the juncture where Ratzinger claims that the theology of Teilhard de Chardin, although limited by its excessively biological focus, has helped unveil Paul's Christological intentions.

> One can safely say that here the tendency of Pauline Christology is in essentials correctly grasped from the modern angle and rendered comprehensible again, even if the vocabulary employed is certainly rather too biological. Faith sees in Jesus the man in whom – on the biological plane – the next evolutionary leap, as it were, has been accomplished; the man in whom the breakthrough out of the limited scope of humanity, out of its monadic enclosure, has occurred; the man in whom personalization and socialization no longer exclude each other but support each other; the man in whom perfect unity – "The body of Christ", says Paul, and even more pointedly "You are all one in Christ Jesus" (Gal. 3:28) – and perfect individuality are one; the man in whom humanity comes into contact with its future and in the highest extent itself becomes its future, because through him it makes contact with God himself, shares in him and thus realizes its most intrinsic possibility. From here onwards faith in Christ will see the beginning of a movement in which dismembered humanity is gathered together more and more into the being of the one single Adam, one single body – the man to come. It will see in him the movement to that future of man when he is completely "socialized", incorporated in one single being, but in such a way that the separate individual is not extinguished but brought completely to himself.[32]

Ratzinger's premise here is that Paul's notion of 'oneness in Christ' implies that Christ and the members of the church now share one being and become together 'a single, united subject.'[33] However, before enquiring into the

---

[30] Ratzinger, *Introduction to Christianity*, p. 176.
[31] Joseph Ratzinger, 'Theologie und Kirche.' *Internationale Katholische Zeitschrift 'Communio'* 15 (1986), p. 519 cited in Volf, *After Our Likeness*, p. 33.
[32] Ratzinger, *Introduction to Christianity*, pp. 178-179.
[33] Volf's succinct summary of Ratzinger's stance. Volf, *After Our Likeness*, p. 34.

soteriological implications of the church's shared subjectivity with Christ we must consider his doctrine of the Trinity which arguably underpins all aspects of his theology.[34]

In *Church, Ecumenism and Politics* we are afforded a glimpse into what is his ultimate conviction about the nature of the Triune God. Put at its starkest, it is that God is not fundamentally an 'I' but a 'We', and this, as we shall see, has significant consequences:

> [T]he deepest reason for Christianity having this "we" character is shown to be the fact that God himself is a we: the God confessed by the Christian creed is not thought thinking itself in solitude, is not an absolute and indivisible ego shut in on itself, but unity in the Trinitarian relationship of I-you-we, so that being we as the fundamental form of God precedes all earthly forms of this relationship and being made in the image of God is from the start referred to this kind of being we.[35]

What constitutes the core difference in God being 'we' as opposed to 'I'? What might this say about the nature of his person and how does this understanding of personhood filter down into Ratzinger's understanding of the church and the manner in which salvation is appropriated? It is at this point that his theology becomes considerably more abstract. At the danger of over-simplification, it would seem that Ratzinger's view of divine personhood is essentially that of 'pure relationality.' This view appears in stark form in *Introduction to Christianity* where he asserts boldly that, 'Person is the pure relation of being related, nothing else. Relationship is not something added to the person, as it is with us; it only exists at all as relatedness.'[36] This concept is given increased clarity when it is related concretely to the *person* of the Father. He states,

> Expressed in the imagery of Christian tradition, this means that the First Person does not beget the Son in the sense of the act of begetting coming on top of the finished Person; it *is* the act of begetting, of giving oneself, of streaming forth. It is identical with the act of giving. Only as this act is it person, and therefore it is not the giver but the act of giving...[37]

In a theological move reflective of what he has already done in his treatment of Jesus as the Last Adam, Ratzinger asserts that the concept of personhood revealed in the Trinity is the model for how human personhood will ultimately be expressed. So although this form of existence has not already been attained among human beings (i.e. a state of pure relations), it is the goal towards which

---

[34] According to Volf, *After Our Likeness*, p. 67, '[A]ll the crucial elements in his ecclesiology and entire theology are rooted in the doctrine of the Trinity.'
[35] Joseph Ratzinger, *Church, Ecumenism and Politics ,Church, Ecumenism & Politics: New Essays in Ecclesiology* (Slough: St Paul Publications, 1988), p. 31.
[36] Ratzinger, *Introduction to Christianity*, p. 131.
[37] Ratzinger, *Introduction to Christianity*, p. 132.

the members of the church are moving and one that will be accomplished at the Eschaton.[38] Indeed, God's engagement with the church in the redemptive process reflects this Trinitarian reality and determines the manner in which salvation is communicated. Thus Christ always acts in concert with his 'body' the church with whom he shares the same subjectivity. His salvific activity is therefore not enacted in splendid isolation but in communion with the church. Moreover, a context of self-enclosed individualism (of the lonely path to God variety) is not the proper setting for the reception of faith. Because existence is essentially communion this has implications for the impartation of faith. It is partly on this basis that Ratzinger is able to make the sort of claims that he does in the conclusion to his homily on the sacraments.[39] Put at its starkest, he is suggesting that our own activity as limited individuals, functioning within the constraints of an *individualist* mindset, cannot be the full measure of our conversion to Christ. Faith itself is a gift and this is received by means of the church which shares in Christ's subjectivity.

Expressed in these terms, Ratzinger's ecclesiology poses a significant challenge to some evangelical conceptions of conversion and faith. I shall explore this crucial issue in the penultimate section of the chapter, but in the interim we must engage Ratzinger's ecclesiology in more general terms and ask whether this close association between Christ and the Church, argued for in a manner that is original to him, is in any way persuasive to evangelicals. However, given that his anthropological and ecclesiological application of the pure relations ontology is idiosyncratic, and would not necessarily garner even the support of other Catholic theologians[40], I have chosen to examine this idea only within the wider context of his more standard Catholic proposal that Christ and the Church share a single subjectivity.

An Evangelical Critique of Ratzinger's Ecclesiology
Christ as One Single Subject with the Church

As stated above, Ratzinger's ecclesiologically-orientated Christology is but one variation of a widely held Roman Catholic view which identifies Christ with the church.[41] De Chirico in a study of evangelical perspectives on Catholicism argues persuasively that the 'Christologically-based self-understanding' of the Church is one of the two determining factors giving shape to the whole Catholic system.[42][43] A major stimulus for such an elevated perception of the

---

[38] Joseph Ratzinger, *Dogma and Preaching* (Chicago: Francisco Herald, 1984), pp. 213, 221 cited in Volf, *After Our Likeness*, p. 69.
[39] In a later discussion we shall see how Ratzinger's views on the catechumenate shed light on the apparent anomalies in the sermon.
[40] For a Catholic alternative to Ratzinger's *pure relations* ontology see Walter Kasper, *The God of Jesus Christ* (London: SCM Press, 1983), p. 284.
[41] It is acknowledged that this identity is not undifferentiated and that the Church does not function as an equal partner in this relationship.
[42] De Chirico, *Evangelical Theological Perspectives*, p. 14.

church is unquestionably Paul's depiction of the church as the body of Christ. This idea not only gave rise to the patristic notion of the *totus Christus* which later influenced de Lubac and Ratzinger, but functioned at various times as a catalyst for renewed confidence in the Church's pre-eminent place in the economy of salvation. A striking example of the latter was the role of nineteenth century Tübingen theologian, Johann Adam Möhler, whose portrayal of the church as the continuation of the Incarnation had a profound impact on Catholic theology. Möhler writes,

> The visible church ... is the Son of God himself, everlastingly manifesting himself among men in a human form, perpetually renovated, and eternally young – the permanent incarnation of the same, as in Holy Writ, even the faithful are called the body of Christ.[44]

Indeed, above and beyond its impact on the work of individual theologians, the image of the Church as the Body of Christ has both informed magisterial teaching (the 1943 encyclical *Mystici corporis Christi*) and been the spur for Communio ecclesiology, a now ecumenically rooted view of the church which conceives Christ's union with the church in strongly realistic terms.[45] Given this latter background, Ratzinger's unique ecclesiology must be seen in the light of a much larger theological movement which shares with him certain core presuppositions.[46] This will mean that the critique will at points extend to a consideration of Commmunio ecclesiology in general rather than being entirely restricted to Ratzinger. As is the case with all of the analysis thus far, I will be employing evangelical theological method and seeking to find out how commensurate Ratzinger's ecclesiology is with some of the core convictions of Evangelicalism. Particular attention will be given to ascertaining whether the theological assumptions undergirding Communio ecclesiology can be accommodated to the evangelical understanding of God and Scripture.

---

[43] The other is the nature-grace relationship which is also deemed by de Chirico as being at odds with classical evangelicalism, (*Evangelical Theological Perspectives* pp. 237-38).

[44] Johann Adam Möhler, *Symbolism or Exposition of the Doctrinal Differences between Catholics and Protestants as Evidenced by their Symbolical Writings*' (London: Gibbings and Co., 1906), p. 259 cited in De Chirico, *Evangelical Theological Perspectives*, p. 253.

[45] See Robert W. Jenson, *Systematic Theology* Volumes 1 and 2. (New York: Oxford University Press, 1997 and 1999) as an example of this outlook within Lutheranism.

[46] For a recent discussion of Ratzinger's place in the wider *Communio* school see Francesca Aran Murphy, 'De Lubac, Ratzinger and von Balthasar: A Communal Adventure in Ecclesiology' in Francesca Aran Murphy and Christopher Asprey (eds), *Ecumenism Today: The Universal Church in the 21st Century* (Aldershot: Ashgate Publishing Company, 2008), pp. 45-80.

Christ as a Corporate Personality in Scripture

While Ratzinger and Communio theologians are highly invested in the notion of Christ as a corporate Personality, it would seem that no consensus obtains amongst New Testament scholars as to whether or not this concept is a fitting category by which to conceptualize believers' union with Christ. All would agree that being 'in Christ' is a hugely significant idea for Paul, emerging as it does about 216 times in his writings[47], but there is dispute over whether we can say very much about the mechanics of this relationship.[48] John Ziesler, a major authority on Paul, has cast doubt on whether corporate personality is a viable explanation for believers' relationship to Christ and sought to explicate Paul's language in non-realist terms.[49] He suggests that the two most prevalent theories seeking to account for Paul's use of the concept have run aground and that we must seek an alternative explanation. The notion that Paul unconsciously exploited the Gnostic Redeemer myth[50] to explain Christ being made complete by the incorporation of believers into himself is dismissed on two counts. First, Paul opposed incipient Gnosticism in some of his writings (1 Corinthians and Colossians) and was therefore unlikely to advocate a variation of it. Second, his conception of the believer's life in heaven consists of that believer not being 'in' Christ but rather being 'with' Christ. This suggests to Ziesler that Christ remained distinct from believers no matter how closely he was related to them.[51]

The other main theory cited by Ziesler is the view that Paul employed the specifically Hebrew notion of 'corporate personality' to make sense of the church's relationship to Christ. Whilst acknowledging the importance of solidarity in the Jewish worldview, Ziesler suggests that there is now 'grave doubt' in scholarly circles over whether such a notion existed in the strong form that we have understood it. His conclusion is that it is extremely uncertain 'whether there ever was a Hebrew idea of corporate personality which could

---

[47] Michael Parsons, 'In Christ' in Paul, *Vox Evangelica Volume XVIII* 1988, p. 25.

[48] C.K. Barrett suggests that our agnosticism on this question arises from Paul's failure to elucidate how exactly he conceived the union between Christ and believers. C.K. Barrett, 'New Testament Eschatology, *Scottish Journal of Theology* (1953) 149 cited in Parsons, 'In Christ', in Paul', p. 25.

[49] John Ziesler, *Pauline Christianity (Revised Edition)* (Oxford University Press: New York, 1990).

[50] Ziesler, *Pauline Christianity*, p. 61, suggests that the Redeemer Myth was related to Pauline thought in the following fashion: Paul is thought to have 'consciously or unconsciously exploit[ed] the idea that the Redeemer is incomplete without the redeemed, that the fragments of divinity imprisoned within human beings since a pre-cosmic fall are needed for the original wholeness to be restored. When the elect know their true nature and turn to the Redeemer, they enter him and in a quite literal sense are *in* him, or at least will be when restoration is complete. Sometimes they are specifically in his *body*.'

[51] Ziesler, *Pauline Christianity*, p. 61.

account for Paul's language.'[52] Ziesler's alternative explanation is to understand Christ as a centre of divine power in Paul's thought, the power of the Spirit, and to view Christ's ministry in the Spirit as the means by which the Body is 'empowered, controlled and defined...'[53] Thus he merges Christology with Pneumatology in order to account for Christ's ubiquitous ministry in the lives and hearts of believers.[54]

Ziesler is not an evangelical and his viewpoint is something of a minority report in terms of Evangelicalism. Indeed, De Chirico characterizes the evangelical reading of Paul's language about the body of Christ as being as realist as the Roman Catholic[55] and Watson goes further by suggesting that Paul's wording 'seems to get very near' the Catholic teaching 'at times,'[56] though always stopping short. Writing in the Hodder *I Believe* series, he articulates an evangelical realist view of the body of Christ which takes seriously the church's agency in the mediation of salvation. According to Watson,

> Paul clearly has in mind something more than the sum of believers in one place [when he refers to the body of Christ]. Had this been his intention he would probably have referred to the body of Christians; but in fact he specifically writes about the body of Christ. It seems clear to me that he is speaking of an *organic unity*, in which Christians not only belong to Christ and to one another within his body; they also abide in him and find life in him. Without Christ, and for that matter without his body, there is no true salvation. This needs once again to be thoroughly grasped by Christians in an age when many see the church as little more than a club...[57]

Given this contrast in outlooks, it is intriguing to note that when scepticism about the notion of corporate personality[58] would arguably sound the death knell for Ratzinger's ecclesiology[59], it is evangelicals who are often that notion's

---

[52] Ziesler, *Pauline Christianity*, pp. 62-63.
[53] Ziesler, *Pauline Christianity*, p. 65.
[54] Whilst the non-realist perspective on corporate personality has been challenged in more recent publications such as J. Louis Martyn, 'Epilogue: An Essay in Pauline Meta-Ethics' in John M.G. Barclay and Simon J. Gathercole (eds), *Divine and Human Agency in Paul and His Cultural Environment* (London: T&T Clark, 2006), pp. 180ff and Daniel G. Powers, *Salvation through Participation: An Examination of the Notion of the Believers' Corporate Unity With Christ in Early Christian Soteriology* (Leuven: VA Peeters, 2001), Ziesler's earlier work still stands as one of the best articulations of the opposing view.
[55] De Chirico, *Evangelical Theological Perspectives*, p. 278.
[56] David Watson, *I Believe in the Church* (London: Hodder & Stoughton, 1977), p. 97.
[57] David Watson, *I Believe in the Church*, pp. 96-97.
[58] A view which is at least current among some leading academics, as demonstrated by Ziesler.
[59] Ratzinger's ecclesiological project would collapse with the demise of the notion of corporate personality as it depends on Christ functioning precisely in that role. See his

chief defenders. We shall now explore the implications of Ratzinger's own realist understanding of the body of Christ and attempt to gauge how evangelicals fare with the notion that Christ and the church constitute a single united subject. Key to these deliberations will be a brief consideration of Ratzinger's *pure relations* ontology which is the cornerstone of his whole ecclesiological project.

In the overview of Ratzinger's ecclesiology (see pp. 144-152), I summarised the argument advanced by him in favour of the church as a single, united subject with Christ. Examining that case now from a critical perspective, I would concur with Volf's judgment that the proposal lacks theological and exegetical grounding.[60] What is ultimately affirmed about Christ's union with the church builds upon Ratzinger's exegetical defence of the 'pure relations' ontology.[61] Without this view of Christ and humanity already in place, he would have struggled to make the additional theological moves required to assert the church's shared subjectivity with Christ. Yet here is the rub. The case for a 'pure relations' ontology derived from the life and ministry of Jesus is relatively weak. Indeed, there is extensive biblical evidence confirming that the Persons of the Trinity stand in relation to one another rather than subsist as pure relations.[62] This failure to sustain the claim that Jesus' life was one of 'pure relationality' must therefore prejudice the subsequent claim made for the church that it was drawn into the same mode of being.[63] Indeed, is the dominical phrase once cited by Ratzinger to justify this anthropology, 'Apart

---

comments in Joseph Cardinal Ratzinger, *Called to Communion: Understanding the Church Today* (San Francisco: Ignatius Press, 1996), p. 36.

[60] Volf, *After Our Likeness*, p. 34.

[61] As a scripturally orientated theologian, Ratzinger seeks to demonstrate that a notion about personhood coming to fruition in Augustine was anticipated in the Christological discourses in John's Gospel as well as by Paul in his Christological hymn in Philippians 2:5-11. See *Dogma and Preaching: Applying Christian Doctrine to Daily Life* (San Francisco: Ignatius Press, 2011), pp. 187ff. and *Introduction to Christianity*, pp. 163ff for an outline of his argument.

[62] For a detailed summary of the evidence see J. Scott Horrell, 'Toward a Biblical Model of the Social Trinity: Avoiding Equivocation of Nature and Order, *Journal of the Evangelical Theological Society* 47/3 (September 2004), pp. 399-421.

[63] Ratzinger's attempt to anchor a *pure relations* ontology within the Gospel accounts of Jesus' union with the Father ultimately fails on two counts. First, while the New Testament indicators of the Trinity presuppose a form of mutuality and inter-dependency between the Persons that transcends human relationships, it is also the case that these same texts present each of the Persons as functioning individually as 'intelligent, purposive centres of consciousness' (Leonard Hodgson, *The Doctrine of the Trinity* (London: James Nisbet, 1943), p. 229. More significantly, Ratzinger has been unable to evade the dialogical nature of the intra-Trinitarian relationship as it unfolds in Scripture, and devotes space in both *Introduction to Christianity* and *Dogma and Preaching* to explicate its importance. However, as Volf has noted, this admission involves him in a fundamental contradiction (see Volf, *After Our Likeness*, p.69). Is it not the case that the phenomenon of dialogue demands persons standing in relation to one another?

from me you can do nothing', not more naturally interpreted in a way which does not allude to or bolster the notion of pure relationality?

The next stage of Ratzinger's argument – the claim that Christ's movement beyond the boundaries of individuality established him as a collective Subject - is similarly difficult to sustain intellectually or exegetically. Volf characterizes it as a theological move lacking both substance and coherence.

> Even the notion of a collective subject, a notion underlying all of Ratzinger's soteriological and ecclesiological thinking, is simply postulated. With great leaps, Ratzinger draws a line from the Hebrew notion of Adam to the Greek idea that 'the human existence of all human beings is ... one (Kirche in die Welt 350) and then tries to express both ideas in the categories of modern personalism. He notes that the modern concept of subject is gradually loosening today, revealing 'that no securely-enclosed self really exists at all, but rather that many different kinds of forces go in and out of us.' (Gemeinschaft, 33) Although this reference certainly prompts us to reconsider the relationship between person and community, it does not suffice to render plausible the idea of a comprehensive personality or a (divine-human) 'super-I', as Ratzinger formulates this elsewhere.[64]

The exegetical case is no less troublesome in that Ratzinger's unfolding argument depends on the accuracy of his interpretation of particular texts. When he cites John 12:32, 'And I, when I am lifted up from the earth, will draw all men to myself', the presupposition is that Jesus has stepped outside humanity's monadic enclosure and summoned others to join with him in a new collective Subject:

> The event of the crucifixion appears there (i.e. John 12:32) as a process of opening, in which the scattered man-monads are drawn into the embrace of Jesus Christ, into the wide span of his outstretched arms, in order to arrive in this union, at their goal, the goal of humanity.[65]

However, the fact remains that this passage can be interpreted in a way which bears no relation to the anthropology that he is promoting.[66] Even if it was acknowledged that being drawn to Christ has the outcome of the individual being incorporated into the mystical unity of the body of Christ, this would not automatically entail a single subjectivity with Christ. To use texts such as John 12:32 in such a manner is special pleading on Ratzinger's part. Indeed, the very

---

[64] Volf, *After Our Likeness*, p. 38.
[65] Ratzinger, *Introduction to Christianity*, p. 179.
[66] See Colin G. Kruse, *Tyndale New Testament Commentary on John* (Leicester: IVP, 2003), p. 272 where those being 'drawn to Jesus' are 'drawn to put their faith in him' as opposed to incorporation into a single unified Subject. For similar conclusions see Raymond E. Brown, *The Gospel According to John I-XII (The Anchor Bible)* (London: Geoffrey Chapman, 1966), p. 277 and Rudolf Schnackenburg, *The Gospel According to John*, Volume 2. Chapters 5-12 (New York: Crossroad, 1982), pp. 392-393.

few other texts alluded to in order to demonstrate the subjective unity of Christ with the church fail to convince unless one approaches them with certain ecclesiological presuppositions already in place.

Ratzinger's use of Galatians 2:20, 'it is no longer I who live, but Christ who lives in me' to demonstrate that 'the self of the believer ceases to be a self-contained subject' but has been 'inserted into a new subject'[67] is a case in point. One might counter that Paul's language could more easily refer to a still self-contained subject having Christ dwell in *him*, rather than refer to the believer being taken out of himself in order to dwell as part of a corporate Christ.[68] This failure at the level of exegesis impacts on any evangelical assessment of Ratzinger. His claim that the church (in union with Christ) confers faith on the individual must be weakened when the evidence he supplies for the two sharing the same subjectivity is unpersuasive.

The situation remains unchanged when Ratzinger's notion of the church's union with Christ is considered from a strictly dogmatic perspective. Evangelical theological method will demand that firm lines of demarcation be drawn between Christ or the Trinity, and the community of redeemed creatures who make up the *ekklesia*. Thus while Christ and the church may be in the most intimate relationship with one another, this relationship is deemed to be asymmetrical.[69] God and the church converge not as equals but as entities divided profoundly at the level of being. However, the legitimacy of this distinction is what evangelicals perceive as being undermined by an approach to ecclesiology which Webster has characterized as ecclesiological hypertrophy.[70]

One avenue to understanding why there is such a divergence dogmatically between an evangelical creaturely ecclesiology (if I may use that terminology) and the one favoured by Ratzinger and Catholicism is their respective hermeneutical approaches to the Ascension.[71] De Chirico observes that Catholic ecclesiology has assumed that there exists a fundamental, if not undifferentiated continuity 'between the incarnation of the Son of God and the extension of that incarnation in the life of the church.'[72] De Lubac gives voice to this ecclesiological self-perception when he states of the church, 'If Christ is the sacrament of God, the church is for us the sacrament of Christ; she

---

[67] Joseph Ratzinger, *Theologie*, p. 519 cited in Volf, *After Our Likeness*, p. 33.
[68] For commentaries that reflect this perspective see J. Louis Martyn, *Galatians (The Anchor Bible Commentary)* (New York: Doubleday, 1997), p. 258 and Raymond K. Fung, *The Epistle to the Galatians (NICNT)* (Grand Rapids: Eerdmans, 1988), p. 124.
[69] See Christoph Schöbel, 'The Creature of the Word: Recovering the Ecclesiology of the Reformation,' in Colin E. Gunton and David W. Hardy (Editors), *On Being the Church: Essays on the Christian Community* (Edinburgh: T & T Clark, 1989), p. 120 cited in Webster, 'The Perfection of God', p. 78.
[70] Hypertrophy: A term meaning 'excessive growth beyond its appropriate dimension.' The reference is made to Communio ecclesiology, in general, but would also apply specifically to Ratzinger. Webster, 'The Perfection of God', p. 78.
[71] I am indebted to the discussion in De Chirico at this point.
[72] De Chirico, *Evangelical Theological Perspectives*, p. 275.

represents him ... She really makes him present.'[73] Evangelicalism, approaching the Ascension from a markedly different perspective, has opted for what might be termed a hermeneutic of discontinuity.[74] De Chirico characterizes that outlook in the following terms:

> The Evangelical system tends to view the ascension in more abrupt, radical ways in that it conceives it as the coming to an end of the earthly ministry of Jesus which cannot be extended or prolonged in any form because of its uniqueness within the economy of salvation and its once for all soteriological significance.[75]

At root the difference between the two perspectives seems to lie in their assessment of the Incarnation and its theological ramifications. Whereas Catholicism has invested the biblical metaphor of the body of Christ with optimum meaning in order to secure an identification between Christ and the Church[76], Evangelicalism has turned to other sources in order to understand the relationship between the two. Although there is no single argument advanced by evangelicals to account for their ecclesiology in light of the challenge mounted by the Communio approach, it may be helpful to draw upon a work produced recently by one of Evangelicalism's most respected academic theologians. Its great advantage is that it exhibits a profound acquaintance with Communio ecclesiology and is not written out of that historical evangelical proclivity towards caricature, particularly when the subject matter is the Roman Catholic church.[77]

Webster and Communio Ecclesiology

John Webster, writing for a symposium on ecclesiology at iconic Wheaton College, goes back to what we might term theological first principles in order to define Christ's relation to the church. His starting point is the doctrine of the perfection of God. This idea is conceived primarily in terms of God's

---

[73] De Lubac, *Catholicism*, p. 29.
[74] This outlook is exemplified in the later theology of Karl Barth who asserts that though the world 'would be lost without Jesus Christ and his saving work', it 'would not necessarily be lost if there were no church.' (CD/IV/3.2, p.826 cited in Ian A. McFarland, 'The Body of Christ: Rethinking a Classic Ecclesiology Model' in *International Journal of Systematic Theology* Volume 7 Number 4 (October 2005)
[75] De Chirico, *Evangelical Theological Perspectives*, p. 276.
[76] De Chirico, *Evangelical Theological Perspectives* p. 276. 'The core of the metaphor [in Catholicism] refers to the indissoluble, organic bond between head (i.e. Christ) and members (i.e. the church) within the unity of a single body so that what can be ascribed to the head can also be attributed in some measure to the members.'
[77] A classically biased evangelical study of Catholicism is Loraine Boettner's widely read *Roman Catholicism* (New Jersey: Presbyterian and Reformed,1962) cf. Karl Keating, *Catholicism and Fundamentalism: The Attack on 'Romanism by Bible Christians* (San Francisco: Ignatius Press, 1988), pp. 27-50.

metaphysical greatness which includes but extends beyond his 'maximal moral goodness.'[78] God's perfection is in fact the utter repleteness of his being. Within his Trinitarian life and activity he is fully realized and finds no lack or imperfection.[79] It is from this blessed state, and as an exercise of his sovereign freedom, that God chooses to bring the created order into existence. Such an eventuality causes Webster to raise a question which alerts us to the direction of his whole argument. 'How are we to conceive the relation between God's perfection and the creaturely realm?'[80] Is his perfection to be defined in *inclusive* as opposed to *exclusive* terms? Webster takes the former to indicate that the perfection of God's being 'includes as an integral element of itself some reality other than God.'[81] The other possibility, that God's perfection should be understood in *exclusive* terms, is taken to intimate that God stands in a different relationship to his creatures. That is, while sharing close fellowship with them he remains sovereignly free and distinct. The issue set out in these terms has an obvious implication for ecclesiology. '[I]s the church, as the assembly of creatures in relation to God, intrinsic to God's perfection, or externally related to God's perfect being and work? Does God's perfect being include the being of the church?'[82]

Webster ultimately takes the view that an exclusive definition of God's perfection is needed as 'the theologies of creation and reconciliation alike require us to conceive of the relation of God and creatures as a relation-in-distinction ...'[83]

Such a resolution to the question has particular ramifications for Christology and ecclesiology. Webster asks whether the notion of the church sharing an ontological unity with Christ 'can be co-ordinated with the perfection of God?'[84] His judgment is that such a view would entail a misunderstanding of the Incarnation. This was a wholly unique action on the part of the Son whereby he united himself not to human nature in general, but to one person in particular.[85] In what could well be taken as a riposte to Ratzinger's claim that Christ is a collective Subject encompassing the whole of humanity, Webster re-casts the Incarnation as a crucicentric event in which Christ's union with human beings functions at an altogether different level:

> He assumes our humanity; but he does not do this by absorbing it into his own and so enabling us to partake of his union with the Father. Rather, he assumes our humanity by freely taking our place, being and acting in our

---

[78] Webster, 'The Perfection of God', p. 79.
[79] Webster, 'The Perfection of God', p. 79.
[80] Webster, 'The Perfection of God', p. 79.
[81] Webster, 'The Perfection of God', p. 79.
[82] Webster, 'The Perfection of God', p. 79.
[83] Webster, 'The Perfection of God', p. 87.
[84] Webster, 'The Perfection of God', p. 93.
[85] Webster, 'The Perfection of God', p. 93.

stead. His humanity only gathers all others into itself as substitute; it includes all in itself only as it excludes them.[86]

Returning to the same theological first principle as animates the rest of his account, Webster interprets Christ's death, resurrection and ascension as enactments of his divine perfection marking the absolute distinction between Christ and the church. His closing comments amount not only to a succinct summary of his position but a specific rejection of the ecclesiology of de Lubac which has played so signal a role in the development of Ratzinger's own unique view of the church. Webster writes,

> All this, then, amounts to a cumulative suggestion that the notion of the *totus Christus* – of Christ's completeness as inclusive of the church as his body – will be impermissible if it elides the distinction between Christ and the objects of his mercy: impermissible on the grounds of the doctrines of incarnation, salvation and the exaltation of Christ. Christ, says Lubac, bears "... all men within himself.... For the Word did not merely take on a human body; his Incarnation was not a simple *corporatio* but ... a *concorporatio*."
> At this point, a responsible Evangelical ecclesiology must beg to differ: any attempted synthesis of Christology and ecclesiology must be broken by "the all-shattering truth of *unus solus creator*."[87]

Whilst some evangelicals might want to find a via media between Webster's conception of the church's relationship to Christ and a full-blown incarnational view of the church[88], there is little doubt that all will affirm Christ's superiority to the church and his capacity to act independently of its ministry. He does not conjoin himself to the church in such a fashion that he is determined by the church's structures and ministrations. Perhaps Ratzinger's great lesson, though, is that we are relational creatures and though capable of independent activity find relationship with God via the ministry of those around us. Salvation is ecclesially mediated if not ecclesially determined.

Baptism, Conversion and Faith in Ratzinger

In the chapter thus far I have sought to identify ecumenical obstacles to rapprochement with Evangelicalism within Joseph Ratzinger's ecclesiology. An interesting discovery from the standpoint of the publication as a whole is that his Augustinian theology plays as great a part in closing doors of ecumenical opportunity as opening them. The previous discussion has illustrated that it was two Augustinian notions in particular, *pure relations* and the *totus Christus*, which gave the bedrock to a theology which evangelicals,

---

[86] Webster, 'The Perfection of God', p. 94.
[87] Webster, 'The Perfection of God', p. 94.
[88] For example, the position articulated by David Watson which allowed for some kind of organic union with Christ whilst affirming his independence from and Lordship over the church.

with virtual unanimity, would find unacceptable. However, there is another issue yet to be addressed which for methodological reasons I have reserved for this penultimate section. This is the notion of faith or conversion as it emerges in Ratzinger's thought. I deem this to have significant ecumenical promise (in contrast with what has gone before) and wish to consider it separately from the other aspects of his ecclesiology/soteriology.

To set his thought in context we must re-visit the papal homily on the sacraments which was the catalyst for the exploration embarked upon in this closing chapter. In that address I had identified what amounted to a seeming contradiction in Ratzinger's thought in that regeneration was presented as involving both the activity of the believing subject and the sacramental ministrations of the church. It was left uncertain within the context of the homily how these two conflicting emphases were integrated in Ratzinger's thought. What I shall now argue is that a genuine tension does exist between a seeming unequivocal endorsement of the sacramental approach to soteriology and a surprising openness to emphases which would more comfortably sit with Evangelicalism. This 'tension' is alluded to by Ratzinger himself in a passage from *Principles of Catholic Theology* where he talks of the 'problem' involved in understanding the relationship between baptism, faith and membership in the church.[89]

> What is the problem here? In the New Testament, there is, as we know, a series of texts that establish a link between man's justification and faith: '... as we see it, a man is justified by faith and not by doing something the law tells him to do' (Rom. 3:28; cf. 5:1; Gal. 2:16; 3:8). But these texts are balanced by others, in the same Pauline epistles, that link man's justification to baptism: "When a man dies, of course, he has finished with sin" (Rom. 6:7; cf. Gal. 3:26-29).[90]

His conclusion is that these two apparently conflicting formulas possess in reality an inner unity.[91] This acknowledgment takes place, however, in a context where Ratzinger seems to place overwhelming emphasis on the church's participatory role in the individual's reception of faith. Thus for Ratzinger 'there is no such thing as a faith that is the decision of an isolated individual',

> acceptance into the believing community is part of faith itself, not just a subsequent juridical act' and 'justification through faith demands a faith that is ecclesial – and that means sacramental – a faith that is received and made one's own.[92]

---

[89] Ratzinger, *Principles of Catholic Theology*, p. 40.
[90] Ratzinger, *Principles of Catholic Theology*, p. 40.
[91] Ratzinger, *Principles of Catholic Theology*, p. 41.
[92] Ratzinger, *Principles of Catholic Theology*, p. 41.

Obstacles to Rapprochement

These statements may be read as an undoing of the admission just made that one element of the New Testament witness talks of justification being associated with the personal act of faith. However, I would maintain that other strands of Ratzinger's thought (i.e. ideas which succeed in shedding a somewhat different light on some of those statements cited above) indicate that there may be more common ground with evangelicals than one might surmise. For amid much adulatory language about the centrality of the church, Ratzinger makes three significant theological moves which the bulk of evangelicals would applaud: he affirms that an essential link should exist between sacramental baptism and the *existential act of faith*; he conceives of *metanoia* in such a way that should his ideas trespass beyond the confines of an academic textbook they would transform Catholic homiletical content; and (on occasion) he couches language about the church's role in the *giving* of faith in terms which would cause little offence to moderate evangelicals. Notwithstanding this, I consider these emphases as only part of Ratzinger's theological vision. His absolute concern to place the church at the heart of the soteriological enterprise blunts the force of some of the significant acknowledgments that he is willing to make. Yet it is in the ambivalences – in those aspects of Ratzinger's output which stir the hearts of evangelicals but seem oddly out of sync with a strongly sacramental ecclesiology – that the first inklings of an ecumenical way forward emerge.

Baptism

What is most notable about Ratzinger's approach to baptism is the strong link that he forges between the administration of the sacrament and the catechumenate.[93] The case for a binding relationship between the two is made so forcefully that Ratzinger ponders whether his readers might understand him to be questioning the validity of infant baptism itself.[94] Whilst that is clearly not his intention[95], the impression remains that he is less than sanguine about what has replaced the catechumenate in contemporary church practice. At the centre of his discussion of baptism is the question of the baptismal formula and its original function within the early church. He notes that a disparity exists between what the ceremony entailed for candidates in the earliest centuries and what its meaning is today. Whilst the baptismal formula had involved an existential act of commitment on the part of the catechumen, this 'I-Thou' relational aspect of the formula is now largely absent from current practice.[96]

---

[93] See the discussion in Ratzinger, *Principles of Catholic Theology*, pp. 34ff.
[94] Ratzinger, *Principles of Catholic Theology*, p. 41. 'The close connection we have discovered between baptism and the catechumenate cannot fail to raise the question of whether there is room in such a view for the baptism of infants.'
[95] See his defence of infant baptism in *Principles of Catholic Theology*, pp. 41-43, where he posits the possibility of the catechumenate functioning as easily as a post-baptismal process.
[96] Ratzinger, *Principles of Catholic Theology*, p. 34.

Ratzinger's vision for baptismal theology is a return to the roots of the sacrament and a re-embracing of insights which helped define its early practice. His proposal opens with an observation about how the earliest baptismal formulas differ from what came later on:

> [I]t will be rewarding first to enquire briefly into the historical context of the baptismal formula. In recent times, it has become no more than a formula recited over the one to be baptized by the priest who administers the sacrament. But this was not always the case. In the early church it had, even into the fourth or fifth century, the form of a dialogue ...[97]

This dialogue, of course, consisted of a series of questions that were addressed to the catechumen and resulted in a confession of faith on his or her part.[98] It is in such a highly personal setting that Ratzinger believes the sacrament finds its ultimate expression. Thus baptism may be viewed as profoundly sacramental and yet simultaneously the exercise of a deeply existential form of faith.

> It is clear from what has been said that the baptismal formula was, in its oldest form, a confession of faith. But the reverse is also true: the confession of faith was, in its oldest form, a part of the sacrament, a concrete expression of the act of conversion, of the new orientation of the catechumen's whole existence to the faith of the Church.[99]

Although Ratzinger does not question the practice of infant baptism in the Catholic church[100], his insistence on the necessary relationship between baptism and the catechumenate does cast doubt on contemporary Catholic practice. That this is the case is demonstrated most vividly by Ratzinger himself when addressing the negative effects of separating what are for him the two essential components of baptism. His words are worth citing in some detail as they also underscore his conviction that the catechumenate is not merely a preparation for baptism *but an essential element of the sacrament itself.*

> It is thus made clear that the administration of baptism points always to something beyond itself and requires the larger context of the catechumenate, which is itself part of the sacrament. This insight is of great importance. On the one hand, it reveals the catechumenate as it is generally understood, as part of the sacrament – not a preliminary course of instruction, but an integral part of the sacrament itself. On the other hand, the sacrament is not just a liturgical act but a process, a long road that demands the individual's whole strength, mind, will and heart. *Here, too, the separation has had disastrous consequences. It has led to the ritualization of*

---

[97] Ratzinger, *Principles of Catholic Theology*, p. 34.
[98] *Principles of Catholic Theology*, p. 34. Ratzinger draws on *The Apostolic Tradition* to illustrate both the dialogical nature of the baptismal formula as well as the common practice of post-catechumenate baptism.
[99] Ratzinger, *Principles of Catholic Theology*, p. 34.
[100] Ratzinger, *Principles of Catholic Theology*, pp. 41-43.

> *the sacrament and a doctrinalization of the word and, in doing so, has obscured a unity that is one of the central components of Christianity.*[101]

These comments illustrate that Ratzinger is deeply uneasy with what we might term a magical view of the sacraments.[102] Indeed, his emphasis on the catechumenate and the personal expression of faith as constituent parts of baptism allow us to understand the apparently contradictory nature of the language employed during the papal homily. In Ratzinger's thought, the sacramental input of the church must always be balanced by its teaching of the faith and the exercise of individual, heartfelt trust on the part of the one being baptized. It is a moot point whether his notion of a postbaptismal catechumenate as easily achieves the same kind of soteriological impact as might a pre-baptismal one.

Conversion/Metanoia

Ratzinger's close identification of baptism with conversion and metanoia[103] prompts us to consider in more depth what he means by conversion and whether this might constitute a meeting point with Evangelicalism. It would appear from his definition of metanoia that there may be considerable potential in this regard. In *Principles of Catholic Theology*, for example, Ratzinger lays great stress on the distinction between metanoia as it was conceived in Greek culture - where it referred to a turning away from isolated acts - and its New Testament usage wherein it is a single all-encompassing act of surrender to God in Christ.[104] This latter interpretation coheres with emphases in evangelical soteriology which portray genuine faith as resting upon an unequivocal and absolute turning of one's whole being to Christ. Insofar as Ratzinger's language carries obvious meaning he seems to affirm both this understanding of conversion and its centrality to an authentic Christian life. Thus he informs his readers that, 'To be a Christian, one must change not just in some particular area but without reservation even to the innermost depths of one's being,'[105] and that 'becoming a Christian depends on one experiencing genuinely

---

[101] Ratzinger, *Principles of Catholic Theology*, p. 36 (italics mine).

[102] Volf, *After Our Likeness,* 40. Volf cites Ratzinger to the effect that without personal engagement the sacraments are meaningless. This outlook is especially prevalent in *Das Neue Volk* (p. 330) where he affirms the 'primacy of conviction, of faith before mere sacramentalism.'

[103] See his discussion in Ratzinger, *Introduction to Christianity*, pp. 54-56 where he treats conversion or metanoia in light of the baptismal dialogue.

[104] Ratzinger, *Principles of Catholic Theology*, p. 58. 'Individual acts of metanoia remain separate acts of repentance or regret; they never combine into a single whole – a single permanent and total turning of one's whole existence into a new way; metanoia continues to be just repentance; it does not become conversion. The notion never suggests itself that one's whole existence, precisely *as* a whole, has need of a total conversion in order to become itself.'

[105] Ratzinger, *Principles of Catholic Theology*, p. 60.

Christian metanoia as it is preached by the prophets or by Jesus.'[106] Indeed, faith itself is 'located in the act of conversion' and is said to 'signif[y] an all-encompassing movement of human existence ... an 'about turn' by the whole person that from then on constantly structures one's existence.'[107] Language of this nature would indicate that, at least at the theoretical level, Ratzinger conceives of conversion in terms that resonate with evangelicals. Perhaps the distinction might lie in Evangelicalism's historical propensity to make this act of metanoia a focal point of preaching and in a very public way the *de facto* beginning of the Christian life. Whilst the logic of Ratzinger's words would suggest that a similar approach might be appropriate in Catholicism (given that the challenge of conversion is so pivotal to the Christian life as he understands it), the general pattern within Catholicism (with the exception of the charismatic movement)[108] seems to be one in which less emphasis is given to 'a single permanent and total turning of one's whole existence into a new way.' It might be suggested that as faith takes on an increasingly nominal hue in Western lands, such an unequivocal presentation of the faith may well be viewed as necessary and essential. Indeed, Evangelicalism's 'know-how' in this regard may be especially beneficial to Catholicism.[109] What would not be in dispute is that homiletic emphasis on conversion, as understood by Ratzinger, would represent significant common ground between the two traditions. However, before one can lay too much weight on this conclusion, it is vital to consider Ratzinger's emphasis on the church's role in the mediation of faith and whether this undermines the potential gains from his theology of conversion.

The Church and the Mediation of Faith

Ratzinger's acknowledgment that conversion is 'a highly personal process' with an 'inalienable individuality'[110] to it, is balanced by what he describes as an essential ecclesial dimension.[111] The question I wish to resolve is whether Ratzinger's understanding of the ecclesial nature of faith may be in any way accommodated by Evangelicalism. What seems clear at the outset is that his language veers away from giving any sense that the church's role in the mediation of faith is purely mechanical or magical. To best understand

---

[106] Ratzinger, *Principles of Catholic Theology*, p. 60.
[107] Ratzinger, *Introduction to Christianity*, p. 55.
[108] For interesting reflections on the central role of conversion in Catholic charismatic thought see Kilian McDonnell OSB, *The Charismatic Renewal and Ecumenism* (Arundel: Pegasaurus Books, 1978) and Ralph Martin, *Unless the Lord Build the House: The Church and the New Pentecost* (Notre Dame: Ave Maria Press, 1971), pp. 39-49.
[109] Arguably this is demonstrated by the employment of the Alpha course in some French dioceses as well as the support given to the course by Ranieri Cantallamessa, preacher to the Papal household.
[110] Ratzinger, *Introduction to Christianity*, p. 55.
[111] Volf cites Ratzinger to the effect that 'conversion can never be realized fully in the inwardness of personal decision.' (*Theologie*, p. 520 cited in *After Our Likeness*, p. 36).

Obstacles to Rapprochement

Ratzinger's account of the process we return to the credal formula of the earliest baptismal liturgies which is key to many of Ratzinger's ruminations on Christian initiation. The dialogue between celebrant and catechumen is said to remind us that 'belief is not the result of lonely meditation in which the 'I' freed from all ties and reflecting alone on the truth, thinks something out for itself; [but is] … the result of a dialogue, the expression of a hearing, receiving and answering …' [112] Paul's reference to 'faith com[ing] from what is heard' (Romans 10:17) is deemed paradigmatic to the whole question of faith's mediation. The apostle's words are not to be understood as randomly chosen but as conveying something of vital relevance to the communication of faith:

> The assertion "faith comes from what is heard" contains an abiding structural truth about what happens here. It illuminates the fundamental differences between faith and mere philosophy … In philosophy the thought precedes the word; it is after all a product of the reflection that one *then* tries to put into words; the words that always remain secondary to the thought … Faith, on the other hand, comes to man from the outside, and this very fact is fundamental to it. It is – let me repeat – not something thought up by itself; it is something said to me, which hits me as something that has not been thought out and lays an obligation on me. This double structure of 'Do you believe? – I do believe!', this form of the call from outside and the reply to it, is fundamental to it. It is therefore not at all abnormal if, with very few exceptions, we have to say: I did not come to believe through the private search for truth but through a process of reception that had, so to speak, already forestalled me. Faith cannot and should not be a mere product of reflection.[113]

This long citation carries echoes of his original thesis on Augustine in which he emphasises the Church Father's movement away from the notion that faith is discovered in lonely isolation. However, the argumentation he employs is largely workable in the context of ecumenical dialogue in that many evangelicals would likewise acknowledge that faith is not normally the outcome of a lone, individual search for God insulated from all outside influences.[114] It is a response to or a reception of that which is presented by the church. Indeed, one might agree with Ratzinger when he says that, 'faith does not come to the individual as an isolated "I"; he receives it from the community

---

[112] Ratzinger, *Introduction to Christianity*, p. 57.

[113] Ratzinger, *Introduction to Christianity*, pp. 57-58.

[114] Volf, *After Our Likeness*, p. 163 comes close to Ratzinger's position when he states, 'The communal character of the mediation of faith implies that, in a limited but significant sense, every Christian does indeed receive faith from the church; for that which a person believes is precisely that which the previously existing communion of believers has believed. By believing, a person appropriates the Spirit-inspired confession of faith of all churches in space and time. There is no other way to believe, unless one was to create one's own religion. The faith with which I believe is shaped by the ecclesially mediated forms in which it is expressed; there is no pure, ecclesially unmediated faith consisting of pure feeling.'

of those who have believed before him and who tell him of God as an accepted reality of their history.'[115] Here we have resonances of not only Paul's 'faith comes from hearing' but the dominical statement wherein Jesus refers to future believers as those who would 'see your [the faith community's] good works and glorify your Father who is in heaven.'[116] What is most striking here is that the church's mediation of faith is to a conscious subject who is impacted by the church's ministrations. It is not merely a mechanical or mysterious action incapable of concrete description. This same understanding of the manner in which faith is mediated occurs both in Ratzinger's discussion of the catechumenate and his treatment of infant baptism. In the former case he links the existential decision for belief to the impact of the witness given by the community of faith.

> As the making of a decision that will affect one's whole life, the catechumenate requires more than the candidates' own efforts. For such a decision means the embracing of an already existing life form ... Consequently, it is not an isolated and autonomous decision of the subject but essentially a reception: a sharing in the already existing decision of the believing community. *The very fact that one is able to turn in this direction is due to the radiance that emanates from it.*[117]

This emphasis on mediation of faith to a conscious subject remains even in his discussion of infant baptism. Not only may the catechumenate function in a post-baptismal context (presumably with no weakening of the theology of conversion which underpins it), but the effectiveness of infant baptism is determined by the life and witness of the parents and godparents. Ratzinger speaks of the child's spiritual life being caught up in the spiritual life of the parents and thus the representative function expressed by sponsors in baptism is not a 'theological fiction' but something which contributes to the ineluctable destiny of the child.[118]

> Beginning with parents and godparents, who represent the infant, the catechumenal rites of the sacrament of baptism serve as an anticipation of the catechumenate. By thus acting for the child, parents and friends hold in their hands not only its biological life but its spiritual life. The spiritual life of the child unfolds *within* the spiritual life of its parents and teachers.... This representation, which bears the weight of the parental love or neglect that will determine the child's life, is, of its very nature, the beginning by anticipation of the course the child will take... *It is obvious...that the meaning of baptism is destroyed wherever it is no longer understood as an anticipatory gift but only as a self-contained rite. Wherever it is severed from the catechumenate, baptism loses its raison d'etre.*[119]

---

[115] Ratzinger, *Principles of Catholic Theology*, p. 30.
[116] Matthew 5:16.
[117] Ratzinger, *Principles of Catholic Theology*, p. 37 (italics mine).
[118] Ratzinger, *Principles of Catholic Theology*, p. 42.
[119] Ratzinger, *Principles of Catholic Theology*, pp. 42-43 (italics mine).

It seems apparent from Ratzinger's approach to the sacrament that its efficacy derives from the manner in which faith is concretely mediated and appropriated. God's intention for the sacrament is that it leads to a personally owned faith and this outcome is facilitated by the faith of those who are especially related to the one being baptized. Whilst Ratzinger may not reach the same conclusions as evangelicals might from such an understanding of the nature of faith and how it is communicated[120], what he does affirm is clearly not in opposition to how many evangelicals understand the mediation of faith. Indeed, evangelicals in the paedo-baptist tradition would identify many points of commonality with his approach.[121] However, the clarity of Ratzinger's theology is obfuscated by the sheer volume of reference to the church in all of his deliberations. Although this does not take away from the important acknowledgments that have been made, the repercussions for mission are not drawn out in ways with which evangelicals might easily identify. To this degree, there is an ambivalence and tension in Ratzinger's theology of conversion which makes it not wholly acceptable. However, the way forward must lie with the mining of these ambivalences, these points of contact where evangelicals might take encouragement from Ratzinger and his willingness to both demystify the church's role in the transmission of faith and emphasise the necessity of fundamental conversion. His belief in the shared subjectivity of Christ and Church, so pivotal to his ecclesiology, is ultimately not an absolute barrier to some measure of rapprochement.

The Critical Reverse Test

The potential for ecumenical convergence within Ratzinger's sacramental theology, as well as his robust anti-Pelagianism outlined in earlier chapters, offer some grounds for optimism with regard to the Catholic-evangelical dialogue. However, it remains the case that certain Catholic beliefs and practices (most notably Purgatory and Mariology) are deemed antithetical to evangelical formulations of the gospel, and it is incumbent upon me to explore whether Ratzinger's adherence to these ideas belie his commitment to a theology of grace and his promotion of a Christocentric spirituality. The following discussion will indicate that Ratzinger's treatment of these controversial themes has enhanced rather than detracted from his ability to be an ecumenical bridge. The reader should note that this analysis of Ratzinger's thought will entail, in the case of Mariology especially, placing his ideas in historical and theological context.

---

[120] This is the case to the extent that he does not publicly emphasise the need for conversion in the way that some evangelicals might feel obliged to do.

[121] For evidence of a common outlook see George Carey's discussion of Christian initiation, 'Christian Beginning' in John Stott (General Editor), *Obeying Christ in a Changing World: 1. The Lord Christ* (Glasgow: Fountain Books, 1977), pp. 137-138.

Purgatory

The potentially radical nature of Ratzinger's understanding of Purgatory is made plain when one reads the following assessment of his thought by Anglican theologian, N.T. Wright.[122] Citing as evidence the publication *Eschatology*, he suggests that Ratzinger has to some degree subverted traditional Roman Catholic teaching about the nature and duration of the purgatorial state. This example of independent thought on Ratzinger's part is said to have mirrored the efforts of Karl Rahner who also re-interpreted the meaning of Purgatory.[123] Wright comments in relation to the two scholars:

> More remarkable still [that is, than the position adopted by Karl Rahner] is the view of Cardinal Ratzinger, now Pope Benedict XVI. Building on 1 Corinthians 3, he argued that the Lord himself is the fire of judgment which transforms us as he conforms us to his glorious, resurrected body. This happens, not during a long-drawn-out process, but in the moment of final judgment itself. By thus linking purgatory to Jesus Christ himself as the eschatological fire, Ratzinger detaches the doctrine of purgatory from the concept of an intermediate state, and breaks the link that, in the Middle Ages, gave rise to the idea of indulgences and so provided a soft target for Protestant polemics. Whatever we think of that, it is clear that two of the most central, important and conservative Roman theologians of the last generation have offered quite a radical climb-down from Aquinas, Dante, Newman and all that went in between.[124]

Few would quibble that such a reading of Ratzinger serves to strengthen the view that his belief in *Sola gratia* has impacted the rest of his theology to a considerable degree. Indeed, if accurate, Wright has shown that Ratzinger has not only challenged long-held views about Purgatory but presented the phenomenon as something quite akin to the momentary eschatological transformation posited by Protestantism. Are there grounds on which we might bring this judgment into question or is Wright's conclusion unassailable given the content of Ratzinger's published writings? The most immediate challenge to Wright's assertions arose from the pen of Richard John Neuhaus who argued that remarks in a homily delivered to priests in 2008 demonstrated that Benedict had in no way abandoned the dogma of Purgatory.[125] Neuhaus comments somewhat acerbically,

> As the pope recently said in a meeting with Italian clergy: "God creates justice. We must keep this in mind. For this reason, it also seemed important to me to write about purgatory in the encyclical [ie. *Spe Salvi*], which for me

---

[122] Tom Wright, *Surprised by Hope* (London: SPCK, 2007).
[123] Karl Rahner, *On the Theology of Death* (New York: Herder & Herder, 1961).
[124] Wright, *Surprised by Hope*, p. 179.
[125] Address by Benedict XVI to the clergy and parish priests of Rome on 7 Feb 2008 http://www.vatican.va/holy_father/benedict_xvi/speeches/2008/february/documents/hf_ben-xvi_spe_20080207_clergy-rome_en.html [accessed 5 December 2012].

is such an obvious truth, so evident and also so necessary and comforting, that it cannot be omitted." It appears that Bishop Wright's tutelage of the pope still has a way to go.[126]

This observation highlights one undeniable feature of the Pope Emeritus' thought on Purgatory. Whatever may be the precise intent of his theology, he has never publicly denied the doctrine nor given the impression that he has dissented in any way from the Church's teaching. This is clear not only from the homily cited by Neuhaus but from sentiments expressed during an interview with Peter Seewald in 2002[127]. To this extent, Wright's rather forthright claim that Ratzinger broke unequivocally with the tradition is seriously prejudiced.

However, more intensive study of Ratzinger's thought on Purgatory indicates that although Wright has perhaps claimed too much for the Pontiff, Neuhaus has been guilty of the opposite error in presuming too little movement or innovation.

Ratzinger's own stated opinions on the subject are found in 16 pages devoted to the theme in *Eschatology*. The first ten pages function as a review of the history of the doctrine and this is followed by a brief section intriguingly entitled, 'The Permanent Content of the Doctrine of Purgatory.' The wording here implies that not all the ideas associated with Purgatory correspond to its core meaning and that, to some degree, the doctrine awaits crystallization so that the enduring aspects of it might be more clearly comprehended. As a scripturally orientated theologian, it is no surprise that he locates the essential core of the doctrine within the biblical text itself (viz. Paul's teaching about eschatological fire in 1 Corinthians 3:10-15). Although this passage has often been treated as a proof text for the dogma[128], Ratzinger concedes that it would be difficult to establish that Paul is presenting 'a naively objective concept of Purgatory'[129] to his readers. However, the work of Catholic exegete, Joachim Gnilka[130], was to stimulate a train of thought in Ratzinger's mind which would result in him viewing 'Purgatory' as the natural explanation of the process which Paul was describing to his Corinthian audience. Citing the passage in question,

> [Each one's work] ...will be revealed with fire, and the fire will test what sort of work each has done. If the work which any man has built on the foundation survives, he will receive a reward. If any man's work is burned

---

[126] Richard John Neuhaus 'The Possibilities and Perils in Being a Really Smart Bishop' *First Things* April 2008. http://www.firstthings.com/article/2008/03/the-possibilities-and-perils-in-being-a-really-smart-bishop-13 [accessed 5 March 2012].
[127] Ratzinger, *God and the World*, pp. 129-131.
[128] See Keating, *Catholicism and Fundamentalism*, p. 193.
[129] Joseph Ratzinger, *Eschatology: Death and Eternal Life* (Washington DC: Catholic University of America Press, 1988), p. 229.
[130] Joachim Gnilka, *1st 1 Kor 3:10-15 ein Schriftzeugnis für das Fegfeuer?* (Düsseldorf: Triltsch, 1955), pp. 27 ff.

up, he will suffer loss, though he himself will be saved, but only as through fire.[131]

he concurs with Gnilka that the testing fire is a picture of Christ himself. However, in contrast to Gnilka and in solidarity with Lutheran exegete Jeremias[132], he affirms that there are grounds for interpreting the text in terms of Purgatory.[133] In language which reflects his search for the kernel of the doctrine, he speaks of 'Purgatory [being] understood in a *properly Christian way* when it is grasped *christologically*, in terms of the Lord himself as the judging fire which transforms us and conforms us to his glorious body.' Thus

> ... *the real Christianising of the early Jewish notion of a purging fire* lies precisely in the insight that the purification involved does not happen through some *thing*, but through the transforming power of the Lord himself, whose burning flame cuts free our closed-off heart, melting it, and pouring it into a new mold to make it fit for the living organism of his body.[134]

Having outlined the background to Ratzinger's appropriation of 1 Corinthians 3 as the paradigmatic text for Purgatory, we are now in a position to better assess whether he has 'detache[d] the doctrine ... from the concept of an intermediate state,'[135] as claimed by N.T. Wright. On the surface, this would seem unlikely given that Ratzinger queries whether Paul's words in the passage can be interpreted as referring only to the Eschaton as a single occasion.

> One can't really object that Paul is only talking here about the Last Day as a unique event: that would be hermeneutical *naivete* ... Man does not have to strip away his temporality in order thereby to become 'eternal'; Christ as Judge is *ho eschatos*, the Final One, in relation to whom we undergo judgment *both* after death *and* on the Last Day.[136]

Ironically, having established the distinction between what we might term the particular and the general judgment, Ratzinger's concept of Christ as 'the Final One' serves to open the door to a possible blurring of the two judgments. He sets about justifying this move on the grounds that in the afterlife the idea of time is a meaningless construct.

> In the perspective we are offered here, these two judgments are indistinguishable. A person's entry into the realm of manifest reality is an entry into his definitive destiny and thus an immersion into eschatological fire. The transforming 'moment' of this encounter cannot be quantified by

---

[131] Ratzinger, *Eschatology*, p. 228.
[132] J. Jeremias, 'geenna', TWNT 1, p. 656.
[133] Ratzinger, *Eschatology*, p. 229.
[134] Ratzinger, *Eschatology*, p. 229.
[135] Wright, *Surprised By Hope*, p. 179.
[136] Ratzinger, *Eschatology*, p. 230.

the measurements of earthly time. It is, indeed, not eternal but a transition, and yet trying to qualify it as of "short" or "long" duration on the basis of temporal measurements derived from physics would be naïve and unproductive. The 'temporal measure' of this encounter lies in the unsoundable depths of existence, in a passing-over where we are burned ere before we are transformed. To measure ... such an 'existential time' , in terms of the time of this world would be to ignore the specificity of the human spirit in its simultaneous relationship with, and differentiation from, the world.[137]

It should be noted that Ratzinger's employment of the term 'moment' (which is cited in inverted commas to illustrate that his meaning is not completely captured by any normal associations one might make on hearing the word) stands at odds with Wright's use of it. In *Surprised By Hope,* Wright uses the word (shorn of inverted commas) to illustrate the fact that in Ratzinger's theology the Lord's fiery judgment happens 'not during a long-drawn-out process, but in the *moment* of final judgment itself.'[138] This clearly was not Ratzinger's intention as his nuanced discussion and judicious use of punctuation should have made clear. However, it cannot be denied that his refusal to speak in terms of short or long duration at least allows for the possibility that the purgatorial process may be instantaneous if described by the standards of temporal time. This would certainly seem to be the view of one leading Catholic apologist who is famed for unstinting loyalty to the magisterium. James Akin, addressing the Protestant assumption that 'the church used to even sell indulgences to shorten your time in purgatory by a number of days' writes in reply,

> ... the Church has never said that purgatory involves the same kind of time as we experience here on earth, or even time at all. Thus Cardinal Ratzinger, no theological liberal, writes that purgatory may involve 'existential' rather than temporal duration. It may be something one experiences, but experiences in a moment, rather than something one endures over time.[139]

The next stage in Ratzinger's argument, having introduced his 'Christological' interpretation of Purgatory, is to demonstrate that such a process of inward transformation is not at variance with the idea of salvation by grace. This is the case because the process itself is an expression of grace.

> [Purgatory] does not replace grace by works, but allows the former to achieve its full victory precisely as grace. What actually saves is the full ascent of faith. But in most of us, that basic option is buried under a great deal of wood, hay and straw. Only with difficulty can it peer out from behind the latticework of an egoism we are powerless to pull down with our

---

[137] Ratzinger, *Eschatology*, p. 230.
[138] Wright, *Surprised By Hope*, p. 179.
[139] James Akin, 'How to explain Purgatory to Protestants.' (1996) http://www.ewtn.com/library/answers/how2purg.htm (accessed 16 March, 2012).

own hands. Man is the recipient of the divine mercy, yet this does not exonerate him from the need to be transformed. Encounter with the Lord *is* this transformation. It is the fire that burns away our dross and re-forms us to be vessels of eternal joy.[140]

Here Ratzinger is able to speak of the purgatorial encounter as an avenue of grace in that the individual has the opportunity to respond in trusting faith to Christ's own dealing with his or her soul.

Having now explored those aspects of Ratzinger's thought which are relatively innovative in terms of the traditional theology, a question-mark remains concerning the standard Catholic assertions that individuals in some way make expiation for their sins by penance in Purgatory and that the prayers of the faithful are required to assist individuals in their journey through the purgatorial experience. How does Ratzinger engage with these themes and does that engagement compromise his otherwise robust defence of salvation by grace? It is precisely here that the critical reverse test becomes most crucial.

The summary answer to that question is that Ratzinger incorporates core data or terminology perennially associated with the dogma into his view of Purgatory (e.g. penance and prayers for the dead), but does so in such a way that what the Reformation divines would have found most offensive about these ideas is largely absent from his own meaning. For example, the term penance seems to function entirely as a synonym for repentance and there are no hints of an older, fuller definition which might be ecumenically hazardous.[141] Thus he can conclude, when describing the essential Christian understanding of Purgatory, that it 'is not, as Tertullian thought, some kind of supra-worldly concentration camp where man is forced to undergo punishment in a more or less arbitrary fashion. Rather it is an inwardly necessary process.'[142] This perspective on the doctrine, he asserts,

> would contradict the doctrine of grace only if *penance* were the antithesis of grace and not its form ... Purgatory follows by an inner necessity from the idea of *penance*, the idea of the constant readiness for reform which marks the forgiven sinner.[143]

The one context where Benedict comes closest to the older language and to speak in some form about the soul's expiation of its own sin is a papal address given on the life of St Catherine of Genoa.[144] However, even on this occasion

---

[140] Ratzinger, *Eschatology*, p. 231.
[141] See Ludwig Ott, *Fundamentals of Catholic Dogma* (Charlotte: Tan Books, 1974), p. 416 in which he defines penance as, '... that moral virtue, which inclines the will to turn away inwardly from sin, and to render atonement to God for it.
[142] Ratzinger, *Eschatology*, p. 230.
[143] Ratzinger,*IEschatology*, p. 231 (italics mine).
[144] Pope Benedict XVI, General Audience, 12 January 2011. 'St Catherine of Genoa.' http://www.vatican.va/holy_father/benedict_xvi/audiences/2011/documents/hf_ben-xvi_aud_20110112_en.html (accessed 16 March, 2012).

the aim seems to be to challenge current perceptions of purgatory by presenting Christ to his audience as the eschatological fire whose interactions with the human soul constitute the real meaning of the doctrine: 'Catherine, however, did not see purgatory as a scene in the bowels of the earth: for her it is not an exterior but an interior fire. This is purgatory: an inner fire.'[145] Later describing the purgatorial experience, he introduces his own very nuanced understanding of expiation. He writes,

> The soul is aware of the immense love and perfect justice of God and consequently suffers for having failed to respond in a correct and perfect way to this love; *and love for God itself becomes a flame, love itself cleanses it from the residue of sin.*[146]

Surely we have here a carefully crafted statement in which the notion of human merit or achievement is made difficult to sustain when the love which cleanses is shown to be utterly derivative of the love that encounters and transforms. The primacy of grace is thus preserved in the midst of a conversation in which one wrong choice of vocabulary on Benedict's part would have summoned the spectre of Pelagianism. We might conclude that as much as possible is being done, given the strictures imposed by historic dogma and practice, to establish Purgatory as an existential encounter with the Lord which is most fundamentally about his work and not the exertions and privations of those undergoing the experience.

The same form of subtle argumentation also characterises Ratzinger's discussion of prayer for the dead. His justification of the practice is premised on the frank admission that the picture he presents of purgatory would seem to leave little scope for such a theological move. He writes,

> One vital question still remains to be cleared up. We saw that prayer for the departed, in its many forms, belongs with the original data of the Judaeo-Christian tradition. But does not this prayer presuppose that Purgatory entails some kind of external punishment which can be remitted through vicarious acceptance by others in a form of spiritual barter? And how can a third party enter into that most highly personal process of encounter with Christ, where the 'I' is transformed in the flame of his closeness? Is this not an event which so concerns the individual that all replacement or substitution must be ruled out? Is not the pious tradition of 'helping the holy souls' based on treating these souls after the fashion of 'having' – whereas our reflections so far have surely led to the conclusion that the heart of the matter is 'being,' for which there can be no substitute?[147]

His answer to these criticisms is that they do not take full account of the interconnectedness of humanity: 'Yet the being of man is not, in fact, that of a

---

[145] Benedict XVI, 'St Catherine of Genoa'.
[146] Benedict XVI, 'St Catherine of Genoa'.
[147] Ratzinger, *Eschatology*, pp. 231-232.

closed monad', he states. 'It is related to others by love or hate, and in these ways, has colonies within them.'[148] The argument is further elaborated in the encyclical *Spe Salvi* where he states,

> The lives of others continually spill over into mine: in what I think, say, do and achieve. And conversely, my life spills over into that of others: for better and for worse. So my prayer for another is not something extraneous to that person, something external, not even after death. In the interconnectedness of Being, my gratitude to the other – my prayer for him – can play a small part in his purification.[149]

The fundamental point to note in these comments seems to be that this ability to spiritually impact another life is not curtailed by the barrier of death. In *Eschatology*, he offers the following justification,

> ... self-substituting love is a central Christian reality, and the doctrine of Purgatory states that for such love the limit of death does not exist. The possibility of helping and giving does not cease to exist on the death of the Christian. Rather does it stretch out to encompass the entire communion of saints, on both sides of death's portals. The capacity and the duty to love beyond the grave might even be called the true primordial datum in this whole area of tradition – II Maccabees 12:42-45 first makes clear.[150]

The reference to the 'true primordial datum' hints at what is probably the most powerful theological motivation involved in Ratzinger's endorsement of prayer for the dead. It seems to this writer that his belief in its legitimacy rests ultimately on its canonical basis (II Maccabees[151]) and the universal voice of church tradition (East and West) for the first fifteen centuries of the Church.[152] A 'man of the tradition', as Hans Küng once designated him, would demur from casting doubt on a common conviction of such longevity. However, his depiction of the practice – resting strongly as it does on a theory about the interconnectedness of Being – lays stress on the impact of that prayer on the internal process of purification rather than its ability to vicariously alleviate any external pain or suffering. Thus it avoids the very form of criticism alluded to at the start of the discussion. Moreover, and this may be the crucial point of vindication for Ratzinger, the aid which is intended by this form of prayer is surely not qualitatively different from earthly prayer that seeks the purification or sanctification of a brother or sister. Can one therefore argue that when the

---

[148] Ratzinger, *Eschatology*, p. 232.
[149] Benedict XVI, *Spe Salvi*, p. 49.
[150] Ratzinger, *Eschatology*, p. 233.
[151] II Maccabees is accorded full canonical status within the Roman Catholic Church.
[152] See Ratzinger, *Eschatology*, p. 232. Ratzinger states, '... this original 'given' has never been in dispute as between East and West. It was the Reformation which called it into question, and that in the face of what were in part objectionable and deformed practices.'

focus of such prayer is changed from an earthly to a post mortem context that it contravenes or undermines the idea of grace or the work of Christ? Evangelicals may feel uncomfortable with the practice and have less confidence in the biblical and ecclesiastical foundation that undergirds it, but Benedict's nuanced discussion of the subject inhibits the reader from seeing it as something fundamentally at odds with the doctrine of grace.

The Place of Mary in Ratzinger's Thought
Theological and Personal Context

Ratzinger's Mariology is best understood when some of the factors which helped determine its shape have been identified. For example, he has acknowledged in his autobiography that he underwent priestly formation in an environment which was lukewarm in its embrace of Mariology.[153] Various Catholic theological faculties worldwide had been canvassed on whether Mary's bodily assumption should be defined as an infallible dogma, and the judgment of the German centres of learning was an emphatically negative one.[154] In a study jointly written with Hans Urs von Balthasar, Ratzinger pondered why one stream of the Church had been unenthusiastic about Mariology whilst another stemming from the same time period had greatly lauded the merits of Marian devotion.[155] His answer is that these two dominant streams (both of them very powerful in the intervening years between the First and Second World Wars) had fundamentally different starting points. On the one hand, those influenced by the liturgical movement (itself complemented by the biblical and ecumenical movements) were Trinitarian in focus and 'sought a piety governed strictly by the measure of the Bible or, at the most, of the ancient Church.'[156] Conversely, the Marian movement, with a more subjective and personal piety, looked to a spirituality which centred on Jesus and Mary and drew more on Medieval and modern sources. Given Ratzinger's own context, it is no surprise that the liturgical movement, especially strong in the German-speaking lands, should have exerted the more dominant influence on him. As he acknowledges to Seewald, 'Personally, my attitude was shaped from the beginning by the strongly christocentric aspect of the liturgical movement, and this has been further strengthened in dialogue with our Protestant friends.'[157]

---

[153] Ratzinger, *Milestones*, pp. 58-59.
[154] Ratzinger, *Milestones*, p. 58-59. For example, Altaner the patrologist from Würzburg and Ratzinger's own doctoral supervisor, Gottlieb Söhngen, were passionately convinced that the textual evidence alone proved that the doctrine was unknown before the fifth century.
[155] Hans Urs von Balthasar and Joseph Ratzinger, *Mary: The Church at the Source* (Ignatius Press:
San Francisco, 1980).
[156] Von Balthasar and Ratzinger, *Mary: The Church at the Source*, p. 20.
[157] Ratzinger, *God and the World*, p. 296.

However, this relative coolness towards Mariology[158] was not an indicator that he had emulated his Tübingen colleague, Hans Küng, in negating Marian piety altogether.[159] Ratzinger in later years has acknowledged that popular devotion to Mary in the form of the May devotions and pilgrimages had always held meaning for him.[160] This devotional outlook was shared and perhaps reinforced by his mentor at the Second Vatican Council, Cardinal Josef Frings. Ratzinger writes with reference to Frings,

> At the Council, when the liturgical, christological, and ecumenical movements opposed the Marian movement, and the two parties threatened to become irreconcilable alternatives, [Frings] addressed an imploring appeal to the Fathers to find the common center. He emphatically rejected a shortsighted, hasty either-or, as if the Church now had to decide whether to become modern, biblical, liturgical, and ecumenical or to remain 'old-fashioned' and Marian. It was his personal concern to join the two streams together, to give the liturgy the heartfelt intensity of Marian piety and to open to Marian piety the breadth of the liturgical tradition.[161]

It would seem from Ratzinger's subsequent writings that he was decisively influenced by Frings' call for a *via media* approach in which Mariology was protected from being overwhelmed by the liturgical and ecumenical tide sweeping through the church. However, this decision seems not to have been at the expense of replacing ecclesiological Mariology – the stance of the liturgical movement at Vatican II – with a Mariology that was correlated with Christology and soteriology. In Ratzinger's opinion, the Council Fathers' decision to discuss Mary in the context of the Church (i.e. in *Lumen Gentium*) and not to have a separate schema which potentially focused on her soteriological significance was the correct approach given dogmatic and other considerations.[162] I shall demonstrate in the next section that this desire to endorse a Mariology which has an essentially biblical and patristic foundation is key to his whole approach.

Ratzinger's Defence of Mariology

As already intimated, the most striking feature of Ratzinger's Mariology is his acknowledgment that its legitimacy depends ultimately on its grounding within Scripture itself. This view was freshly articulated in a 2003 article published in

---

[158] In *The Ratzinger Report* (p. 105) he speaks of his early unease with certain aspects of Mariology: 'As a young theologian in the time before (and also during) the Council, I had, as many did then and still do today, some reservations in regard to certain ancient formulas, as, for example, that famous *De Maria nunquam satis*, "concerning Mary one can never say enough." It seemed exaggerated to me.'
[159] See Küng, *My Struggle for Freedom*, pp. 154-156.
[160] Ratzinger, *God and the World*, p. 296.
[161] Von Balthasar and Ratzinger, *Mary: The Church at the Source*, p. 17.
[162] Von Balthasar and Ratzinger, *Mary: The Church at the Source*, p. 27.

Communio wherein he raised the question of whether Mary's maternity could still be deemed to have any theological significance. His reply was in the affirmative but he added this very significant proviso.

> We must avoid relegating Mary's maternity to the sphere of biology. But we can do so only if our reading of Scripture can legitimately presuppose a hermeneutics that rules out just this kind of division and allows us instead to recognise the correlation of Christ and his Mother as a theological reality.[163]

The style of hermeneutics required for the legitimation of Mariology is thought to exist within the ecclesiology developed by the Church Fathers.[164] This was the case because the relationship of Christ and the Church was understood by them to be the central facet of Scripture and the hermeneutical key to unlock its riches. From this foundation, so to speak, it was considered possible to construct a theologically viable Mariology. He summarises the Church Fathers' interpretive model in these terms,

> Briefly put, the burden of this hermeneutics is that the salvation brought about by the triune God, the true center of all history, is 'Christ and the Church' – Church here meaning the creature's fusion with its Lord in spousal love, in which its hope for divinization is fulfilled by way of faith.[165]

The immediate issue arising from the hermeneutical model just sketched out is the manner in which a doctrine of Mary might potentially emerge from it. The solution Ratzinger advances is heavily dependent on an ancient style of biblical interpretation which he and other *ressourcement* theologians had sought to revive within the life of the Church. His essential point is that employment of this long-neglected hermeneutic carves a legitimate foothold for Mariology proper in the text of Scripture. He sets out his case in the following way:

> If, therefore, Christ and *ecclesia* are the hermeneutical center of the scriptural narration of the history of God's saving dealings with man, then and only then is the place fixed where *Mary's motherhood becomes theologically significant as the ultimate personal concretization of Church.*[166]

The term 'ultimate personal concretization of the church' reveals the centrality of typology within Ratzinger's hermeneutic. It is by this means, rather than by historical critical enquiry, that he is able to identify Mary as the personification or figure of the Church. The following citation highlights some of the weighty

---

[163] Joseph Ratzinger, 'Retrieving the Tradition: Thoughts on the Place of Marian Doctrine and Piety in Faith and Theology as a Whole.' *Communio* 30 (Spring 2003), p. 155.
[164] Ratzinger, 'Retrieving the Tradition', p. 154.
[165] Ratzinger, 'Retrieving the Tradition', p. 154.
[166] Ratzinger, 'Retrieving the Tradition', p. 155 (italics mine).

Mariological claims made possible for Ratzinger on account of this style of interpretation. Here he is reflecting upon Mary's submissive response to the will of God and the theological implications involved in that choice.

> At the moment when she pronounces her Yes, Mary is Israel in person; she is the Church in person and as a person. She is the personal concretization of the Church because her *Fiat* makes her the bodily mother of the Lord. But this biological fact is a theological reality, because it realizes the deepest spiritual content of the covenant God intended to make with Israel ... We can therefore say that the affirmation of Mary's motherhood and the affirmation of her representation of the Church are related as *factum* and *mysterium facti*, as a fact and the sense that gives the fact its meaning. The two things are inseparable: the fact without its sense would be blind; the sense without the fact would be empty. Mariology cannot be developed from the naked fact, but only from the fact as it is understood in the hermeneutics of faith.[167]

What is the precise nature of this hermeneutics of faith? Perhaps the best way to understand his defence of Mariology is to examine his interpretive model in practice. An example from the Gospel of Luke may suffice. Here he cites Luke's account of the Annunciation as the basis of New Testament Mariology. Whilst he offers a cursory account of this passage's significance in his book, *Daughter Zion*[168], a fuller consideration is given in the work co-authored with von Balthasar. Here it is suggested that the angel's greeting to Mary, 'Rejoice, full of grace. The Lord is with you', is more than a formulaic greeting common to the Greek-speaking world. Examined against the background of the Old Testament, it is said to carry a profound theological significance. This is indicated by the fact that the same word used by Luke in the Gospel account appears four times in the Septuagint, and on each of these occasions it is an announcement of messianic joy (Zeph. 3:14; Joel 2:21; Zech. 9:9 and Lam. 4:21). Thus it is the case that 'Mary is not greeted in some vague or indifferent way; that God greets her and, in her, greets expectant Israel and all of humanity is an invitation to rejoice from the innermost depth of our beings.'[169] This identification of Mary with Israel – not immediately apparent from a non-Catholic reading of the text - derives its justification from the passages already cited, particularly Zephaniah. Ratzinger articulates their significance for Mariology in the following manner.

> These texts invariably contain a double promise to the personification of Israel, daughter Zion: God will come to save, and he will come to dwell in her. The angel's dialogue with Mary reprises this promise and in so doing makes it concrete in two ways. What in the prophecy is said to daughter Zion is now directed to Mary: She is identified with daughter Zion, she is

---

[167] Ratzinger, 'Retrieving the Tradition', pp. 155-156.
[168] Ratzinger, *Daughter Zion*, pp. 42-43.
[169] Von Balthasar and Ratzinger, *Mary: Source of the Church*, p. 64.

daughter Zion in person. In a parallel manner, Jesus, whom Mary is permitted to bear, is identified with Yahweh, the living God.[170]

It is Ratzinger's ultimate view that the identification of Mary with Daughter Zion, which he portrays as the deliberate intent of Luke the theologian, 'leads us ... into the depths.'[171] In other words, this linkage is not to be perceived as a superficial and temporary connection, but as the assertion that God has enabled his covenant people to be represented by a responsive agent who, in her own person, embodies the faith of Israel. Such an association of Mary with the church, partially derived as it is from the 'anonymous but personally shaped ecclesiology'[172] of the Fathers, lays the platform for the high view of Mariology embedded in Catholic tradition. Arguably, though, the typological argument developed by Ratzinger to undergird such a Mariological reading of the passage functions more by way of assertion than evidence. By employing the same exegetical method as the patristic writers, he is exposing himself to the same charge levelled against them (viz. that their exegesis is based on unwarranted interpretive leaps). The citation below illustrates how Ratzinger uses allegory to defend Mary's identification with Daughter Zion.

> This manner of connecting the Old and New Testaments is much more than an interesting historical construction by means of which the Evangelist links promise and fulfilment and reinterprets the OT in the light of what has happened in Christ. Mary is Zion in person, which means that her life wholly embodies what is meant by "Zion". She does not wish to be just this one human being who defends and protects her own ego...Her life is such that she is transparent to God, 'habitable' for him. Her life is such that she is a place for God. Her life sinks her into the common measure of sacred history, so that what appears in her is, not the narrow and constricted ego of an isolated individual, but the whole, true Israel.[173]

Whilst Ratzinger's Mariology extends beyond his depiction of Mary in her role as Daughter Zion, this undoubtedly remains its defining image. Indeed, it is on the basis of the typology that made such an association possible that he sets out to defend other key beliefs such as the perpetual virginity of Mary[174] and the Immaculate Conception.[175] His rationale for the justification of the latter doctrine offers a very clear window into his whole method.

> One need not search very far for a typological identification grounding Mary's freedom from original sin. The Epistle to the Ephesians describes the new Israel, the bride, as 'holy', 'immaculate', 'luminously beautiful' ... Patristic theology further developed this image of the *Ecclesia immaculate*

---

[170] Von Balthasar and Ratzinger, *Mary: Source of the Church*, p. 65.
[171] Von Balthasar and Ratzinger, *Mary: Source of the* Church, p. 66.
[172] Von Balthasar and Ratzinger, *Mary: Source of the Church*, p. 28.
[173] Ratzinger, *Daughter Zion*, p. 67.
[174] Ratzinger, *God and the World*, p. 303.
[175] Ratzinger, *Daughter Zion*, pp. 67-68.

in passages of lyrical beauty. Consequently, from the very beginning there is a doctrine about the *Immaculata* in Scripture and especially in the Fathers, even if it concerns the *Ecclesia Immaculata*. Here the doctrine of the *Immaculata*, like the whole of later Mariology, is first anticipated as ecclesiology. The image of the Church, virgin and mother, is *secondarily* transferred to Mary, not vice versa. So if the dogma of the Immaculate Conception transferred to the concrete figure of Mary those assertions which primarily belong to the antithesis new-old Israel, and are in this sense a typologically developed ecclesiology, this means that Mary is presented as the beginning and the personal concreteness of the Church.[176]

Whatever judgment one might want to make of Ratzinger's justification of Mariology, it cannot be gainsaid that his instinct was to build a Scriptural case for the practice. He is unwilling to lay any of the weight of Mariology on the shoulders of tradition. However, the irony may be that it is the powerful but subtle influence of tradition that has driven him to find a biblical justification for the practice in the first place. The admission that it 'cannot be developed from the naked fact [of the biblical text]' does not instil confidence that an allegorical interpretation, deemed highly dubious by the majority of historical critics, will make the doctrine any more palatable to those not otherwise convinced.

On the other hand, it should be acknowledged that his Mariology is an ecclesiological Mariology in which Mary's role is defined by her membership in the church and her identity as a believer. She does not take on the features of the Mary venerated by those who would seek to have her defined as Coredemptrix. However, even given this, the vast majority of evangelicals will still be uncomfortable that the place accorded to Mary by Ratzinger is dependent on the slender stem of Old Testament typology. This perceived excess in his theology may be somewhat ameliorated by the claim that he is at least seeking to take Mary's role in the Incarnation with the seriousness that it deserves. Arguably, this is a goal to which Protestant exegesis has too rarely aspired. Reformed theologian, Herman Bavinck, exerts a charity towards Roman Catholics which might be applied appropriately to Joseph Ratzinger on this matter. He writes,

> Mary is the most blessed among women; she received a privilege which is given to no other creature. Through unmerited grace she is elevated above all men and angels. Rome has rightly maintained this, and anyone who denies it is not taking the incarnation of God seriously.[177]

---

[176] Ratzinger, *Daughter Zion*, pp. 67-68.
[177] Herman Bavinck, *Gereformeede Dogmatik*, III, p. 261 cited in G.C. Berkouwer, *The Second Vatican Council and the New Catholicism* (Grand Rapids: Eerdmans, 1965), p. 233.

Obstacles to Rapprochement

Ratzinger's Mariology and Evangelicalism

Having sought to articulate the core of Ratzinger's Mariology, the issue now facing us is whether this Marian outlook fundamentally undermines the doctrine of grace and the centrality of Christ? My aim will be to demonstrate that Ratzinger's approach is sufficiently circumscribed so as not to be a threat to either of these themes.

Mary as Co-redemptrix

Protestant commentators on Mariology often hold that the Rubicon which no Christologically responsible reading of Mary should cross is adoption of the doctrine of Co-redemptrix.[178] Indeed, it was in anticipation of the promulgation of this dogma that Karl Barth spoke scathingly of Mariology as the 'one heresy of the Roman Catholic Church which explains all the rest.' According to him, 'The 'mother of God' of Roman Catholic dogma is quite simply the principle, type and essence of the human creature co-operating servantlike in its own redemption on the basis of prevenient grace, and to that extent the principle, type and essence of the Church.'[179] This unease that a maximalist Mariology masks a flagrant Pelagianism has been echoed in some Roman Catholic circles as well. A further issue of concern with Catholic commentators is that the traditional teaching about Christ's two natures is compromised by the dogma.[180] Berkouwer helpfully summarises some objections voiced by Edward Schillebeeckx which encapsulate the apprehensions of both Catholics and Protestants alike. He writes,

> Schillebeeckx ... disowns the idea that Mary adds a complementary function to the incarnation such as would suggest that she, as a human being, participates actively in the work of salvation by adding something to the work of Christ. Were Mary truly active and creative in this sense, says Schillebeeckx, human cooperation would be an ontologically necessary component of the incarnation. And we would be ascribing to Mary the human being what was in fact accomplished by Christ. But this cannot be the import of Mary's position in the work of salvation, for if it were, the suggestion would be unavoidable that Mary provides the human side of salvation while Christ provides the divine side – and this leads to the heresy of monophysitism. For monophysitism creates a vacuum where the humanity of Christ should be – a vacuum too easily filled by Mary.[181]

---

[178] See the discussion in Berkouwer, *The Second Vatican Council and the New Catholicism*, pp. 233- 246.
[179] Karl Barth, *Church Dogmatics.*, *1, 2*, (p. 157) cited in Berkouwer, *The Second Vatican Council and the New Catholicism*, pp. 235-36.
[180] Berkouwer, *The Second Vatican Council and the New Catholicism*, p. 236.
[181] Edward Schillebeeckx, *Theologische Wordenboek, II*, 3146 cited in Berkouwer, *The Second Vatican Council and the New Catholicism*, p. 36.

Conversely, Marian maximalists are deeply suspect of the Mariology promoted by minimalists such as Schillebeeckx and Ratzinger. Protestant objections to ecclesiological Mariology are virtually replicated within the pro-Marian camp. These traditional supporters of Mariology see their opponents as defending the Marian dogmas by a theological leap rather than by irresistible logic. 'How, it is asked, can it be shown that the immaculate conception and the assumption into heaven are implicit in the idea of Mary as type of the Church?'[182] For them, the implication is that 'the minimalist Mariology is intrinsically an aberration in Catholicism.'[183] Ratzinger's observation that the immediate outcome of the victory of the minimalists at Vatican II was 'the collapse of Mariology altogether'[184] lends an interesting credence to the traditionalist voice. One might speculate that a Mariological approach which does nothing to enhance that burgeoning Mariology of pre-Vatican II times and which is based on theological premises alien to high Mariology is no threat either to a theology of grace or the centrality of Christ.

The most telling evidences that Ratzinger's Mariology is too nuanced and Christologically rooted to undermine either *Sola gratia* or *Solus Christus* are his own published statements. I shall show that at key moments in his career he has been implacably opposed to any development in Mariology which would prejudice either the doctrine of grace or the unique role of Christ in devotion and spirituality. The following two examples reflect both the early and later Ratzinger and witness to a fundamentally consistent outlook. Indeed, I shall suggest that when Mariology crosses a certain line and threatens Christology that Ratzinger is prepared to take unusual steps in defence of a Christ-centred spirituality.

Perhaps Ratzinger's most definitive statements regarding Mariology appear in *Introduction to Christianity* wherein he lays out certain parameters for an appropriate Mariology. The context for his statements is a discussion about the symbolic significance of the virgin birth. While the following citation is lengthy it absolutely confirms that for him Mariology must not extend beyond the faith of the New Testament and become a duplicate form of Christology. Mary cannot function as a devotional focus in any way that detracts from Christ nor can she be conceived as an agent in her own salvation. Rather, as a figure of the Church, she represents a humanity which is redeemed on the basis of grace alone. He writes,

> The meaning of the divine symbol of the virgin birth, if properly understood, indicates at the same time the proper theological place for a devotion to Mary that lets itself be guided by the faith of the New Testament. Devotion to Mary cannot be based on a Mariology that represents a sort of miniature second edition of Christology – such a duplication is neither right nor justifiable on the evidence. If one wanted to indicate a department of

---

[182] Berkouwer, *The Second Vatican Council and the New Catholicism*, p. 240.
[183] Berkouwer, *The Second Vatican Council and the New Catholicism*, p. 240.
[184] Von Balthasar and Ratzinger, *Mary: Source of the Church*, p. 24.

theology to which Mariology belonged as its concrete illustration, it would probably be the doctrine of grace, which of course goes to form a whole with ecclesiology and anthropology. As the true 'daughter of Zion', Mary is the image of the Church, the image of believing man, who can only come to salvation and to himself through the gift of love – through grace. The saying with which Bernanos ends his *Diary of a Country Priest* – "Everything is grace" – a saying in which a life which is full of weakness and futility can see itself as full of riches and fulfilment – truly becomes in Mary, 'full of grace' (Luke 1.28), a concrete reality. She does not contest or endanger the exclusiveness of salvation through Christ; she points to it.[185]

This plea for a conscious limiting of the boundaries of Mariology, spoken at the beginning of his career, is reprised in the most unexpected of contexts over thirty years later in a statement produced by the Congregation for the Doctrine of the Faith. The title of the document is *The Message of Fatima*[186] and the background fact to bear in mind is that the Mariology emanating from this source is one that would arguably elevate Mary to a place rivalling Christ. Its content is summed up in a letter written by Sr Lucia (one of the children involved in the events) in which she records the three secrets allegedly revealed by the apparition in 1917.

How does Ratzinger deal with the theological content of this account? His comments are too dense to engage with in detail but reflections made at the beginning of the commentary on the distinction between public and private revelation, as well as his exegesis of the message itself, reveals an instinctive motivation not to allow any diminution of the place of Christ.

We are given an intimation of Ratzinger's standpoint early in the commentary when he contrasts the binding nature of public revelation against any illumination of that public revelation which might be vouchsafed through private revelation. Thus, he asserts that '[i]n Christ, God has said everything, that is, he has revealed himself completely, and therefore Revelation came to an end with the fulfilment of the mystery of Christ as enunciated in the New Testament'.[187] We find here a reiteration of his early position in *Introduction to Christianity* where he makes the New Testament normative and private revelation subject to an already complete revelation. However, in the light of later statements he makes about the content of this Marian revelation, his criterion for identifying private revelations which fall short or in some manner contravene the public revelation is particularly instructive. He writes,

> The criterion for the truth and value of a private revelation is therefore its orientation to Christ himself. When it leads us away from him, when it becomes independent of him or even presents itself as another and better plan of salvation, more important than the Gospel, then it certainly does not

---

[185] Ratzinger, *Introduction to Christianity*, pp. 212-13.
[186] Congregation for the Doctrine of the Faith, *The Message of Fatima* (2000) http://www.ewtn.com/library/curia/cdfatima.htm (accessed 13 March, 2012).
[187] CDF, *The Message of Fatima*.

come from the Holy Spirit, who guides us more deeply into the Gospel and not away from it.[188]

These words are prescient as we now consider Ratzinger's exegesis of the Fatima message. An early clue to his unease with the content is his registering of surprise at the description given of the way of salvation. He writes, 'To reach this goal [i.e. salvation], the way indicated —surprisingly for people from the Anglo-Saxon and German cultural world—is devotion to the Immaculate Heart of Mary.' The words taken in their original context and accorded the meaning traditionally associated with such language amount to a massive endorsement of high Mariology. Her Immaculate Heart is to be the centre of devotion and she is the way to salvation. However, exercising hermeneutical ingenuity, Ratzinger succeeds in inverting this message and making it an entirely Christocentric one.

> A brief comment may suffice to explain this [i.e. Salvation through devotion to the Immaculate Heart of Mary]. In biblical language, the "heart" indicates the centre of human life, the point where reason, will, temperament and sensitivity converge, where the person finds his unity and his interior orientation. According to Matthew 5:8, the "immaculate heart" is a heart which, with God's grace, has come to perfect interior unity and therefore "sees God". To be "devoted" to the Immaculate Heart of Mary means therefore to embrace this attitude of heart, which makes the *fiat*—"your will be done"—the defining centre of one's whole life. It might be objected that we should not place a human being between ourselves and Christ. But then we remember that Paul did not hesitate to say to his communities: "imitate me" (*1 Cor* 4:16; *Phil* 3:17; *1 Th* 1:6; *2 Th* 3:7, 9). In the Apostle they could see concretely what it meant to follow Christ. But from whom might we better learn in every age than from the Mother of the Lord?[189]

This style of hermeneutical leap – used in this case to deflate rather than enhance Mariology – is employed again towards the end of the document in order to reinterpret a statement which in its original intention only makes sense if Mary is Co-redemptrix. He writes,

> I would like finally to mention another key expression of the "secret" which has become justly famous: "my Immaculate Heart will triumph". What does this mean? The Heart open to God, purified by contemplation of God, is stronger than guns and weapons of every kind. The *fiat* of Mary, the word of her heart, has changed the history of the world, because it brought the Saviour into the world—because, thanks to her *Yes,* God could become man in our world and remains so for all time.[190]

---

[188] CDF, *The Message of Fatima.*
[189] CDF, *The Message of Fatima.*
[190] CDF, *The Message of Fatima.*

One must ask what is motivating Ratzinger to engage in what gives the impression of being a process of hermeneutical subterfuge and dissimulation. Is it dissatisfaction with a theology that diverges significantly from Scripture but from which he cannot publicly demur? This would appear to be the case, given comments addressed to Peter Seewald on why Mary's status should not be raised to that of Co-redemptrix. He states, 'The formula "Co-redemptrix" departs to too great an extent from the language of Scripture and of the Fathers and therefore gives rise to misunderstandings.'[191] Is this shorthand for the acknowledgment that such a theology is deeply at odds with the received revelation? Evangelicals may not be entirely sanguine about Ratzinger's approach to Mariology but they may be assured it is sufficiently boundaried so that the centrality of grace, and indeed of Christ, are protected.

---

[191] Ratzinger, *God and the World*, p. 306.

Conclusion

The proposal of Joseph Ratzinger as an ecumenical resource for the dialogue between Catholicism and Evangelicalism will have caused some to register surprise. His authorship of the controversial Vatican document *Dominus Iesus* serves only to reinforce the impression of a senior ecclesiastical figure who is intolerant of other traditions and their claims to be valid embodiments of the church.[1] The further possibility that his powerful institutional role within Catholicism came at the expense of earlier liberal convictions helps make him even less appealing as a subject for ecumenical enquiry. However, the reality of Ratzinger's life is more nuanced and multi-faceted than some caricatured accounts of it would suggest. Those who know his career well testify that no fundamental theological *volte-face* occurred[2], even if his ecclesiological outlook hardened into something rigid and defensive where previously it had not been.[3]

A helpful vantage point from which to view Joseph Ratzinger is the Second Vatican Council. This critical event in ecclesiastical history both locates him as a theologian and accounts for some of the radical choices he made in its wake. Prior to John XXIII's decision to summon an Ecumenical Council, Ratzinger was unquestionably part of the reformist wing of the church. However, his dissatisfaction with the status quo lay primarily with the neo-scholastic hegemony in the theological faculties and never extended to a full-scale questioning of fundamental Catholic dogma. The choice of St Augustine as theological mentor, which itself was preceded by an investment in Romano Guardini's negative assessment of certain aspects of the historical critical method, helped set his thought on a fundamentally conservative trajectory. The embrace of Augustine was also to involve the embrace of an emerging school of theology (*ressourcement*) which took Scripture and the Fathers with the utmost seriousness and attempted to find stimulus for church renewal in these neglected sources. In this respect, Ratzinger, de Lubac and other representatives of this school were substantially different from the so-called Council liberals who sought not *ressourcement* but *aggiornamento*. The Italian term spoke of a catching up with the times and allowing contemporary thought and the current voice of the Spirit to determine theology as much as the past had done. It was awareness that the theological presuppositions undergirding *ressourcement* were at odds with the aims of what became post-conciliar liberalism that ultimately presaged a parting of the ways. Ratzinger's withdrawal from the board of *Concilium* and his role in the formation of the more conservative journal *Communio* marked a clear distinction in outlook between those who

---

[1] This is particularly the case in his native Germany where there was a hostile public reaction to the claims made for the Church in *Dominus Iesus*.
[2] Note the perspective of Francis Schüssler Fiorenza who encountered Ratzinger during his early days at Münster when he was identified with the liberal camp at Vatican II.
[3] See the comments of Miroslav Volf at the close of chapter one.

Conclusion

saw the church's direction being determined largely by an engagement with contemporary culture and those who invested the traditional sources of the church's life with the ultimate authority.

Ratzinger's long-term theological conservatism, as it may be adduced from a biographical overview, does not of itself establish him as a credible dialogue partner with the evangelical tradition. To sustain this claim one would be aided greatly by being able to demonstrate that his conservatism was deeply rooted and that even in the most 'liberal' phase of his career there were surprising resonances with Evangelicalism in his theological outlook. Three converging pieces of evidence have lent credence to these claims. The first is with regard to theological method. Ratzinger's thought seems always to have been a merging of reason *and* revelation with revelation functioning as the dominant partner. This was the case because reason functioned not as an expression of Enlightenment rationalism whereby it was judge and arbiter of the claims of Scripture and tradition; but as Augustinian or neo-Platonic partner to the revelation, explicating and enunciating it in philosophical terms. Unsurprisingly, given this starting premise, Ratzinger took a consciously diachronic approach to matters of truth, seeing truth as resident in the definitive voice of Scripture and the magisterium. However this commitment to the magisterium was subtle and imaginative as opposed to naïve and uncritical. Thus it seems always to have been tempered by a marked emphasis on the authority of Scripture and the testimony of the early Fathers.

Alongside theological method, there is significant biographical evidence of a core theological conservatism in Ratzinger. His reaction to the so-called Halbfass affair - a dispute involving the Tübingen faculty and its response to the withdrawal of the *Missio canonica* from an erring local theologian in 1967 - revealed a visceral and deep-seated orthodoxy which placed him publicly at odds with members of the faculty and student body. This telling event is complemented by an insightful memoir written by one of his postgraduate students from the Münster period, Francis Schüssler Fiorenza. What makes this account credible is that while the author is not a theological conservative, his memories of the time confirm that Ratzinger's later outlook was thoroughly consistent with what had gone before. Writing of the Münster days, Schüssler Fiorenza concludes that Ratzinger's theological emphases visible then continued to be central to his theological project.

However, the major piece of evidence, both for Ratzinger's conservatism and his appropriateness as a potential dialogue partner with the evangelical tradition, is his best-selling publication from the Tübingen period, *Introduction to Christianity*. His colleague Hans Küng interpreted the work as a polemical assault on modern approaches to Christology and that criticism itself vouches for the essentially conservative nature of Ratzinger's approach. However, what is more striking from the standpoint of the study is his characterization of 'belief'. Here the notion is presented as an act of deep personal commitment to Christ and one into which the bulk of Catholics in the Medieval period had not entered! This understanding of the radical nature of conversion has significant commonalities with the evangelical tradition as Ratzinger's further reflections in *Principles of Catholic Theology* demonstrate.

His exploration of the key articles of the Apostles Creed in *Introduction to Christianity* afforded the opportunity to identify points of correlation between his theological outlook and that of historic Evangelicalism. This was achieved by a comparison of the so-called five fundamentals of the 1920s Fundamentalist Controversy and Ratzinger's thought as it is outlined in the *Introduction* and other sources. Three observations are made with regard to that exercise. First, Ratzinger shares with evangelicals an unequivocal commitment to three of the five fundamental beliefs deemed to be essential to conservative Christianity (i.e. the deity of Christ, his virginal conception, and the bodily resurrection and Second Coming of Christ at the end of time).[4] The study noted that Ratzinger defended these ideas in a vocabulary that was often foreign to evangelicals and on occasion drew on sources which many of them would have deemed suspect (most notably Teilhard de Chardin). However, it was shown that Ratzinger did not compromise essential orthodoxy by adopting this approach, even if his methodology would have been unsettling to evangelicals. Second, while not affirming biblical inerrancy as it was defined in the 1920s controversy, it is nonetheless clear that Ratzinger is strongly committed to Scripture's inspiration and that he promotes a biblical hermeneutic not substantially dissimilar to that of certain contemporary evangelicals. Thus he is an ally in the bid to develop a nuanced but ultimately conservative approach to the biblical text. Third, while dismissing Catholic caricatures of Anselm's satisfaction theory of atonement and not being thoroughly convinced by even the most nuanced expression of that view, Ratzinger ultimately promotes a notion of atonement which has some form of substitution at its core. Drawing on the work of Jean Daniélou, he expresses a view of the cross which centres around the love of the Trinity being expressed in Christ's costly spanning of the void separating God and sinful humanity. This is not the exact equivalent of the traditional substitutionary atonement affirmed in the Fundamentalist Controversy, but it suggests a possible meeting point between the two perspectives.

At the core of any attempt to establish a bridge between Ratzinger and the evangelical tradition is the towering figure of St Augustine who is Ratzinger's major theological inspiration. It is shown that mainstream Evangelicalism attaches great importance to Ratzinger's embrace of Augustinian theology and that he is currently the pre-eminent representative of that tradition within Catholicism. While some scholars have sought to soften his Augustinianism, it would seem clear that it bears the same adversative, *contra mundum* stance as that of the Reformers. The main distinction, perhaps, is that his outlook is tempered by a regard for reason to which Protestant Augustinianism tends not to give much place. Notwithstanding this, the

---

[4] The author is aware that mainstream Catholic and Orthodox theology would concur with Evangelicalism at this point. What lends particular weight to the comparison is Ratzinger's near embrace of the other two fundamentals as well.

Conclusion

similarity with Protestant Augustinianism is supremely evident in Ratzinger's doctrine of sin which at points seems to be as robust as that of the Reformers. It should be noted, however, that this profound emphasis on sin does not extend to a belief in predestination which modern Catholic Augustinians such as de Lubac and Ratzinger reject definitively.

The major scholarly work undertaken on Augustine by Ratzinger is his original doctoral thesis on Augustine's view of the church. This was to influence much of his subsequent thought though our study focuses primarily on his treatment of Augustine's idea of conversion. Here his main objective is to endorse Augustine's negation of a highly individualized understanding of salvation derived from the mystical writings of the neo-Platonist, Plotinus. Rather than being the outcome of a lone and independent journey (arguably the model in some expressions of Evangelicalism), salvation is seen as being communicated through the ministry of the church as she fulfils her maternal role in the life of the believer. This essentially ecclesial view of salvation is presented later in a more nuanced form by Ratzinger in *Principles of Catholic Theology*.

Ratzinger's early work on Vatican II is perceived by some scholars as influenced definitively by a strict Augustinian outlook. While Tracey Rowland takes issue with such a judgment, it is my view that Ratzinger's comments on both *Dei Verbum* and *Gaudium et Spes* are not only markedly Augustinian but at times seem even to reflect a Reformed or Lutheran perspective. Thus he is resistant to the soteriological optimism that he believes undergirds parts of *Dei Verbum* and replies to it with a spirited defence of the law/gospel dialectic so redolent of Lutheranism. Moreover, his general response to *Gaudium et Spes* seems to be an unequivocal anti-Pelagianism which finds later expression in his papal homilies on the apostle Paul. Thus Augustine's theology of grace and his denigration of works are quite fundamental to Ratzinger's critique of two major conciliar documents.

Reflections on the Augustinian theme of the love of God are among the most ecumenically suggestive of all of Ratzinger/Benedict's writings. In his first encyclical as Pope, *Deus Caritas Est,* the love an individual has for God is portrayed as the antidote to a religion centred on ethical demands. This radical orientation towards 'religion as relationship' is reinforced by the acknowledgment that some expressions of Catholic faith have been motivated more by the pathological fear of damnation than the willing embrace of communion with Christ. However, the triune God is far divorced from the stern figure imagined by those in the grip of Pelagian religion. He is the one whose love is utterly gratuitous and whose attitude to the world is most perfectly displayed in the cross of Christ. Indeed, it is at the cross where this God of overwhelming love turns against himself in order to be gracious towards the objects of his love.

Having given an overview of Ratzinger's general engagement with Augustine, the study seeks to explore what contribution Protestant Augustinianism might offer to the task of rapprochement with Catholicism. Particular attention is paid to the nineteenth century American church historian,

Philip Schaff, who is deemed to speak most tellingly of Augustine's role vis-à-vis the two traditions. His view is that Augustine has the potential to stand above both Catholicism and Protestantism and be the model of a spirituality which would transcend their differences. In particular, he highlights Augustine's anti-Pelagianism and his embrace of inward piety over and above the mechanics of ritualised religion. In these aspirations there is a meeting point with Ratzinger who is himself thoroughly anti-Pelagian and not well-disposed towards a superficial, externalized religion. Neither Schaff, Ratzinger nor the bulk of the evangelical tradition accredit anything which would amount to ecumenical merit to Augustine's doctrine of election.

Given Augustine's prioritization of *Sola gratia*, it is no surprise that Ratzinger's own soteriology is suffused by grace. This is underscored by the historic intervention on his part which enabled the possibility of a Joint Lutheran/Roman Catholic Declaration on the Doctrine of Justification. The key statement of the agreement neatly presages what can be affirmed unequivocally about Ratzinger's own understanding of justification: 'By grace alone, in faith in Christ's saving work and not because of any merit on our own part, we are accepted by God and receive the Holy Spirit, who renews our hearts while equipping us and calling us to do good works.'

A vital factor in understanding the particular shape of Ratzinger's soteriology must be Augustine's own doctrine of justification. It is argued that Augustine's stance is essentially summed up by the Catholic *fides caritas* formula and that the Reformation doctrine of imputed righteousness is a genuine theological novum in terms of church tradition. Thus it was Augustinian emphases on sovereign election and free grace which led to a false identification of Augustine with the Reformed tradition in the matter of justification. Ratzinger's first foray into the justification debate was a 1958 review of Küng's classic study. Here he was less optimistic about the latter's ecumenical achievement than many other Catholic commentators though he maintained the hope that full agreement would one day be reached. His engagement with the Conciliar statements relating to justification (as already intimated and now more thoroughly explicated) reveal strongly anti-Pelagian tendencies as well as a soteriological vocabulary more akin to Reformation discourse than anything one might associate with Catholicism. Most striking is his upholding of the Lutheran law-gospel dialectic (albeit in slightly modified form) as the core of the divine revelation: 'To be sure, one has to view justification as radical and deep as [Luther] did, that is, as a reduction of the entire anthropology and thus of all matters of doctrine to the dialectic of Law and Gospel.' However, he is distanced from aspects of Luther's approach such as the heightened emphasis on the individual and the making of love into a work in the economy of salvation. Here his commitment to *fides caritas* is complete as is his sense that Luther's perspective is somewhat flawed by a dialectical view of God.

A certain ambivalence emerges when he explores the concept of faith in the teaching of St Paul. Here he speaks of it as a radically individual decision in a manner more reminiscent of Evangelicalism than Catholicism. He does,

Conclusion

nevertheless, also affirm the communal nature of faith in the same general context. This ambivalence is most marked in a homily on the sacraments where he *appears* to present regeneration as involving both the active response of the believing subject as well as an entirely passive reception of the sacramental ministrations of the Church. The language taken at face value suggests a contradiction at work but this is partially resolved later when Ratzinger's concept of passivity is explored at the close of the study.

The final chapter focuses on those elements in Ratzinger's theology which might present a barrier to ecumenical rapprochement. Ecclesiology and the doctrine of baptism are the initial foci of this examination and it is discovered that while core elements in his ecclesiology are troubling from an ecumenical perspective, his theology of baptism/conversion is surprisingly helpful. Ironically, it is two Augustinian themes undergirding his ecclesiology (*pure relations* and the *totus Christus*) which are deemed to be most problematic for evangelicals. The notion of 'pure relations' applied to ecclesiology was not only deemed to be idiosyncratic but also lacking any coherent exegetical foundation, despite Ratzinger's best efforts.

The second Augustinian theme, the *totus Christus*, is adjudged a particularly Catholic reading of Christ's corporate relationship with the church which evangelicals find generally unconvincing. Webster's wide-ranging critique of Communio ecclesiology is used to demonstrate why evangelicals balk at the kind of ecclesiological project promoted by Ratzinger et al. However, it is also recognized that while salvation is not ecclesially determined, it is nevertheless ecclesially mediated. Ratzinger's evangelical interlocutor, Miroslav Volf's embrace of a more communally-orientated soteriology was to provide some of the intellectual stimulus for this judgment.

The penultimate section of the final chapter explores Ratzinger's soteriological ecclesiology in relation to his understanding of baptism, conversion and faith. It is discovered that a genuine tension exists in Ratzinger's thought between a *seemingly* unequivocal endorsement of the sacramental approach to soteriology and a surprising openness to emphases which would sit more comfortably within Evangelicalism. Most notably, he affirms that an essential link should exist between baptism and the existential act of faith. Indeed, the latter is so vitally important that the catechumenate (the context in which the act of faith takes place) is interpreted as an essential element in baptism. Ratzinger further argues that baptism so understood may be identified with conversion and metanoia. In language reminiscent of his discussion in *Introduction to Christianity* he speaks of conversion as a 'single, total and permanent turning of one's existence into a new way.' Here there is a tremendous commonality with Evangelicalism and the conversionist theology of the charismatic renewal. While Ratzinger ultimately seeks to combine the heavily sacramental with the experiential and perceives no problem therein, evangelicals will acknowledge an element of contradiction or unresolved paradox in the action. However, the ecumenical way forward will involve mining the ambivalences.

The discussion concludes on the positive note that Ratzinger's language about the church's role in the mediation of faith veers away from the magical and the mechanical. His argumentation is deemed workable in an ecumenical context in that some contemporary evangelicals will concede that faith is not normally the outcome of a lone, individual search for God isolated from all outside influences. Indeed, some may agree with Ratzinger when he says that 'faith does not come to the individual as an isolated "I"; he receives it from the community of those who have believed before him and who tell him of God as an accepted reality of their history.'

The concluding section of the chapter consists of a critical reverse test where Ratzinger's perspective on two Catholic doctrines deemed to be antithetical to Evangelicalism (Purgatory and Mariology) is measured against his stated views on the priority of grace and the centrality of Christ. It is shown that Ratzinger's nuanced perspective avoids the pitfalls of Pelagian religion and presents Purgatory and Mariology in terms which are unfamiliar but not necessarily unwelcome to moderate evangelicals. Thus there are substantial meeting points between the two traditions and Ratzinger's emphasis on grace, combined as it is with a downplayed sacramentalism, is ecumenically hopeful and full of potential.

Future Pathways

Four key avenues of investigation suggest themselves as a result of my research into the ecumenical potential of Joseph Ratzinger's theology. First, his embrace of the *fides caritas* formula functions as a challenge to evangelicals to reconsider certain Catholic attempts at integrating this idea into the *Sola fide*. In particular, more attention should be paid to Calvin's positive assessment of the Regensburg agreement on justification. Second, Ratzinger's soteriology challenges narrowly individualistic notions of salvation and invites evangelicals to develop a soteriological model which has some place for an essential ecclesial dimension. Miroslav Volf's work in *After Our Likeness* is a helpful model for approaching this task. Third, Ratzinger's strong emphases on conversion and anti-Pelagianism would provide an arresting starting point for any future Catholic-evangelical dialogue on the nature of mission. The work of Kilian McDonnell on the theme of soteriology stands out as another thoughtful Catholic contribution to such a discussion. Fourth, Ratzinger's theologically rigorous engagement with Purgatory and Mariology offers a measured Catholic perspective on these themes which takes serious account of Protestant concerns. Future ecumenical dialogue may be greatly aided by such a nuanced papal contribution to the discussion.

Bibliography

Allen Jr. John L., *Cardinal Ratzinger: The Vatican's Enforcer of the Faith* (New York: Continuum, 2000).

Allen Jr., John L., *The Rise of Benedict XVI: The Inside Story of How the Pope Was Elected and Where He Will Take the Catholic Church* (New York: Doubleday, 2005).

Althaus, Paul, *The Theology of Martin Luther* (trans. Robert C. Schultz; Philadelphia: Fortress Press, 1981).

Atkinson, James, *Martin Luther and the Birth of Protestantism* (London: Marshall, Morgan & Scott, 1968).

Atkinson, James, *Martin Luther: Prophet to the Church Catholic* (Grand Rapids: Eerdmans Publishing Company, 1983).

Augustine, Saint, *Confessions* (trans. R.S. Pine-Coffin, London: Penguin Books, 1961).

Augustine, St, *Enchiridion on Faith, Hope and Love* (trans. J.B. Shaw; Washington, DC: Regnerry Publishing Inc, 1996).

Augustine, 'The Spirit and the Letter' in *Library of Christian Classics Volume VIII, Augustine: Later Works* (trans. John Burnaby; London: SCM Press, 1955).

Balisuriya, Tissa, 'Companion to the Encyclical of Pope Benedict XVI on "God is Love."' *Crosscurrents* Summer (2006): pp. 229-260.

Balthasar, Hans Urs von and Joseph Cardinal Ratzinger, *Mary: The Church at the Source* (trans. Adrian Walker; San Francisco: Ignatius Press, 2005).

Balz, Horst and Gerhard Schneider, eds. *Exegetical Dictionary of the New Testament* (2 vols; Grand Rapids: Eerdmans, 1981).

Barrett, C.K., 'New Testament Eschatology'. *Scottish Journal of Theology* Spring (1953): pp. 225-243.

Barth, Karl, *Church Dogmatics* 1:2 (trans. G.W. Bromiley; Edinburgh: T & T Clark, 1980).

Bauder, Kevin T., 'Fundamentalism.' Pages 19-49 in *Four Views on the Spectrum of Evangelicalism* (ed. Stanley N. Gundry, Andrew David Naselli and Colin Hansen; Grand Rapids: Zondervan, 2011).

Bebbington, David, *Evangelicalism in Modern Britain: A History from the 1730s to the 1980s* (Grand Rapids: Baker Book House, 1992).

Benedict XVI, *Caritas in Veritate (Charity in Truth)* (Dublin: Veritas, 2009).

Benedict XVI, *Deus Caritas Est: First Encyclical Letter* (London: Catholic Truth Society, 2006)

Benedict XVI, *Great Christian Thinkers: From the Early Church Through the Middle Ages* (trans. Vatican Library Press; London: SPCK, 2011).

Benedict XVI and Peter Seewald, *Light of the World: The Pope, the Church and the Signs of the Times* (trans. Michael J. Miller and Adrian Walker; San Francisco: Ignatius Press, 2010)

Bibliography

Benedict XVI, Pope, *Saint Paul: General Audiences July 2, 2008-February 4, 2009* (trans. *L'Osservatore Romano*; San Francisco: Ignatius Press, 2009).

Benedict XVI, *Spe Salvi: Encyclical Letter on Christian Hope* (London: Catholic Truth Society, 2007).

Berkouwer, G.C., *The Conflict With Rome* (trans. David H. Freeman; Philadelphia: Presbyterian and Reformed, 1958)

Berkouwer, G.C., *The Second Vatican Council and the New Catholicism* (trans. Lewis B. Smedes; Grand Rapids: Eerdmans, 1965).

Berkouwer, G.C., *A Half Century of Theology: Movements and Motives* (trans. Lewis B. Smedes; Grand Rapids: Eerdmans, 1977).

Bockmuehl, Marcus, *Black's New Testament Commentary on Philippians* (London: A&C Black,1997).

Boettner, Loraine, *Roman Catholicism* (New Jersey: Presbyterian and Reformed, 1962).

Boeve, Lieven and Gerard Mannion, eds. *The Ratzinger Reader: Mapping a Theological Journey* (London: T&T Clark, 2010).

Bonner, Gerald, *St Augustine of Hippo: Life and Controversies. Library of History and Doctrine* (London: SCM Press, 1963).

Bouyer, Louis, *The Spirit and Forms of Protestantism* (London: Harvill Press, 1956).

Brown, Raymond E., *The Gospel According to John I-XII* The Anchor Bible (London: Geoffrey Chapman, 1966).

Buchanan, James, *The Doctrine of Justification* (Reprint Edinburgh: Banner of Truth Trust, 1997).

Calvin, John, *The Institutes of the Christian Religion* (The Library of Christian Classics, vols xx and xxi; trans. Ford Lewis Battles; ed. John T. McNeill; Philadelphia: Westminster, 1960).

Calvin, John, 'Letter to Farel 1541' in 'Letters of John Calvin, Vol. 1', *Corpus Reformatorum* 39.215, (Halle: C.A. Schwetschke, 1834-1900; reprint New York: Johnston Reprint, 1964).

Carey, George, 'Christian Beginning.' Pages 123-141 in *Obeying Christ in a Changing World: 1. The Lord Christ* (ed. John Stott; Glasgow: Fountain Books, 1977).

Carey, George, 'Justification in Roman Catholicism.' Pages 120-136 in *Here We Stand: Justification by Faith Today* (ed. J.I. Packer et al; London: Hodder and Stoughton, 1986).

Carson, D.A., *Right with God: Justification in the Bible and the World* (Carlisle: Paternoster Press,1992).

Carson, D.A., *The Pillar New Testament Commentary on John* (Leicester: Apollos, 1991).

Cary, Philip, 'Why Luther is Not Quite Protestant: The Logic of Faith in a Sacramental Promise.' *Pro Ecclesia* Vol. XIV, No.4 (2005): pp. 447-467.

Chadwick, Henry, *Augustine: A Very Short Introduction* (Oxford: Oxford University Press, 1986).

Chirico, Peter, 'Hans Küng's Christology: An Evaluation of its
   Presuppositions.' *Theological Studies*, 40. No.2 Je (1979): pp. 256-
   272.
Colson, Charles and Richard Neuhaus S.J. ed. *Evangelicals and Catholics
   Together: Working Towards a Common Mission* (London: Hodder &
   Stoughton, 1996).
Corkery, James, *Joseph Ratzinger's Theological Ideas: Wise Cautions and
   Legitimate Hopes* (New York: Paulist Press, 2009).
Cranfield, C.E.B., *A Shorter Commentary on Romans* (Edinburgh: T&T Clark,
   1985).
De Chirico, Leonardo, *Evangelical Theological Perspectives on post-Vatican II
   Roman Catholicism* (ed. James M.M. Francis; Bern: Peter Lang, 2003)
De Chirico, Leonardo, 'The Dignity of the Human Person: Towards An
   Evangelical Reading of the Theology of Personhood of Vatican II',
   Evangelical Quarterly 77.3 (2005): pp. 249-259.
Del Colle, Ralph, 'Communion and the Trinity: The Free Church Ecclesiology
   Of Miroslav Volf – A Catholic Response.' *PNEUMA, The Journal of
   the Society for Pentecostal Studies*, Vol.22, No. 2, Fall (2000): pp.
   303-327.
Denzinger, H. and A. Schonmetzer, *Enchiridion Symbolorum Definitionum et
   Declarationum de rebus fidei et morum* (Freiburg, 1967).
DiNoia O.P., J. Augustine, 'The Church in the Gospel: Catholics and
   Evangelicals in Conversation.' *Pro Ecclesia* Vol. XIII No.1 (2004):
   pp. 58-69.
Dorrien, Gary, *The Remaking of Evangelical Theology* (Louisville:
   Westminster John Knox Press, 1998)
Duffy Eamon, ' "I": Urbi, but not Orbi ... the Cardinal, the Church and the
   World.' *New Blackfriars* 66, 780 (1985): pp. 272-78.
Duffy, Eamon, *The Stripping of the Altars: Traditional Religion in England
   1400-1580* (London: Yale University Press, 1992).
Dunn, James D. G., *The Theology of Paul the Apostle* (T&T Clark: London,
   1998).
Dupuis, S.J., Jacques, *Towards a Christian Theology of Religious Pluralism*
   (Maryknoll, NY: Orbis Books, 2002).
Ellingsen, Mark, 'Joseph Ratzinger (1927-) 'How Conservative is Benedict
   XVI?' *Theology Today* 62, No.3 (2005): pp. 388-398.
Ellingsen, Mark, *The Richness of Augustine: His Context and Pastoral
   Theology* (Louisville: Westminster John Knox Press, 2005).
England, R.G., *Justification Today: The Roman Catholic and Anglican Debate*
   (Oxford: Latimer House, 1979)
Evans, William B., *Imputation and Impartation: Union with Christ in American
   Reformed Theology* (Milton Keynes: Paternoster, 2008).
Fee, Gordon, *Paul's Letter to the Philippians (NICNT)* (Grand Rapids:
   Eerdmans, 1995).
Fischer, H.J., *Pope Benedict XVI: A Personal Portrait* (New York: Crossroads
   Publishing Company, 2005).

Bibliography

Fitzmyer, Joseph A., *Romans: The Anchor Bible Commentary* (New York: Doubleday, 1993).

Frame, John M., *The Doctrine of God: A Theology of Lordship* (New Jersey: P&R Publishing, 2002).

Fung, Raymond K., *The Epistle to the Galatians (NICNT)* (Grand Rapids: Eerdmans, 1998).

Geisler, Norman and Ralph E. MacKenzie, eds. *Roman Catholics and Evangelicals: Agreements and Differences* (Grand Rapids: Baker Books, 1998).

Geisler, Norman, *Thomas Aquinas: An Evangelical Appraisal* (Eugene: Widf & Stock Publishers, 2003).

George, Timothy, 'Evangelicals and Catholics Together: A New Initiative (An Evangelical Assessment)' in *Christianity Today* (December 8, 1997): pp. 34-35.

George, Timothy and Richard John Neuhaus et al, 'Evangelicals and Catholics Together: The Gift of Salvation.' in *Christianity Today* (December 8, 1997): pp. 35-38.

George, Timothy, 'The Promise of Benedict,' *Christianity Today* Vol.49, No. 6, June 2005.

Gerrish, B.A., 'The Place of John Calvin in Christian Theology.' Pages 289-304 in *The Cambridge Companion to John Calvin* (ed. Donald McKim; Cambridge: Cambridge University Press, 2005).

Gibson, David, *The Rule of Benedict: Pope Benedict XVI and His Battle with the Modern World* (New York: HarperSanFrancisco, 2006).

Gillies, Donald, *Revolt from the Church* (Belfast: Christian Journals Ltd, 1980).

Grudem, Wayne, *Systematic Theology: An Introduction to Biblical Doctrine* (Leicester: Inter Varsity Press, 1994).

Guardini, Romano, *The Conversion of Augustine* (trans. Elinor Briefs; London: Sands & Co., 1960).

Gunton, Colin E. and Daniel W. Hardy, eds. *On Being the Church: Essays on the Christian Community* (Edinburgh: T&T Clark, 1989).

Gunton, Colin E., *The Promise of Trinitarian Theology* (London: T&T Clark, 1991).

Hahn, Scott and Kimberley Hahn, *Rome Sweet Home* (San Francisco: Ignatius Press, 1993).

Hawthorn, Gerald and Ralph P. Martin, *Philippians (WBC)* (Waco: Word, rev. edn, 2004).

Heckel, Matthew C., 'Is R.C. Sproul Wrong About Martin Luther? An Analysis of R.C. Sproul's *Faith Alone: The Evangelical Doctrine of Justification* With Respect to Augustine, Luther, Calvin and Catholic Luther Scholarship.' *JETS*, 47/1 March (2004): pp. 89-120.

Heim, Maximilian Heinrich, *Joseph Ratzinger: Life in the Church and Living Theology : Fundamentals of Ecclesiology with Reference to Lumen Gentium* (San Francisco: Ignatius Press, 2007).

Hill, Wesley, 'Divine Persons and their 'Reduction' to Relations: A Plea for Conceptual Clarity.' *International Journal of Systematic Theology* Volume 14 Number 2 April (2012): pp. 148-160.

Hodge, Charles, *Systematic Theology* (3 vols; Grand Rapids: Eerdmans, 1993).

Horrell, J. Scott, 'Toward a Biblical Model of the Social Trinity: Avoiding Equivocation of Nature and Order,' *JETS* 47/3 [September] (2004): pp. 399-421.

Horton, Michael, *The Christian Faith: A Systematic Theology for Pilgrims for Pilgrims on the Way* (Grand Rapids: Zondervan, 2011).

Horton, Michael, 'What Still Keeps Us Apart.' Pages 245-268 in *Roman Catholicism and Protestants: What Divides and Unites Us* (ed. John Armstrong; Chicago: Moody Press, 1994)

Husbands, Mark and Daniel J. Treier, ed. *Justification: What's at Stake in the Current Debates* (Leicester: Apollos, 2004).

Husbands, Mark and Daniel J. Treier, eds. *The Community of the Word: Toward an Evangelical Ecclesiology* (Apollos: Leicester, 2005).

Kasper, Walter, *The God of Jesus Christ* (trans. Matthew J. O'Connell; New York: Crossroad, 1991).

Keating, Karl, *Catholicism and Fundamentalism: The Attack on 'Romanism' by 'Bible Christians'* (San Francisco: Ignatius Press, 1998).

Kerkhofs, Jan, ed. *Europe Without Priests* (London: SCM Press, 2003).

Kilby, Karen, 'Perichoresis and Projection: Problems with Social Doctrines of the Trinity,' *New Blackfriars*, October (2000): pp. 432-445.

Kittel, Gerhard, ed. *Theological Dictionary of the New Testament* (3 vols; trans. Geoffrey W. Bromiley; Grand Rapids: Eerdmans Publishing Company, 1978).

Kruse, Colin G., *Tyndale New Testament Commentary on John* (Leicester: IVP, 2003).

Küng, Hans, *Disputed Truths: Memoirs* (trans. John Bowden; New York: Continuum, 2008).

Küng, Hans, *Justification: The Doctrine of Karl Barth and a Catholic Reflection* (trans. Edward Quinn; London: Burns & Oates, 1981).

Küng, Hans, *My Struggle for Freedom: Memoirs* (trans. John Bowden; Grand Rapids: Eerdmans, 2003).

Küng, Hans, *On Being A Christian* (trans. Edward Quinn; London: Fount, 1977).

Küng, Hans, *The Catholic Church: A Short History* (trans. John Bowden; London: Weidenfeld & Nicholson, 2001).

Küng, Hans, *The Church* (trans. Ray and Rosaleen Ockenden; London: Search, 1968).

Ladd, George Eldon, *The New Testament and Criticism* (Grand Rapids: Eerdmans, 1970).

Lancel, Serge, *St Augustine* (trans. Antonia Nevill; London: SCM Press, 2002).

Lane, Anthony N.S., 'Calvin's Use of the Fathers and the Medievals.' *Calvin Theological Journal* 16 (1981): pp. 149-205.

Bibliography

Lane, Anthony N.S., *Justification by Faith in Catholic-Protestant Dialogue: An Evangelical Assessment* London: T & T Clark, 2002).

Lennan, Richard, 'Communion Ecclesiology: Foundations, Critiques and Affirmations,' *Pacifica* 20, February (2007): pp. 24-39

Levering, Matthew, 'Providence and Predestination in Al Ghazali,' *New Blackfriars*, Vol. 92, Number 1027 January (2011): pp. 55-70.

Lewis, C.S., *Mere Christianity* (London: Fount, 1983).

Lindars, Barnabus, *The Gospel of John: New Century Bible* (London: Oliphants, 1972).

Lohse, Bernhard, *Martin Luther: An Introduction to His Life and Work* (trans. Robert C. Schultz; Edinburgh: T & T Clark, 1986).

Lohse, Bernhard, *Martin Luther's Theology: Its Historic and Systematic Development* (trans. Roy A. Harrisville; Edinburgh: T&T Clark, 1999).

De Lubac, Henri, *Augustinianism and Modern Theology* (trans. Lancelot Sheppard; New York: The Crossway Publishing Company, 2000).

De Lubac, Henri, *Catholicism: Christ and the Common Destiny of Man* (trans. Lancelot Sheppard and Sr. Elizabeth Englund, OCD; San Francisco: Ignatius Press, 1988).

De Lubac, Henri, *Teilhard Explained* (trans. Anthony Buono; New York: Paulist Press, 1968).

Luther, Martin, *Luther's Works* Volume 26: Lectures on Galatians 1535 Chapters 1-4. (trans. Jaroslav Pelikan; St Louis: Concordia Publishing, 1963).

MacCullough, Diarmaid, *Reformation: Europe's House Divided* (London: Penguin, 2004).

McCormack, Bruce L. ed. *Justification in Perspective: Historical Developments and Contemporary Challenges* (Grand Rapids: Baker Academic and Rutherford House, 2006).

McDonnell OSB, Killian, *The Charismatic Renewal and Ecumenism* (Arundel: Pegasaurus Books, 1978).

McDonnell OSB, Kilian, 'The Kasper/Ratzinger Debate: The Universal Church and Local Churches,' *Theological Studies* 63 (2002): pp. 227-250.

McFarland, Ian A., 'The Body of Christ: Rethinking a Classic Ecclesiology Model.' in *International Journal of Systematic Theology* Volume 7 Number 4 October (2005): pp. 225-245.

McGrath, Alister, *Christianity's Dangerous Idea: The Protestant Revolution – A History From The Sixteenth Century to the Twenty-First* (San Francisco: Harper One, 2007).

McGrath, Alister E., 'Forerunners of the Reformation? A Critical Investigation For Evidence of Precursors to the Reformation Doctrines of Justification,' *Harvard Theological Review*, 75:2 (1982): pp. 219-242.

McGrath, Alister, 'Justification: Barth, Trent and Kung', *Scottish Journal of Theology* 34 (1981): pp. 517-529.

McGrath, Alister, 'Justification – 'Making Just' or 'Declaring Just', *Churchman*, Vol.96, No.1 (1982): pp. 44-52.

McGrath, Alister E., *Iustitia Dei: A History of the Christian Doctrine of Justification* (Cambridge: Cambridge University Press, rev. edn., 2005).

McGrath, Alister E. (1993) *Reformation Thought: An Introduction* (Oxford: Blackwell, rev. edn., 1993).

Metzler, Norman, 'The Trinity in Contemporary Theology: Questioning the Social Trinity.' *Concordia Theological Quarterly* Volume 67:3/4 July/October (2003): pp. 270-287.

McGuckin, John A., *The SCM Press A-Z of Patristic Theology* (London: SCM Press, 2005)

McKim, Donald ed. *The Cambridge Companion to Martin Luther* Cambridge: Cambridge University Press, 2004).

Martin OSA, Thomas F., *Our Restless Heart: The Augustinian Tradition* London: Darton, Longman & Todd, 2003).

Marsden, George, *Fundamentalism and American Culture: The Shaping of Twentieth Century Evangelicalism 1870-1925* (Oxford: Oxford University Press, 1999).

Matheson, P., *Cardinal Contarini at Regensburg* (Oxford: Oxford University Press, 1972).

Meeking, Basil and John Stott, *The Evangelical Roman Catholic Dialogue on Mission 1977-1984* (Exeter: Paternoster Press, 1986).

Mohler Jr., R. Albert, 'Confessional Evangelicalism.' Pages 68-96 in *Four Views on the Spectrum of Evangelicalism* (ed. Stanley N. Gundry, Andrew David Naselli and Colin Hansen; Grand Rapids: Zondervan, 2011).

Moltmann, Jürgen, 'A Critique of Spe Salvi: Horizons of Hope', *Christian Century,* May 20, 2008.

Moltmann, Jürgen, *The Trinity and the Kingdom of God* (trans. Margaret Kohl; London: SCM Press, 1981).

Morris, Leon, *The Gospel According to John (NICNT)* (Grand Rapids: Eerdmans, rev. edn., 1971).

Moule, C.F.D., *Origin of Christology* (Cambridge: Cambridge University Press, 1977).

Murphy, Francesca Aran, 'De Lubac, Ratzinger and von Balthasar: A Communal Adventure in Ecclesiology.' Pages 45-80 in *Ecumenism Today: The Universal Church in the 21st Century* (ed. Francesca Aran Murphy and Christopher Asprey; Aldershot: Ashgate Publishing Company, 2008).

Nichols OP, Aidan, *The Thought of Pope Benedict XVI: An Introduction to the Theology of Joseph Ratzinger* London: Burns & Oates, 2007).

Noll, Mark A., *Between Faith and Criticism: Evangelicals, Scholarship and the Bible* (Grand Rapids: Baker, 1991).

Noll, Mark A., 'History of the Encounter: Roman Catholics and Protestant Evangelicals.' Pages 81-114 in *Evangelicals and Catholics Together: Working Towards A Common Mission* (ed. Charles Colson & Richard Neuhaus SJ; London: Hodder & Stoughton, 1996).

Bibliography

Noll, Mark A. and Carolyn Nystrom, *Is the Reformation Over? An Evangelical Assessment of Contemporary Roman Catholicism* (Grand Rapids: Baker Academic, 2005).
O'Callaghan, Paul, *Fides Christi: The Justification Debate* (Dublin: Four Courts Press, 1997).
Oden, Thomas C., *The Justification Reader* (Grand Rapids: Eerdmans, 2002).
Olson, Roger E., *The SCM Press A-Z of Evangelical Theology* (London: SCM Press, 2005).
Ott, Ludwig, *Fundamentals of Catholic Dogma* (Charlotte: Tan Books, 1974).
Packer, J.I., 'Justification in Protestant Theology.' Pages 84-102 in *Here We Stand: Justification by Faith Today* (ed. J.I. Packer et al; London: Hodder and Stoughton, 1986).
Parsons, Michael, 'In Christ' in Paul.'*Vox Evangelica* Volume XVIII (1988): pp. 25-44.
Pascal, Blaise, *Provincial Letters* (London: Penguin Classics, 1988).
Partee, Charles, *The Theology of John Calvin* (Louisville: Westminster John Knox Press, 2008).
Pelikan, Jaroslav, *The Riddle of Roman Catholicism* (London: Hodder and Stoughton, 1960).
Perriman, Andrew, 'The Corporate Christ: Re-Assessing the Jewish Background', *Tyndale Bulletin* 50:2 (1999): pp. 239-263.
Piper, John, *The Future of Justification: A Response to N.T. Wright* (Leicester: IVP, 2008).
Plantinga, Cornelius, 'The Threeness/Oneness Problem of the Trinity' in *Calvin Theological Journal*, 23, no.1 April (1988): pp. 37-53.
Przywara, Erich, *An Augustinian Synthesis* (London: Sheed and Ward, 1991).
Rahner, Karl, *On the Theology of Death* (New York: Herder & Herder, 1961).
Rahner, Karl, 'Towards a Fundamental Theology of Vatican II,' *Theological Studies 40* December (1979): pp. 726-727.
Ratzinger, Joseph, 'Augustine's Conversion', *L'Osservatore Romano* (English Edition) 5 March, 2008.
Ratzinger, Joseph, *Behold the Pierced One: An Approach to a Spiritual Christology* (trans. Graham Harrison; San Francisco: Ignatius Press, 1986).
Ratzinger, Joseph Cardinal (1991) *Called to Communion: Understanding the Church Today* (trans. Adrian Walker; San Francisco: Ignatius Press, 1991).
Ratzinger, Joseph, *Church, Ecumenism & Politics: New Essays in Ecclesiology* (trans. Robert Nowell; Slough: St Paul Publications, 1988).
Ratzinger, Joseph Cardinal, *Daughter Zion* (trans. John M. McDermott, S.J.; San Francisco: Ignatius Press, 1983).
Ratzinger, Joseph, *Dogma and Preaching: Applying Christian Doctrine to Daily Life* (trans. Michael J. Miller and Matthew J. O'Connell; San Francisco: Ignatius Press, 2011).
Ratzinger, Joseph, *Eschatology: Death and Eternal Life* (trans. Michael Waldstein; Washington DC: Catholic University of America Press,

1988).
Ratzinger, Joseph, 'Europe in the Crisis of Cultures', *Communio* 32, no. 2 (2005): pp. 345-356.
Ratzinger, Joseph and Peter Seewald, *God and the World* (trans. Henry Taylor; San Francisco: Ignatius Press, 2002).
Ratzinger, Joseph, *God is Near Us: The Eucharist, the Heart of Life* (trans. Henry Taylor; San Francisco: Ignatius Press, 2003).
Ratzinger, Joseph, 'Hans Küngs *Rechtfertigung*', Jahrgang 54, *Theologische Review* Nr.1 (1958): pp. 30-36.
Ratzinger, Joseph, 'Homily for Msgr Luigi Giusanni', *Communio International Review*, 31 (2004): pp. 685-687.
Ratzinger, Joseph Cardinal, *Introduction to Christianity* (trans. J.R. Foster; San Francisco: Ignatius Press, 1990).
Ratzinger, Joseph, *'In the Beginning...': A Catholic Understanding of the Story of Creation and the Fall* (trans. Boniface Ramsay, O.P.; Grand Rapids: Eerdmans, 1995).
Ratzinger, Joseph, 'Is the Eucharist A Sacrifice?', *Concilium*, Volume 4 Number 3 April (1967): pp. 35-40.
Ratzinger, Joseph, *Jesus of Nazareth:From the Baptism in the Jordan to the Transfiguration* (trans. Adrian J. Walker; New York: Doubleday, 2007).
Ratzinger, Joseph, *Jesus of Nazareth Part Two: Holy Week: From the Entrance into Jerusalem to the Resurrection* (trans. Vatican Secretariat of State; San Francisco: Ignatius Press, 2011).
Ratzinger, Joseph, 'Luther and the Unity of the Churches', *Communio International Review* 11 (1984): pp. 210-226.
Ratzinger, Joseph, *Milestones: Memoirs 1927-1977* (trans. Erasmo Leiva-Merikakis; San Francisco: Ignatius Press, 1998).
Ratzinger, Joseph, 'Origin and Background to the Dogmatic Constitution on Divine Revelation' (pp. 155-166), 'Preface' (pp. 167-169), Chapter 1, 'Revelation Itself' (pp. 170-180), Chapter 2, 'The Transmission of Divine Revelation' (pp. 181-198) in *Commentary on the Documents of Vatican II* (ed. Herbert Vorgrimler; 5 vols (3); London: Burns & Oats/Herder and Herder, 1966).
Ratzinger, Joseph, *Principles of Catholic Theology: Building Stones for a Fundamental Theology* (trans. Sr Mary Frances McCarthy, SND; San Francisco: Ignatius Press, 1987).
Ratzinger, Joseph, 'Retrieving the Tradition: Concerning the Notion of Person in Theology'. *Communio* 17, no.3 (1990): pp. 439-54.
Ratzinger, Joseph Cardinal, *Salt of the Earth: The Church at the End of the Millennium : An Interview with Peter Seewald* (trans. Adrian Walker, San Francisco: Ignatius Press, 1997).
Ratzinger, Joseph 'The Dignity of the Human Person'. Pages 115-163 in *Commentary on the Documents of Vatican II* (ed. Herbert Vorgrimler; 5 vols (5); London: Burns & Oats/Herder and Herder, 1966).

Bibliography

Ratzinger, Joseph, 'The Ecclesiology of Vatican II,' *L'Osservatore Romano*, Weekly Edition in English, 23 January 2002.

Ratzinger, Joseph, *Theological Highlights of Vatican II* (trans. Henry Traub SJ, Gerard C. Thormann and Werner Barzel; New York: Paulist Press, 1966. Re-issued with an Introduction by Thomas P Rausch copyright 1979).

Ratzinger, Joseph, 'The Pastoral Implications of Episcopal Collegiality,' *Concilium International Review* (Dogma) 1, New Jersey: Paulist (1964): pp. 39-67.

Ratzinger, Joseph and Messorri, Vittorio, *The Ratzinger Report* (trans. Salvator Attanasio and Graham Harrison; San Francisco: Ignatius Press, 1985).

Ratzinger, Joseph, 'The Renewal of Moral Theology: Perspectives on Vatican II and *Veritatis Splendor*, *Communio International Review*, 32 (2005): pp. 357-69.

Ratzinger, Joseph, *The Spirit of the Liturgy* (trans. John Saward; San Francisco: Ignatius Press, 2000).

Ratzinger, Joseph, *The Theology of History in St. Bonaventure* (trans. Zachary Hayes, O.F.M.; Chicago: Francisco Herald Press, 1989).

Ratzinger, Joseph, 'The Unity of the Church – The Unity of Mankind', *Communio International Review* 1(1972): pp. 53-57.

Ratzinger, Joseph, 'Thoughts on the Place of Marian Doctrine and Piety in Faith and Theology as a Whole', *Communio* 30 No.1 (2003): pp. 147-160.

Ratzinger, Joseph, *To Look on Christ: Exercises in Faith, Hope and Love* (trans. Henry Taylor; New York: Crossroad Publishing, 1991).

Ratzinger, Joseph, *Truth and Tolerance* (trans. Henry Taylor, San Francisco: Ignatius Press, 2004).

Ratzinger, Joseph, *Volk und Haus Gottes in Augustins Lehre von der Kirche* (Seiten: Eos Verlag, 1992).

Ratzinger, Joseph, *What It Means To Be A Christian* (trans. Henry Taylor; San Francisco: Ignatius Press, 2006).

Ratzinger, Joseph, 'What Unites and Divides Denominations: Ecumenical Reflections', *Communio: International Catholic Review* 1 No.2 (1972): pp. 115-118.

Rausch, Thomas P., *Pope Benedict XVI: An Introduction to his Theological Vision* (New York: Paulist Press, 2009).

Reid, G. ed. *The Great Acquittal: Justification by Faith and Current Christian Thought* (London: Collins, 1980).

Reno, R.R., 'Theology After The Revolution'. *First Things* May 2007.

Reumann, John, *Philippians: The Anchor Yale Bible* (New Haven: Yale University Press, 2008).

Ridderbos, Herman, *Paul: An Outline of His Theology* (trans. John Richard De Witt; Grand Rapids: Eerdmans, 1975).

Rist, John, 'Faith and Reason in Augustine.' Pages 26-39 in *The Cambridge Companion to Augustine* (ed. Eleonore Stump and Norman Kretzman; Cambridge: Cambridge University Press, 2001).

Root, Michael, 'Catholic and Evangelical Theology', *Pro Ecclesia*, Vol XV, No.1: 9-16 (2006): pp. 9-16.
Root, Michael, 'Is the Reformation Over? And What If It Is? *Pro Ecclesia* Vol XVI, no.3 (2007): pp. 334-344.
Rowland, Tracey, *Benedict XVI: A Guide for the Perplexed* (London: T & T Clark, 2010).
Rowland, Tracey, *Ratzinger's Faith: The Theology of Pope Benedict XVI* (Oxford: Oxford University Press, 2008).
Sanders, Fred, 'The State of the Doctrine of the Trinity in Evangelical Theology' in *Southwestern Journal of Theology*, Volume 47, No. 2 Spring (2005): pp. 153-175.
Saucy, Mark, 'Evangelicals, Catholics, and Orthodox Together: Is the Church an Extension of the Incarnation?' *JETS* 43/2 June (2000): pp. 193-212.
Schaff, Philip, 'Prolegomena: St Augustine's Life and Work' in *A Select Library of the Nicene and Post-Nicene Fathers of the Christian Church*, Vol. 1. (Buffalo: The Christian Literature Co.,1886).
Scheffczyk, Leo, *On Being A Christian:The Hans Küng Debate* (Dublin: Four Courts Press, 1982).
Schleiermacher, Friedrich, *The Christian Faith* (trans. and ed. H.R. Mackintosh and J.S. Stewart; Edinburgh: T&T Clark, 1999).
Schlier, H., 'A Brief Apologia.' Pages 193-214 in *We Are Now Catholics* (ed. K. Hardt S.J. et al; Cork: Mercier Press, 1958).
Schnackenburg, Rudolf, *The Gospel According to John. Volume 2: Chapters 5-12* (New York: Crossroad, 1982).
Schulze, Manfred, 'Martin Luther and the Church Fathers.' Pages 573-626 in *The Reception of the Church Fathers in the West: From the Carolingians to the Maurists* (2 vols (2); ed. Irena Backus; Leiden/Boston: Brill Academic, 2001).
Seewald, Peter, *Benedict XVI: An Intimate Portrait* (trans. Henry Taylor and Anne Englund Nash; San Francisco: Ignatius, 2008).
Sexton, Jason S., 'The State of the Evangelical Trinitarian Resurgence,' *JETS* 54.4 December (2011): pp. 787-805.
Shortt, Rupert, *Benedict XVI: Commander of the Faith* (London: Hodder & Stoughton, 2005).
Silva, Moisés, *Philippians (ECNT)* (Grand Rapids: Baker House, 1992).
Sproul, R.C., *Faith Alone: The Evangelical Doctrine of Justification* Grand Rapids:Baker, 1995).
Stackhouse, John G., 'Generic Evangelicalism.' Pages 116-142 in *Four Views on the Spectrum of Evangelicalism* (ed. Stanley N. Gundry, Andrew David Naselli and Colin Hansen; Grand Rapids: Zondervan, 2011).
Suenens, Leon-Joseph Cardinal, *A New Pentecost?* (London: Darton, Longman and Todd, 1975).
Thompson, John, 'Modern Trinitarian Perspectives.' *Scottish Journal of Theology* Vol. 44 (1991): pp. 349-365.
Thornton, John F. and Susan B. Varenne, eds. *The Essential Pope Benedict*

Bibliography

XVI: His Central Writings and Speeches (New York: HarperSanFrancisco, 2007) .
Thurston, Bonnie B. and Judith M. Ryan, *Phillipians and Philemon (SP)* (Collegeville, Minnesota: Liturgical Press, 2005).
Tilley, Robert, *Benedict XVI and the Search for Truth* (Leominster: Gracewing, 2007).
Toon, Peter, *Evangelical Theology: A Response to Tractarianism* (London: Marshall, Morgan and Scott, 1979).
Toon, Peter, *Justification and Sanctification* (London: Marshall, Morgan & Scott, 1983).
Toon, Peter and James D. Spiceland, eds. *One God in Trinity: An Analysis of the Primary Dogma of Christianity* (London: Samuel Bagster, 1980).
Twomey, D. Vincent, *Pope Benedict XVI: The Conscience of our Age* (San Francisco: Ignatius Press, 2005).
Van Bavel, Jan, 'The "Totus Christus" Idea: A Forgotten Aspect to Augustine's Spirituality.' Pages 84-94 in *Studies in Patristic Christology* (ed. Thomas Finan and Vincent Twomey; Dublin: Four Courts Press, 1998).
Vanhoozer, Kevin J., *Remythologizing Theology: Divine Action, Passion and Authorship.* Cambridge: Cambridge University Press, 2010).
Van Oort, Johannes, 'John Calvin and the Church Fathers' Pages 661-700 in *The Reception of the Church Fathers in the West: From the Carolingians to the Maurists* (2 vols (2); ed. Irena Backus; Leiden/Boston: Brill Academic, 2001)
Voderholzer, Rudolf, *Meet Henri de Lubac: His Life and Work* (San Francisco: Ignatius Press, 2008).
Volf, Miroslav, *After Our Likeness: The Church as the Image of the Trinity* (Grand Rapids: Eerdmans,1998).
Volf, Miroslav, 'Benedict's Challenge: Changing and Changeless.' *Christian Century*, May 17 2005.
Volf, Miroslav, 'The Trinity is our Social Program": The Doctrine of the Trinity and the Shape of Social Engagement', *Modern Theology* Volume 14, Issue 3, July (1998) pp. 403-423.
Wainwright, Geoffrey, 'Dispensations of Grace: Newman on the Sacramental Mediation of Salvation', *Pro Ecclesia* Vol. XII, No.1 (2003): pp. 61-88.
Wainwright, Geoffrey, 'Reflections on Pope Benedict XVI's First Encyclical, *Deus Caritas Est*', *Pro Ecclesia* Vol. XV, No.3 (2006): pp. 263-266.
Warfield, B.B., *Calvin and Augustine* (Philadelphia: Presbyterian and Reformed, 1956).
Watson, David, *I Believe in the Church* (London: Hodder & Stoughton, 1977).
Webster, John, 'The Church and the Perfection of God.' Pages 75-95 in *The Community of the Word:Toward an Evangelical Ecclesiology* (ed. Mark Husbands and Daniel J. Treier; Leicester: Apollos, 2005).
Weigel, George, 'An Open Letter to Hans Küng', *First Things* April 21, 2010.
Weigel, George, *God's Choice: Benedict XVI and the Future of the Catholic*

Church (New York: Harper Collins, 2005).
Wendel, François, *Calvin* (trans. Philip Mairet; London: Collins, 1976).
Wiltgen, S.V.D., Ralph M, *The Rhine Flows into the Tiber: The Unknown Council* (New York: Hawthorn Books, 1967).
Wright, David F., 'Justification in Augustine.' Pages 55-72 in *Justification in Perspective* (ed. Bruce L. McCormack; Grand Rapids: Baker Academic and Rutherford House, 2006).
Wright, N.T., '*Harpagmos* and the Meaning of Philippians 2:5-11,' *Journal of Theological Studies* 37 (1986).
Wright, Tom, *Surprised By Hope* (London: Hodder & Stoughton, 2007).
Ziesler, John, *Pauline Christianity* (New York: Oxford University Press, rev. edn., 1990).

Online Bibliography

Allen, John L. 'Attack on Ratzinger: Italian book assesses Benedict's papacy.' *National Catholic Reporter* (2010), http://ncronline.org/blogs/all-things- *catholic/attack-ratzinger-italian-book-assesses-benedicts*-papacy (accessed 2 October 2010).
Allen, John L. 'Keeping the record straight on Benedict and the crisis.' *National Catholic Reporter* (2011) http://ncronline.org/blogs/all-things-catholic/keeping-record-straight-benedict-and-crisis (accessed 28 January, 2011).
Akin, James. 'How to explain Purgatory to Protestants.' *Catholic Answers* (2011) http://www.ewtn.com/library/answers/how2purg.htm (accessed 16 March, 2011].
Banks, Edelle. 'Conservative Evangelicals Say New Pope Speaks Their Moral Language.' *Religious News Service* (2005) http://www.christianitytoday.com/ct/2005/aprilweb-only/33.0b.html (accessed 10 June, 2009).
Benedict XVI. 'Address to the clergy and parish priests of Rome on 7 Feb 2008.' (2008) http://www.vatican.va/holy_father/benedict_xvi/speeches/2008/februar y/documents/hf_ben-xvi_spe_20080207_clergy-rome_en.html (accessed 5 December 2012).
Benedict XVI. Regensburg address on 'Faith, Reason and the University: Memories and Reflections.' (2008) http://pontificateofpopebenedictxvi.blogspot.ie/2008/08/regensburg-address- faith-reason-and.html (accessed 6 July, 2009).
Benedict XVI. 'Papal Address, 12 January 2011 on St Catherine of Genoa.' (2011) http://www.vatican.va/holy_father/benedict_xvi/audiences/2011/docu ments/hf_ben-xvi_aud_20110112_en.html (accessed 16 March, 2011).
CDF 'Dominus Iesus.' Declaration on the Unicity and Salvific Universality of

Bibliography

Jesus Christ and the Church'. (1999) http://www.vatican.va/roman_curia/congregations/cfaith/documents/rc_con_cfaith_doc_20000806_dominus-iesus_en.html (accessed 20 January 2009).

CDF 'Instructions on Certain Aspects of the Theology of Liberation.' (1984) http://www.vatican.va/roman_curia/congregations/cfaith/documents/rc_con_cf aith_doc_19840806_theology-liberation_en.html (accessed 6 June, 2010).

CDF 'Joint Declaration on Justification by the Lutheran World Federation and the Catholic Church.' (1999) http://www.vatican.va/roman_curia/pontifical_councils/chrstuni/documents/rc _pc_chrstuni_doc_31101999_cath-luth-joint-declaration_en.html [accessed 20 January 2009].

CDF 'Letter to the Bishops of the Catholic Church on the Pastoral Care of Homosexuals.' (1984) http://www.vatican.va/roman_curia/congregations/cfaith/documents/rc_con_cfaith_doc_19861001_homosexual-persons_en.html [accessed 8 November, 2008].

CDF 'The Message of Fatimah.' (2000) http://www.ewtn.com/library/curia/cdfatima.htm (accessed 13 March, 2011).

Dulles, Avery Cardinal. 'From Ratzinger to Benedict.' *First Things* (Feb 2006) http://www.firstthings.com/article/2008/08/from-ratzinger-to-benedict---17 (accessed on 10 June 2011).

Ehlers, Fiona et al. 'The Failed Papacy of Benedict XVI', *Der Spiegel* (2010) http://www.spiegel.de/international/germany/0,1518,687374,00.html (accessed 26 March, 2011).

Fletcher, Patrick James. 'Resurrection and Platonic Dualism: Joseph Ratzinger's Augustinianism.' *Doctoral thesis, Catholic University of America* (2011). http://aladinrc.wrlc.org/bitstream/handle/1961/9306/Fletcher_cua_0043A_10172display.pdf;jsessionid=1BF05443C19B8E3336747EA69F0A1621?sequence=1 (accessed 12 November, 2012).

George, Timothy. 'Symposium on the Declaration *Dominus Iesus*.' *Pro Ecclesia* Vol. X No.1 (2001) http://content.ebscohost.com.queens.ezp1.qub.ac.uk/pdf9/pdf/ddd/rfh//atla0001461845.pdf?T=P&P=AN&K=ATLA (accessed June 7, 2011).

Horton, Michael. 'The Differences Between Rome (Infusion) and Geneva (Imputation) in Justification.' *White Horse Inn: For a Modern Reformation* (2000) http://www.monergism.com/thethreshold/articles/onsite/infusionimputation.ht ml (accessed 1 February, 2010].

Horton, Michael S. (2005) 'What Can Protestants Expect From The New Pope' *White Horse Inn: For A Modern Reformation* (2005) http://www.christianitytoday.com/ct/2005/aprilweb- only/33.0b.html (accessed 12 June, 2009).

Jesson, Nicholas A. 'Where Two or Three are Gathered: Miroslav Volf's Free Church Ecclesiology' *University of St Michael's College, Toronto paper.* (2003) http://ecumenism.net/archive/jesson_volf.pdf (accessed 12 March, 2012).

Küng, Hans. 'Open Letter to Catholic Bishops.' *Irish Times* (2010) 'http://fratres.wordpress.com/2010/04/20/full-text-open-letter-to-bishops- by-hans-kung/ (accessed 4 November, 2010).

Neuhaus, Richard. 'The Possibilities and Perils in Being a Really Smart Bishop' *First Things* (April 2008).
http://www.firstthings.com/article/2008/03/the-possibilities- and-perils-in-being-a-really-smart-bishop-13 (accessed 5 March, 2011).

Pollock, Patrick J. '101 Heresies of Antipope Benedict XVI,' (2005) http://www.patrickpollock.com/101heresiesofbenedictxvitract2.html (accessed May 10, 2008).

Ratzinger, Joseph. 'Biblical Interpretation in Crisis: On the Question of the Foundations and Approaches of Exegesis Today.' *First Things* (1988). http://www.firstthings.com/web-exclusives/2008/04/biblical-interpretation-in-cri (accessed on Jan 13, 2010).

Ratzinger, Joseph (2005) 'Jesus Christ: "The Measure of True Humanism",' Translation online 'Cardinal Ratzinger's Homily in Mass Before Conclave'
Zenit. http://www.zenit.org/article-12791?l=english (accessed 10 June, 2010).

Ratzinger, Cardinal Joseph. 'On the Occasion Of The Centenary Of The Death Of Cardinal John Henry Newman'. Rome, 28 April 1990.
http://www.vatican.va/roman_curia/congregations/cfaith/documents/rc_con_cf aith_doc_19900428_ratzinger-newman_en.html (accessed 15 July, 2009).

Ricossa, Rev. Francesco. 'Ratzinger: 99% Protestant'. *traditionalmass.org* (2006)
http://www.traditionalmass.org/articles/article.php?id=62&catname=15 (accessed 15 June 2009).

Scanlon, Michael J. 'Martin Luther: The Separated Son of Augustine.' *Villanova Magazine* Winter 1999.
http://www.heritage.villanova.edu/vu/heritage/allthings/1999Wa.htm (accessed 10 Sept, 2010).

Schüssler Fiorenza, Francis. 'From Theologian to Pope: A Personal View Back, Past the Public Portrayals.' *Harvard Divinity Bulletin* Vol. 33, No. 2. (Autumn 2005) http://www.hds.harvard.edu/news-events/harvard-divinity- bulletin/articles/from-theologian-to-pope (accessed 9 October, 2009).

Vermes, Geza (2011) Review of *Jesus of Nazareth Vol. 1* in *The Guardian*, 12 March 2011.
http://www.guardian.co.uk/books/2011/mar/12/jesus-nazareth-pope-benedict- review?INTCMP=SRCH (accessed 28 March, 2011).

Index of Names

Akin, J. 24 fn.85, 175.
Altaner, B. 179 fn.154.
Allen Jr, J.L. 5, 9-10, 19 fn.60, 23, 34-36, 60 fn134.
Anderson, G. 111.
Anselm 46-47.
Aquinas, T. 11, 73, 74, 89, 102, 172
Arnaldez, R. 99 fn.109.
Augustine, A. 3-4, 13, 19, 34, 71, 73, 74, 75, 77, 78, 79, 80, 81, 82, 83, 84, 85, 86, 88, 92, 103, 104, 105, 111, 112, 113, 114-119, 169.

Backus, I. 103 fn.116.
Balisuriya, T. 20.
Balthasar von, H.U. 18, 45, 46 fn.82, 72, 93, 98, 179, 182.
Banks, Edelle 70 fn.8
Barclay, J. M. G. 157 fn.54.
Barrett, C.K. 156 fn.48.
Baron Münchhausen 39.
Barth, K. 45, 121, 122, 123, 125, 161 f n.74, 185.
Basil of Caesarea 119.
Bauder, K. T. 2 fn.4.
Bavel, van, T. J. 148 fn.17.
Beyerhaus, P. 92.
Bavinck, H. 184.
Bebbington, D. W. 2, 145.
Berkouwer, G. 62.
Boettner, L. 161 fn.77.
Boeve, L. 149 fn.22, 150 fn.25.
Boff, L. 20.
Bokenkotter, T. 11-12.
Bonaventure 14-15
Brown, R. E. 159 fn.66.
Brunner, E. 29.

Buchanan, J. 3 fn.11, 112, 118.
Bultmann, R. 34, 39, 54, 149.
Calvin, J. 3, 74, 76, 77, 103, 104, 110, 112, 137 fn.80.
Cantallamessa, R. 168 fn.109.
Carey, G. 171 fn.121.
Casel, O. 72.
Catherine of Genoa, 176-177.
Chadwick, H. 92.
Clement of Alexandria 148.
Colson, C. 2 fn.3.
Congar, Y. 17 fn.54.
Constable, D. 137 fn.80.
Contarini, G. 137 fn.80.
Corkery, J. 29, 74, 75.
Curran, C. 20.
Cyril of Alexandria 148-149.

Daeke, S. M. 57.
Danielou, J. 49, 72.
Dante 172.
De Chirico, L. 146, 154, 157, 161, 161.
Defregger, M. 10 fn.22.
Denzinger, H. 31 fn.19, 31 fn.20.
Döpfner, J. 16.
Duffy, E. 103.
Dulles, A. 24 fn.80, 64, 74.
Duns Scotus 100.
Dupuis, J. 20-21.

Einstein, A. 11.
Ellingsen, M. 105.
Ehlers, F. 22 fn.72.
Ezekiel 96.

Faber, G. S. 119.
Farel, G. 136 fn.80.
Fichte, J. G. 149.

Fitzer, J. 104 fn.120.
Finan T. 148 f n.17.
Fletcher, P. J. 53 fn.113, 56 fn.122.
Frings, J. 16, 180.
Fung, R. K. 160 fn.68.

Garrigou-Lagrange, R. 89.
Gathercole, S. J. 157 fn.54.
Geisler, N. 102.
George, T. 70, 110 fn.3.
Gibson, D. 9 fn19, 11 fn.24, 21 fn.70.
Giussani, L. 92, 93 fn.79.
Gnilka, J. 173.
Gnosticism 156.
Gottschalk of Orbais 105.
Grudem, W. 86 fn.64.
Guardini, R. 12-13.
Gundry, S.N. 2 n. 4.
Gunton, C. E. 160 fn.69.
Gutièrrez, G. 1 fn. 1.

Hahn, B. 1 fn.1.
Hahn, S. 1 fn.1.
Haight, R. 20.
Halbfass, H. 27.
Hamer, J. 20.
Hansen, C. 2 fn 4.
Hardt, K. 34 fn.32.
Hardy, D. W. 160 fn.69.
Häring, H. 8-9.
Harnack von, A. 31, 39-40, 78, 100.
Heckel, M. C. 137 fn.80.
Hegel, G.W.F. 58, 151 fn.28.
Heisenberg, W. 11.
Henrici, P. 94 fn.82.
Hilary of Poitiers 147.
Hitler, A. 7.
Hodgson, L. 156 fn.63.
Hoeffner, J. 74.
Hofmann, F. 78.
Horrell, J. S. 158 fn.62.

Horton, M. 71.
Hosea 96.
Husbands, M. 145 fn.5.

Ibn Hazm 100.

Jansen, C. 105.
Jenson, R. W. 155 fn.45.
Jeremias, J. 174 fn.132.
John, St 147-148.
John XXIII 61, 90.
John Paul II 1, 19, 23-24, 92.

Kant, I. 77, 100, 101.
Kasper, W. 18, 53 fn.113, 64, 152 fn.40.
Keating, K. 161 fn.77, 171 fn.128.
Kerkhofs, J. 98 fn.102.
Kershaw, I. 6.
Khoury, A. T. 99 fn.107.
Kierkegaarde, S. 36.
Knitter, P. 1 fn. 1.
König, F. 21.
Kratzl, H. 60 fn.134.
Kretzman, N. 99 fn.105.
Kruse, C. G. 159 fn.66.
Küng, H. 1, 4, 8-9, 16-18, 24 fn.85, 26 fn.1, 28, 35-36, 39, 61, 117, 118, 121-125, 134, 178, 180.

Labourdette, M. 89.
Lane, A. T. C. 47 fn.87, 124 fn.44, 125, 137 fn.80.
Latomus, J. 113,
Lehman, K. 18.
Lewis, C. S. 48 fn.97.
Lubac de, H. 13, 18, 58, 72, 77, 88, 140, 145, 146-149, 160, 163.
Luke, St 104 fn.122, 182, 183.
Luther, M. 3, 74, 77, 91, 99 fn.106, 103, 104, 107, 110, 112, 113, 114, 120, 125, 127, 128-131, 133.

Index of Names

MacAfee Brown, R. 16.
MacCullough, D. 103-104.
McCormack, B. L. 119 fn.33.
MacDonald, C. 35.
McDonnell, K. 168 fn.108.
McFarland, I. A. 161 fn.74.
McGrath, A. 112, 113, 114-116, 125, 135, 137 fn.80.
Maier, F. W. 12.
Mannion, G. 149 fn.22, 148 fn.25.
Marsden, G. 41 fn.67, 42 fn.69.
Matheson, P. 137 fn.80.
Martin, R. 168 fn.108.
Martyn, J. L. 157 fn.54, 160 fn.68.
Melanchthon, P. 112, 114.
Messori, V. 75.
Metz, J.B. 17 fn54, 18-19.
Möhler, J. A. 155.
Mohler Jr, R.A. 2 fn.4.
Moltmann, J. 151 fn.28.
Murphy, F. A. 155 fn.46.

Naselli, A.D. 2 fn. 4.
Neuhaus. R. 172, 173.
Newman, J. H. 23, 79, 172.
Nichols, A. 16, 30, 78 fn.37, 79, 84, 87, 88.
Nietzsche, F. 95.
Noll, M.A. 2, 42 fn.71, 43 fn.72.

Oden, T. C. 112 fn7.
Orr, J. 41, 42.
Osiander, A. 113.
Ott, L. 176 fn.141.

Paleologos II, M. 99.
Parson, M. 156 fn.47.
Paul, St 100, 131-136, 138.
Pelagius 114.
Piper, J. 3 fn. 10.
Planck, M. 11.
Plotinus 80.
Phaedo 102.

Pollock, P.J. 6 fn. 6.
Pryzwara, E. 73.

Rahner, H. 72.
Rahner, K. 1, 15, 29, 30 fn.12, 71, 73, 89, 172.
Ratzinger, J. Subject of Work.
Ratzinger, G. 18.
Rausch, T. P. 74.
Reuter, H. 78, 85 fn.61.
Ricossa, F. 73 fn.15.
Rist, J. 99 fn.105.
Ritschl, A. 117.
Rodari, P. 22 fn.74.
Rowland, T. 6, 66, 69, 73, 74, 75, 76, 77, 87, 89, 93, 94, 110, 111 fn.4.

Saigh, M. 65.
Scanlon, M. J. 107.
Schaff, P. 106-107.
Scheffczyk, L. 61 fn.137.
Schillebeeckx, E. 61.
Schleiermacher F. 144.
Schlier, H. 33-34.
Schmaus, M. 12, 14-15.
Schnackenburg, R. 159 fn.66.
Schonmetzer, A. 31 fn.19, 31 n.20.
Schöbel, C. 160 f n.69.
Schulze, M. 103 fn.116.
Schüssler Fiorenza, E. 33-34.
Schüssler Fiorenza, F. 27.
Seewald, P. 15, 22 fn 73, 28, 108, 179.
Seper, F. 20.
Sgorbati, L. 98 fn.103.
Shortt, R. 6 fn.4, 20.
Simplicianus 114.
Smits, L. 104.
Socrates 102.
Söhngen, G. 13-14, 179 fn.154.
Sproul, R. C. 134 fn.72, 137 fn.80.
Stackhouse Jr, J. G. 2 fn.9.

Stelzle, J. 7-8.
Stott, J. 47 fn.87, 171 fn.121.
Stump, E. 99 fn.105.
Suenens, L.J. 1 fn. 2.

Teilhard De Chardin, P. 51, 54, 55, 56, 57, 58, 59, 152.
Tertullian 99, 176.
Toon, P. 117.
Treier, D. 145 f n.5.
Twomey, V. 13, 15, 28-29, 32, 75, 148 fn.17.
Tornielli, A. 22 fn. 74.

Vanhoozer, K. 47 fn.87.
Vermes, G. 24 fn.87.
Volf, M. 68 fn.156, 145, 149, 150, 152 fn.33, 158, 159, 167 fn.102, 169 fn.114.
Vorgrimler, H. 89, 125.

Wainwright, G. 96.
Warfield, B.B. 85, 104, 105.
Watson, D. 157.
Webster, J. 145, 161-163.
Weigel, G. 24.
Wendell, F. 103 fn.116.
Wenzel, A. 11 fn.26.
Wesley, J. 107 fn129.
Wickert, U. 92.
Williamson, R. 22.
Wiltgen, R. M. 16 fn.44.
Witte, J. L. 124.
Witvliet, J. 70.
Wright, D.F. 119 fn.33.
Wright, N.T. 53, 54 fn.113, 172, 173, 174, 175.

Zephaniah 182.
Ziesler, J. 156-157.

Index of Subjects

activism 2, 143.
Adam 159.
Aggiornamento 17, 37, 38, 88.
alien righteousness 112, 116, 119, 121.
Alpha Course, French 168 fn.110.
Anselm's Satisfaction Theory 46-47.
anti-Pelagianism 113, 133, 171.
Ascension 160-161.
Assumption of Mary 179.
Augustinianism 3-4, 24, 29, 32, 69, 71, 72, 73, 76, 107, 150-154, 163-164, 192.
avant-garde theology 9, 18, 29.

Bamberg Catholic Congress 17.
baptism 144, 145, 165-167, 171.
Barthian *extra nos* 121, 122, 122.
Barthian *intra nos* 122, 123.
biblicism 2, 145.
bodily resurrection 34-35, 50-54.
Bonn, University of 16, 29.

Calvinism 107, 119.
caritas 83, 84, 129.
catechumenate 166-167.
charismatic movement 1, 168.
child abuse crisis 23.
Christianity Today 70.
Christology 39-41, 42.
Church Dogmatics 123, 161 fn.74.
collegiality 62-64, 65.
Communio 18, 72, 181.
Communio Ecclesiology 155, 161-165.
complexification 55, 56.
Concilium 6, 18.
Confessions 78-80.
CDF 6, 10, 19-21, 120.

conversion 38, 86, 167-168.
conversionism 2, 146.
corporate personality 148, 156-161.
Council of Jerusalem, 30 fn.12.
Council of Trent 121, 124, 125.
crucicentrism 2, 147.

Daughter Zion 182-184.
dehellenization 101.
deification, concept of 116.
Dei Verbum 87, 90, 125, 126.
De Magistro 82-83.
demythologization 38.
Der Spiegel 22.
De Trinitate 115, 135, 136.
Deus Caritas Est 94, 95-98.
Dominus Iesus 110.
Donatist Controversy 83-84.
doubt 37.

Eastern Orthodox soteriology 84.
Ecclesiasticus 127.
ecclesiology 60-68, 77-86, 143, 144, 153.
Eros 50, 95-96.
eucharist 120.
Evangelicalism 1-2, 26, 27, 69, 73, 78, 134, 144, 145, 149, 155, 157, 161, 164, 168.
Evangelical Lutheran Church of America 111.
evil 57.
existential act of faith 163.
existentialism 18, 37.

Fatima 32 fn.27, 185-187.
Fides Caritas 123, 129, 133, 134, 138.
Final Judgment 54-56, 174-175.

First Vatican Council 31.
forensic justification 118, 121, 124.
freedom of the will 108.
Freising 12, 15-16, 74.
Fundamental Theology 15, 16, 30, 32.
Fundamentalism 43.
Fundamentalist controversy 41-43.
Furrow, The 17 fn.51.

Gaudium et Spes 16-17, 32, 57, 65, 69, 73, 87-92, 126, 127.
Gnosticism 154.
God's Perfection 161-163.
Greek rationality 29.

Habilitationschrift dispute 14-15.
Hans im Glück 18.
Harvard Divinity Bulletin 33.
Harvard Theological Review 111.
historical critical exegesis 8-9, 12-13, 33, 34.
historicism 38.
history of dogma 31.
history of religions 37.
Holocaust 22.
homosexuality 20.

Idealism 55, 58, 149, 150.
Immaculate Conception 183, 184.
Immaculate Heart of Mary 188.
imparted righteousness 116-117.
imputed righteousness 3, 113, 116 fn.24, 134, 137 fn.80.
individualism 149-154.
inspiration of Scripture 42-43.
Introduction to Christianity 6, 36-60.
Islam 22-23.

Jansenism 105.
Jehovah's Witnesses 9.
Jesus of Nazareth 24.
Joint Declaration 70, 110-111.

justification 25, 110, 111, 114-144.
Jews, prayers for conversion of 23-24.

Lamentabili 31.
La Nouvelle Théologie 34, 71.
Law Gospel dialectic 125, 126, 130.
legalism 93-94.
liberal genie 65.
liberal theological method 12-13, 26, 33, 43, 149.
Liberation Theology 77.
Liturgy, The 7-9.
Lumen Gentium 120, 180.
Lutheranism 111, 113.
Lutheran World Federation 111.

II Maccabees 176.
Maktub 108.
magisterium 31, 125.
Mariology 120, 146, 171, 179-189.
Marxism 18, 38-39.
merit 124.
mediation of faith 168-171.
Middle Ages 14, 37, 138.
Milestones 8, 16.
mission 35.
modernism 12, 61.
moralism 93-94.
Munich, University of 12.
Münster sermons 92 fn.77.
Münster, University of 12, 27, 33.
Mystical Body of Christ 148, 155, 159.

National Catholic Reporter 23.
neo-Platonism 29.
neo-scholasticism 11, 12, 15, 19, 60, 67, 71, 89.
Nijmegen Declaration 17.

Index of Subjects

omega point 56.
Ordinariate 22.
Original Sin 71.

papacy 120.
papal election 21.
parable of the clown 36-37.
pathological religion 93.
Pelagianism 115, 127, 128, 134, 177, 185.
penance 176.
perfect Penitent 48 fn.97.
personalism 11, 66, 139.
Pontifical Council for Christian Unity 111.
prayers for the dead 176, 177-178.
predestination 77, 107-108, 119.
pure relations ontology 150-154, 163.
purgatory 146, 170-179.

rationalism, hegemony of reason 28, 98-102.
regeneration 116, 140-144.
Regensburg address 22,
Regensburg, University of 18
relativism 21.
Ressourcement 12, 17, 88, 181.
resurrection appearances 52-53.
reverse test 123, 146.
Reutlingen *Hochschule* 34.
revelation 14-15, 28, 29, 31.
righteousness (see imputed and imparted)
Roman Grand Inquisitor 8.

Salvation History 15.
sanctification 116, 124.
Scripture 130, 131, 145.
Second Epistle of Clement 59.
Second Vatican Council 27, 29, 30, 32, 60, 72, 120, 180.
secularist hegemony 22.
Septuagint 95, 101.

sin 57, 71.
Social Trinity 158 fn.62.
Society of St. Pius X 22.
Sola Fide 136.
Sola gratia 146, 172.
Solus Christos 146.
Sola Scriptura 15, 32.
Song of Songs 50, 95.
Sonship of Christ 41.
Spe Salvi 172.
Spirit, Holy 140.
student disturbances 18.
substitutionary atonement 41.
Süddeutsche Zeitung 19 fn.61.

Teilhardism 56, 57, 58, 76.
Theologia crucis 74.
theological evolutionism 31.
theological training in Germany 11-12.
The Letter and the Spirit 115, 116 fn.23.
The Tablet 21.
totalitarianism 10.
Totus Christos 148, 155, 163.
tradition 15, 38, 120.
transcendentals 93.
Traunstein 8, 10.
Tridentine Mass 24.
Trinitarian theology 150-154.
truth 29, 31-32.
Tübingen, University of 17, 27, 33.
two sources of revelation 15.
typology 181-184.

Union Theological Seminary 42 fn.68.
unity of the human race 147.
Ut Unum Sint 110 fn.8.

virginal conception 42, 43-46.

www.ingramcontent.com/pod-product-compliance
Lightning Source LLC
Chambersburg PA
CBHW050442240426
43661CB00055B/2476